Celebrating Tongues and Interpretation, Our Heirloom from the Bridegroom:

A Practice Manual for Home, Church, and the World

Black and White Edition

Corinna Craft

Copyright © 2022 Corinna Craft

Celebrating Tongues and Interpretation, Our Heirloom from the Bridegroom: A Practice Manual for Home, Church, and the World
by Corinna Craft

All rights reserved by the author. Except for the antique art, poetry, and song lyrics that are in the public domain, no part of this book may be reproduced or reprinted in any form by any means without written permission of the author. Please consult copyright holders of Bible translations for their unique usage rules.

Softcover Black and White Edition ISBN: 978-1-7377543-3-6

The author has taken reasonable precautions to ensure that the antique art reproduced in this book is in the public domain or is under a license that permits reproduction for commercial use. Contemporary artwork is by kind permission of Eddy Cutrera (https://Christolution.weebly.com), Andre Dial (https://oyacreativearts.com; oyacreativearts@gmail.com), Cassandra Donnelly (https://www.facebook.com/CreativePassages; https://fineartamerica.com/profiles/cassandra-donnelly), Jill Eulo (https://www.facebook.com/jill.eulo; jilleulo@gmail.com), and Alison Webster (https://www.instagram.com/allyblingart; https://www.facebook.com/allyblingcouture).

Cover Art: Cleansing the Harvest by Alison Webster (2017). Instagram: https://www.instagram.com/allyblingart. FaceBook: https://www.facebook.com/allyblingcouture.

Unless otherwise indicated, scripture quotations are taken from the NKJV: *New King James Version*®. Copyright © 1982 by Thomas Nelson. Used by permission. All rights reserved. / *The New Scofield® Study Bible, New King James Version*, ed. C.I. Scofield, Nashville Tennessee: Thomas Nelson Publishers, Copyright ©1989. The Scofield Reference Bible, Copyright © 1909,1917, 1937, 1945, 1967 by Oxford University Press, Inc.

Scripture quotations taken from other Bible translations are identified by the following abbreviated titles:

AMP: *Amplified Bible* Copyright © 2015 by The Lockman Foundation, La Habra, CA 90631. All rights reserved. AMPC: *Amplified Bible, Classic Edition* Copyright © 1954, 1958, 1962, 1964, 1965, 1987 by The Lockman Foundation. CEB: *Common English Bible*, copyright © 2011. CEV: *Contemporary English Version* Copyright © 1995 American Bible Society. CSB: *Christian Standard Bible*. Copyright © 2017 by Holman Bible Publishers. Used by permission. Christian Standard Bible®, and CSB® are federally registered trademarks of Holman Bible Publishers, all rights reserved. ERV: *Easy-to-Read Version* Copyright © 2006 Bible League International. ESV: *The Holy Bible, English Standard Version*. ESV® Text Edition: 2016. Copyright © 2001 by Crossway Bibles, a publishing ministry of Good News Publishers. EXB: *Expanded Bible*, Copyright © 2011 Thomas Nelson Inc. All rights reserved. GNT: *Good News Translation*, Copyright © 1992 by American Bible Society. KJV: *King James Version*. Public Domain. MSG: *The Message* Copyright © 1993, 2002, 2018 by Eugene H. Peterson. NASB:*New American Standard Bible* Copyright © 1960, 1962, 1963, 1968, 1971, 1972, 1973, 1975, 1977, 1995 by the Lockman Foundation. NIV: *Holy Bible, New International Version*® NIV® Copyright © 1973, 1978, 1984, 2011 by Biblica, Inc.® Used by permission. All rights reserved worldwide. / *Holy Bible, New International Version Study Bible*, ed. Kenneth Barker, Grand Rapids, Michigan: Zondervan, Copyright © 1985. Scripture quotations marked NIV are from the HOLY BIBLE, NEW INTERNATIONAL VERSION. Copyright © 1973, 1978, 1984 International Bible Society. Used by permission of Zondervan Bible Publishers. All rights reserved. NLT: *Holy Bible, New Living Translation*, copyright © 1996, 2004, 2015 by Tyndale House Foundation. Used by permission of Tyndale House Publishers, Inc., Carol Stream, Illinois 60188. All rights reserved. NRSV: *New Revised Standard Version Bible* Copyright © 1989 The Division of Christian Education of the National Council of Churches of Christ in the United States of America. Used by permission. All rights reserved. TLB: *Living Bible* Copyright © 1971 Tyndale House Foundation. Used by permission of Tyndale House Publishers, Inc. Carol Stream, Illinois 60188. All rights reserved. TPT: *The Passion Translation®: The New Testament with Psalms, Proverbs, and Song of Songs*, 2nd ed.,trans. Brian Simmons, Savage, Minnesota: BroadStreet Publishing® Group, LLC, Copyright © 2018. / Scripture quotations marked TPT are from The Passion Translation®. Copyright © 2017, 2018 Broadstreet Publishing® Group, LLC. Used by permission. All rights reserved. ThePassionTranslation.com. VOICE: *The Voice Bible* Copyright © 2012 Thomas Nelson, Inc. The Voice™ translation © 2012 Ecclesia Bible Society All rights reserved.

To Pastor Ray Boetcher who first entrusted me with the freedom and responsibility to teach.

TABLE OF CONTENTS

Introduction. 1

The Shantung Revival: "Lord, Do It Again, and Begin in Me!" 11

"A Mega Pentecost" 27

Speaking in Tongues Testimony 45

Speaking in Tongues: Impartation and Activation 57

Singing in Tongues Testimony 83

Singing in Tongues Practice 95

Interpreting Tongues Testimony 107

Interpreting Tongues Practice 121

Case Studies: God's Counsel and Comfort Through Interpretation 169

Appendix: The Enneagram, an Occult Block to the Holy Spirit. 203

Endnotes. 221

Works Cited 232

Index 240

About Corinna Craft. 261

INTRODUCTION

A friend of mine, Philip Botts, texted me this:

> So I've noticed that when I pray in English my mind is going and constantly distracting me. I have to fight day dreams and stuff but when I switch to tongues my mind clears, like it goes blank and all the head noise is gone. Does that mean anything?[1]

Here was my response:

> I don't have a brilliant answer for you, Philip, only the obvious one: you need to pray in tongues to clear your mind! This doesn't surprise me at all. We are in a season where we need to pray more in tongues. We need to let the Spirit of God lead, even in prayer. So pray in tongues and when you get clarity, pray in English, and then go back to tongues again.

Don't worry that you're not contributing anything "meaningful" (as you understand it!). His yoke is easy; His burden is light (Matt 11:30). Better to babble in tongues than to rave or whine or dribble in English: "Out of the mouths of babes and nursing infants, You have ordained strength, You have perfected praise, to silence the enemy and the avenger" (Ps 8:2).[2]

Like so many others, Philip had much to do and much to contend with after the turn of the year 2020, not counting all the spastic convulsions the United States was passing through at the time: the impeachment proceedings, the COVID-19 pandemic, mask mandates, the lockdown and its lingering pall of urban mental blight, the strange police killing of George Floyd,[3] and the protests, vandalism, and removal of historic monuments that flared up on account of it.[4] Since that time, troubles in our society seem to be increasing in frequency, intensity, and duration, calling to mind Jesus's prophecy about the end times: "But all these things are merely the beginning of the birth pangs [of the intolerable anguish and the time of unprecedented trouble]" (Matt 24:8 AMP).

On the home front, Philip requested several extensions to finish his thesis for a Master of Divinity degree while he continued to work for Navy, volunteer as an assistant pastor at a church, and supervise a growing family of three children. His wife Amy had just passed through a medical crisis during pregnancy. She was afflicted with intolerable itching and diagnosed with cholestasis, a liver condition that required inducing birth to avoid complications. Immediately afterward, she developed excruciating shoulder pain and was diagnosed with gall stones and advised to have her gallbladder removed. The surgery was scheduled, but her mother and friends were deeply disturbed by the prospect of organ removal in such a young woman and prayed warring prayers for her recovery. Philip texted me saying, "Just got the doctor report back for Amy. Her liver levels are normal".[5] They cancelled the surgery with relief, only to reschedule it again later.

No wonder Philip had a distracted state of mind! No wonder he could not seem to line up his thoughts in rank order to pray. This is one of the reasons God gave us tongues, as the Apostle Paul explains:

"Door of Hope, Gray Scale" (April 6, 2020), Cassandra Donnelly.[6]

> Also, the Spirit helps us with our weakness. We do not know how to pray as we should [or what we ought to pray for]. But the Spirit himself speaks to God for us [intercedes] with deep feelings [groanings] that words cannot explain [or that are inexpressible; unspoken; too deep for words]. God can see what is in people's hearts and knows what is in the mind of the Spirit, because the Spirit speaks to God [intercedes; appeals] for his people in the way God wants [or in harmony with God].—Romans 8:26-27 EXB (abridged)

Through tongues, the Holy Spirit goes on duty for us! Time praying in tongues is downtime in the Spirit; it's time out—a mental health break; it's one less problem to solve; one less question to answer; one less interference to run; one less fire to extinguish from that infernal pyromaniac. But tongues are not just a prayer language: they are so much more!

The "more" of tongues is explored in the companion Bible study to this practice manual. The study explains dimensions of the gift that some might consider controversial or subversive: tongues in fellowship, in church, and in public. To me, this only proves how far we have deviated from Book of Acts Christianity, the kind of Christianity that inspires sound conversions, even mass conversions. The exercises and assignments in this practice manual are applications of those Bible teachings. Unless you believe that the Bible is an up-to-date manual for modern life, you might have reservations about some of the training drills in this practice manual. Many believers are accustomed to modern church culture, which marginalizes, minimizes, neglects, and even excludes the vocal gifts. Why is this? I can only speculate. Fear of disorder or loss of control in church services, fear of laity limelighting or upstaging clergy, intellectualism, contempt for the gifts of the Holy Spirit or for those who operate in the gifts, programmatic strictures to spontaneous expressions of faith, and personal agendas or religious protocols may all factor into the suppression of the vocal gifts. Some leaders overemphasize Paul's teaching on church order to the point of extinguishing the fire and power of the Holy Spirit. But Paul said, "Do not forbid to speak with tongues," and "Do not quench the Spirit" (1 Cor 14:39; 1 Thess 5:19).

Some believers have been misled by the cessationist doctrine taught in some seminaries and Bible colleges in the United States. What is Cessationism? It is the false teaching that the supernatural aspects of the Christian faith such as the gifts of the Holy Spirit, including tongues and interpretation, ceased with the death of the Apostles, or with the death of the disciples of the Apostles, or with the canonization of scripture. This doctrine is unBiblical in the extreme.[7] In fact, Cessationism is a heresy that deserves to be buried six feet under the gates of Hades, which the church now possesses (Matt 16:15-19). Cessationism will not be raised from the dead, but we will!

Let's return to Philip. Philip is a trophy of God's grace. As "a Southern Baptist from the womb," Philip went to an independent fundamental Baptist grade school, middle school, high school, and college, but he now speaks in tongues.[8] This is remarkable because the Baptist denomination in America has long boycotted the gifts of the Spirit, especially tongues. Until May 13, 2015, the International Mission Board of the Southern Baptist Convention automatically disqualified any missions applicant who spoke in tongues.[9] It is painful to consider that under this policy the Board would have blacklisted the Apostle Paul who spoke in tongues "more than you all" and who evangelized a good deal of real estate on his many missionary journeys! (1 Cor 14:18)

One might well wonder why the Mission Board repealed its anti-tongues policy since doing so comes close to admitting that the policy was never Biblical to begin with. Apparently Baptist missionaries in Africa, Asia, and South America were at a distinct disadvantage in missions work due to the denomination's suppression or denial of the supernatural aspects of the Christian faith. Baptist missionaries had difficulty "competing for converts" in those parts of the world where Pentecostal churches are dominant, "charismatic experiences are normative," and new converts are "enthusiastically embracing the practice" of tongues (and where, I would add, the Satanic supernatural is recognized as a menacing reality that must be confronted). Adding to the pressure to go charismatic, membership in the Southern Baptist denomination in America has declined in recent years, which means that the denomination must recruit from non-Caucasian populations to boost their numbers and revitalize their organization. The repeal is a step in the right direction, but it does not ensure that the Board will commission missionaries who speak in tongues; it simply means that the Board will not automatically reject an admitted tongues speaker.[10] We hope that this concession will lead to greater acceptance of the Spirit and greater liberty for Baptists, for "where the Spirit of the Lord is, there is liberty" (2 Cor 3:17).

Whatever the fate of a tongues speaking applicant, the Baptist Mission Board still considers tongues a "private prayer language," not for fellowship or church service, contrary to Paul's statement that "God has appointed these in the church: varieties of tongues," right alongside church leaders such as apostles, prophets, teachers, and right alongside essential church functions such as miracles, healings, helps, and administrations (1 Cor 12:28). The Board definitely does not consider tongues appropriate for public display, contrary to Jesus' statement, "These *signs* will follow those who believe: in My name they will speak with new tongues" and contrary to Mark's report of "The Lord confirming the word [gospel preaching] through *the accompanying signs*," including tongues (Mk 16:7, 20, italics mine).[11] A sign must be displayed in public for it to serve as a sign. No one hides a sign in a closet. Paul also observed that "tongues are a sign for unbelievers" (1 Cor 14:22: Isa 28:11-13). His statement requires some explanation, which you can read in the companion Bible study.

A related Baptist policy that remains intact is the policy of terminating any missionary who emphasizes "any specific gift of the Spirit as normative for all" or "to the extent such emphasis becomes "disruptive".[12] This leaves open the question of what exactly is disruptive. Would the Board consider Jesus publicly expelling a demon that caused a boy to collapse, convulse, wallow on the ground, foam at the mouth, gnash his teeth, and look dead as disruptive? (Mk 9:14-29) How about 120 disciples speaking in tongues simultaneously and attracting a massive crowd of bewildered temple goers who were diverted from their religious observances and duties by the strange spectacle for which they had no interpreter prepared? (Acts 2:1-42)

The Baptist Board view of tongues as non-normative or not the norm or not applicable to all is incorrect. I need only quote Peter, the leader of the early church, who quoted the prophet Joel, who quoted God: "I will pour out My Spirit on *all flesh*" (Acts 2:17; Joel 2:28). All flesh means all flesh. It does not mean some flesh or certain types of flesh. Not one disciple was excluded from the outpouring of the Holy Spirit and the manifestation of tongues on the day of Pentecost. Jesus' command to "wait for the Promise of the Father" to "receive power" to be His witnesses the world over is a command to every disciple down through the ages (Acts 1:4-5, 8; Lu 24:49). The Father's Promise is for all, to make all spiritually effective in evangelism, not just the first century church. Together, the Father's Promise, Jesus' command, and the Holy Spirit's inclusive outpouring make tongues the norm of the faith, not an anomaly.

Back to Philip, a trophy of God's grace. Philip was first introduced to tongues in college through his drum teacher who drummed for an Apostolic Pentecostal church. The two of them attended a revival meeting where participants spoke in tongues. Philip was fascinated with the gift. The man behind him kept rocking and saying over and over, "Shalom, shalom, shalom". His drummer friend jokingly said, "He must not be advanced yet". Based on that experience, Philip started to "broaden my theology". Then a series of disturbing events and circumstances drove him to seek God's power.[13]

Philip served for an entire year aboard a Navy ship—the IKE or USS Eisenhower—during which time maintenance errors caused a landing aircraft momentum-arresting cable to snap, which nearly plunged a Navy plane (an E-2C Hawkeye) and its crew into the ocean, injured eight sailors who had to be medically evacuated, and caused $200,000 worth of damages to the carrier and other aircraft on deck.[14] That year a baby was born aboard the ship, and numerous Bible studies were rolling, indicating that the stress level of the sailors was high (since when do sailors attend Bible studies?!). Philip reached critical mass, and one night he completely surrendered his life to the Lord. As often happens when a person fully commits to God, his former life fell apart. When he got home from deployment, he became in his own words, "a Navy cliché": despite his earnest prayers and efforts at counseling, his wife filed for divorce.[15] Aside from the personal agony of rejection and the distress of managing two boys as a single parent, he feared his status as a divorcee would adversely affect his credibility and aspiration for the ministry.

In desperation, Philip attended a charismatic "Power Surge" meeting at a Baptist church whose lead pastor of 30+ years had crossed the bridge to the supernatural side of the faith. Philip sat at the back, determined to observe only. He refused to respond to an altar call for healing "just out of principle—I don't know what principle that is!" but he ended up on the floor, completely undone, and received a physical healing in his body that night. Not long after that, he was baptized in the Holy Spirit and spoke in tongues. He told the Lord that he did not want to speak "gibberish"; he wanted to speak "a real language that I can look up and figure out what it means". So the Lord gave him phrases in other languages, most of them names of God.[16]

"Door of Hope, Colorful Burst of Sunlight" (April 6, 2020), Cassandra Donnelly.[17]

One day Philip got a word that he couldn't translate. It sounded "like something out of a Tolkien book, like *Lord of the Rings*". At the next Power Surge meeting, he asked a friend from Regent University, an international student from Turkey,

> "Hey, does this word mean anything in your language?"
> "Yeah," he said, "It means, 'HE HAS WON' in reference to God."
> "WOW!" Philip said, both stunned and stoked.

Around this time a missionary to India, a very mature woman who ministers in dangerous regions to indigenous pastors, prayed over Philip and asked him,

> "Do you speak in tongues?"
> "Yes, ma'am, I do."
> "You need to because this is what's going to sustain you through this time."

Philip concedes that the missionary to India was "absolutely correct".[18] Tongues were what sustained him in integrity and honor through the painful divorce proceedings.

Along with the baptism in the Spirit, Philip also began to have "what Charles Finney calls liquid love experiences". He has had numerous liquid love experiences, all of them in his car. One day while driving on the Navy base, he felt he was "literally drowning in love". He couldn't breathe. He said, "God, You've got to stop this". But then he said, "I want all You have for me". Since that time, Philip started doing power evangelism in the marketplace and witnessing healings of those he prays for. After the divorce was finalized, God graciously brought Philip another wife, a spiritually vibrant woman—Amy—who shares his commitment to the faith and is eager to colabor with him in ministry.[19]

Philip considers himself "an oddity within my own denomination," but his story is not that odd for a Baptist. In fact, his trajectory toward the supernatural is becoming more common. I know many Baptists, including an entire Baptist church, who have turned charismatic or Pentecostal—Bapticostal—as Randy Clark puts it.[20] What is odd is not the individual Baptist's discovery that his faith has power, but the denomination's historic resistance to manifestations of the Holy Spirit. What is odd is the denial of the plain meaning of scripture, which contravenes the denomination's esteem for the Bible as the Word of God. What is odd is the downplaying or censoring of field reports of Baptist missionaries about salvations through charismatic phenomena, which opposes the denomination's zeal to evangelize the world for the Lord. All of these tensions and contradictions within the denomination are odd, not the "rogue" Baptist who realizes that "the Promise of the Father" has no expiration date and the gifts of the Spirit don't spoil (Lu 24:49; Acts 1:4).

The official position of the North American Mission Board (NAMB) on spiritual gifts looks orthodox on paper, but may not be in practice. Here is the paper policy:

> The Holy Spirit "cultivates Christian character, comforts believers, and *bestows the spiritual gifts* by which they serve God through His church."

> "A New Testament church of the Lord Jesus Christ is an autonomous local congregation of baptized believers, associated by covenant in the faith and fellowship of the gospel; observing the two ordinances of Christ, governed by His laws, *exercising the gifts*, rights, and privileges invested in them by His Word, and seeking to extend the gospel to the ends of the earth."[21] (italics mine)

Although the official statement affirms spiritual gifts, the Mission Board refuses to identify which spiritual gifts are still valid and currently in use and which "gifts may have passed away".[22] Through this ambiguity, the Board continues to accommodate cessationist theology and defend an indefensible position that erroneously claims that the gifts expired long ago.

Nevertheless, one of the greatest revivals in Baptist history—if not the greatest—is the Shantung Revival in Northeast China (1927-1937), which was distinguished by charismatic phenomena, including tongues. Philip, who has been a life-long Baptist, only learned about the Shantung Revival a couple years ago from a retired pastor friend. Later he heard Randy Clark lecture on it.[23] Let's read about it, for it foreshadows a mega Pentecost that is to come. Hopefully this piece of Baptist history will encourage Baptists and other reluctant denominations to accept the plain meaning of scripture that "the kingdom of God is not in word but in power" (1 Cor 4:20; see also 1 Thess 1:5).

"Door of Hope, Collage Element" (April 6, 2020), Cassandra Donnelly.[24]

THE SHANTUNG REVIVAL: "LORD, DO IT AGAIN, AND BEGIN IN ME!"

Prophesies about a coming revival, about a great harvest of humanity of a magnitude unlike anything before are becoming more and more prevalent and urgent. Have you noticed? The baptism in the Spirit and the gifts of the Spirit have been integral to past revivals. We know (at least intuitively) that we should no longer live just for ourselves but for others. Jesus said:

> "Most assuredly, I say to you, unless a grain of wheat falls into the ground and dies, it remains alone; but if it dies, it produces much grain. He who loves his life will lose it, and he who hates his life in this world will keep it for eternal life."—John 12:24

Elsewhere Jesus used wheat fields as a metaphor for evangelism:

> Then He said to them, "The harvest truly is great, but the laborers are few; therefore pray the Lord of the harvest to send out laborers into His harvest."—Luke 10:2 (see also Matthew 9:38 and John 4:35)

Our spiritual lives are meant to reproduce. If we are not reproducing spiritually, we have a problem, for we are not born for ourselves but for others. Spiritual reproduction can only occur through the power of the Spirit who operates through the gifts of the Spirit in a believer. The Spirit is the life giver; we are not. He is the one who attracts; we do not. He draws people in ways that are alluring, not boring, and in ways that are personally meaningful and impactful, not doctrinaire. The days of pitching an appeal for Christ through polemics are over. Now is the day of His Presence and power.

The Shantung Revival in China (1927-1937) is a great case in point. It seems to be a historic lesson more relevant to our present condition than past revivals in America. Why? Because this move of God profoundly affected the American Baptists, a denomination that has historically suppressed or denied the gifts of the Spirit, including (and perhaps especially) tongues. Also, the accounts of developments leading up to the revival indicate that God's people were the first in line for a spiritual makeover, for regeneration and upgrade, or there would have been no revival among the Chinese. The days of American optimism that rests on what we can do—the self-made, Rosie the Riveter attitude—are over. We need God. What can God do?

CONTEXT

God uses ordeals to drive humanity to the altar. Before, during, and after the Shantung revival, China was in a state of upheaval as several oppositional forces contended for control over the nation. Missionaries in China suffered through the War Lords, the Nationalist Revolution led by Marshal Chiang Kai-shek in 1927, the Japanese invasion and occupation of China in 1931, the Sino-Japanese War (1937-1945), the steady rise of communism and the communist takeover by Mao Tse-tung in 1949.[1] Conscientious missionaries attributed these conditions and events in part to their own failed efforts to bring Christ's redemption to the people of the land:

> "The local wars, the Communist-inspired unrest, bandit raids, and other incidents showed us how little progress had actually been made in evangelizing China".[2]

Rather than blame the parade of troubles on a hopelessly evil era or some other agent, the missionaries felt responsible for failing to execute a sacred trust committed to them by God. They felt that they and the church in China were no inspiration to others:

> "We realized the foundations needed to be re-examined. First we probed deeply into our own spiritual lives. Then we looked with disillusionment upon the Chinese churches".[3]

According to missionaries, Chinese churches were "cold" or "dead". They languished under lack of ownership and investment by Chinese Christians. Church membership had declined steadily from 1919 onward. Some churches were shut down completely; others were vacant during farming seasons or operational only when missionaries visited. One well-known Baptist missionary regretted that "more than 1,000 church members had been converted to Christianity, not to Christ," for there was little to no evidence of personal transformation after conversion. Professing Christians, either clueless or careless about the moral imperatives of the Bible and their covenant with God, led lackluster lives no different from their unsaved neighbors. Smoking opium, maintaining concubines, and winebibbing were common vices practiced by church members. Anti-foreign sentiment undermined missionary efforts to share the gospel and co-labor with Chinese in ministry. Indifference and apathy in matters of faith forced more than half of all missionaries to work secular jobs, primarily in education. Many missionaries resigned. Defeatism and depression were the dominant milieu.[4] A verse from Isaiah sums up the situation:

> We have, as it were, brought forth wind; We have not accomplished any deliverance in the earth.—Isaiah 26:18

PRAYER GROUPS, MARIE MONSEN, AND REPENTANCE

Mary Crawford, a Baptist missionary who compiled reports on the Shantung revival, attributed the revival to "prayer groups, definitely asking for revival, some dating back as far as 1925".[5] C.L. Culpepper, the president of the North China Baptist Theological Seminary, credited Marie Monsen, a Norwegian Lutheran missionary, for kickstarting the revival. Through Monsen's ministry, Culpepper's wife Ola was miraculously healed of optic neuritis, a painful degenerative condition of the optic nerve that caused loss of vision in one eye. The healing took place at an "electric" prayer meeting led by Monsen in 1927 in the port city of Chefoo (now Yantai), where the missionaries had been temporarily relocated as refugees by the American consul in the event evacuation should become necessary due to the Nationalist Revolution. Two male Chinese cooks who were on site felt compelled to join the meeting and were moved to renounce their animosity toward each other and to be reconciled and saved. This was one of many preludes to revival.[6]

Marie Monsen (1878-1962).[7]

Monsen was ahead of the curve in her disenchantment with religiosity and her longing for God's presence and power. About fifteen years prior, after years and years of teaching the Bible, Monsen had become convinced that most church members were not born again. She had also "recognized her own shallowness and longed for the spiritual power necessary to witness effectively," which compelled her to seek the baptism in the Spirit. Culpepper recognized that "God had raised her up to expose the spiritual apathy and weakness" of the church in China.[8]

In 1927 Monsen hosted a series of meetings in Chefoo to prepare missionaries for revival. Her messages focused on the gravity of sin; the necessity of the new birth; spiritual commitment and zeal; prayer for moral awakening in China; reverence for God's word; and restoration of ruptured relationships. After each meeting, Monsen stood at the exit and asked those who were filing out—missionaries, evangelists, deacons, preachers, and Chinese alike—"Have you been born again?" Many were unnerved or irked by the question but later felt convicted. Some reported that her words "felt like the thrust of a sword" or "like lightening-bolts". Some responded with absurd and evasive answers such as "I've preached for years" and "One cannot know until death". Monsen's meetings and others spearheaded by a few like-hearted, like-minded individuals produced a vanguard of zealous missionaries and Christian leaders baptized in the Spirit who toured China, challenging local churches and Christians in ministry to get saved and Spirit-filled, hot for God and gung ho about kingdom business.[9]

Toward the end of 1930, Monsen prophesied that "a great revival is coming soon and it will begin in the North China Mission". When Culpepper asked her how she could be so sure, Monsen replied, "Because God has a covenant with His people, and it is as true today as it was when He made it":

> If My people who are called by My name will humble themselves, and pray and seek My face, and turn from their wicked ways, then I will hear from heaven, and will forgive their sin and heal their land.— 2 Chronicles 7:14

Monsen observed that God's people had finally done their part to fulfill the conditions for revival.[10]

Repentance mainly consisted of admitting wrongdoings and rectifying them, if at all possible. The examples that follow illustrate the breadth and depth of repentance. Some are on the order of a revelation about the sin nature of humanity. Others are a jolt about specific offenses committed, many of which might be considered trivial by contemporary standards of Christianity, which are abysmally low:[11]

- A missionary nurse felt convicted by a childhood memory of stealing 25 cents from a neighbor and lying to her mother about it. At first fear of punishment as a child and later pride and shame as an adolescent had kept her from confessing and making restitution. Finally, as an adult she apologized in a letter and sent $1 restitution to the neighbor, after which the Bible became eye-opening to her and she felt like a new person.[12]

- A pastor returned money to the Southern Seminary for funds he had obtained by falsifying his financial needs.[13]

- Culpepper (the president of the Baptist theological seminary) felt convicted of a forgotten debt. Years prior, he had worked as a student at a cafeteria register at Baylor University. One day a man at the head of the line had given him $10 so that his family could eat, but the bill only amounted to $6. Since there was no money in the till, they agreed that Culpepper would repay him after other transactions had filled the till with money. But the man left without claiming his refund. Some time later, one of Culpepper's sisters died, and he spent the $4 for a train ride home and back. He fully intended to repay the debt but then forgot about it. The Holy Spirit convicted him to write the president of Baylor University and confess, but Satan insinuated that the president would tell the mission board, and the mission board would terminate him, and he and his family would be stranded without income in China. He wrote the letter anyway, offering the retraction of his diploma. As it turned out, the president was pleased with his effort to make amends. Then Culpepper had great peace, and the experience became a spiritual turning point in his life.[14]

- The principal of a boys' school and deacon of a church whose wife vehemently opposed his faith felt convicted of lying to her about his income in order to hide the 20% tithe that he regularly gave to his church. He also felt convicted about deceiving her about his activities in his spare time. He would pretend to go to market, but he actually attended church services. He maintained this double life to capitulate to his wife and appease her but also to conceal his miserable home life from other church members, for his wife was the sort of demonstrative person who would not hesitate to stalk him and stage a raging fit at church in order to "disgrace" him. He had justified deception as the right thing to do under the circumstances. When he confessed his wrongdoing and duplicity to his wife, to his shock she said, "Well, if Jesus Christ can make you confess your sins to me, then I want to know about Him, too. I have a lot of sins myself." Prior to his confession, he had witnessed to his wife many times in vain.[15]

- A Chinese pastor's wife who knew the Bible well, who had graduated from the mission's high school, and who had several years of seminary training, discovered she was not actually saved. She also "realized the sin of hate for her first child because she had wanted a diploma more than a baby". She publicly repented before her congregation of pride, deceit, worldliness, and hate. Afterward, she felt as if she were walking on air.[16]

- An elderly classics teacher at a girls' school was suspicious that Ms. Monsen operated in "hypnotic power". Later he figured that "she knew psychology" and was using psychological techniques to manipulate and control people. Finally, he wanted to know the truth, whether he was really a sinner, for he fancied himself sin-free. In the middle of the night he was convicted of his sins and felt prompted to itemize them on paper, after which he repented and got peace.[17]

Aside from repenting of pride, envy, criticism, hatred, hypocrisy, and other sins of the heart, repentance also consisted of renouncing intellectualism or head knowledge about Christ and living a life led by the Holy Spirit, not by human reason:

- A well known educator, a graduate of an American college, said he had been a "naotzu" (brain) Christian for 10 years before being saved.[18]

The result of all this soul-searching was that all the faculty at North China Baptist Theological Seminary and Bible School were baptized in the Holy Spirit, as well as many members of the staff at Warren Memorial Hospital.[19]

REPENTANCE AMONG THE PEOPLE

Repentance among God's people had a cascade effect on the populations they served. Conviction swept through a girls' school in Hwanghsien. Girls felt acute remorse for cheating on exams, stealing peaches from the school orchard, lying to their parents and others, and stealing pencils, pens, and money. The same conviction descended on a boys' school. An impromptu revival meeting broke out and lasted ten days, during which 600 girls—the entire female student body—made professions of faith, and 900 boys—the majority of the male student body—made professions of faith.[20]

At the boys' school, a secret communist cell of approximately 10 members was exposed and disbanded. One boy from the secret cell thought the concept of God was sheer foolishness. In private he had threatened to murder Culpepper and all of the missionaries, to incinerate the schools, and obliterate Christianity. Upon learning about the revival, he assumed that the missionaries were hypnotizing the students. He stood up on a bench to challenge Culpepper but was struck down and knocked underneath it (presumably by an angel or by the Holy Spirit). A dreadful conviction seized him as he cowered beneath the bench, but he mistakenly assumed that he was beyond redemption. The staff pleaded with him to give his heart to God, but he left the next morning, and one week later he was dead.[21]

At another meeting, another boy from the same secret cell lay stretched out on a seat, gnashing his teeth and clenching his fists, saying repeatedly, "Take me home! I'm going to die". He confessed that during one winter break when he had no money and had seen Christians buying bread, he had wanted to kill all Christians and confiscate their money and distribute their money to the poor. Like the other communist boy, he wanted to massacre the missionaries, cremate the churches, and annihilate Christianity. He even wanted to climb into heaven and kill God. After this confession, he went limp. He was dazed for several days, but accepted Christ. Culpepper marveled at the logical inconsistencies of communism and the atheist spirit supercharging it: those who claimed that God did not exist still had an irrational drive to "kill God". Culpepper described the communist students as "so poisoned by hatred and unbelief that they were nearly insane". Yet half of the boys from the secret cell accepted Christ. The other half left the school because the revival atmosphere was intolerable to them. Following this spiritual awakening, students and faculty were organized into preaching bands and traveled to nearby villages on the weekends to hold Bible classes and witness.[22]

Hospitals also became revival centers. Doctors and nurses formed evangelistic teams. They prayed and witnessed to every patient. They also preached in nearby villages during their free time. One older Buddhist man's testimony illustrates the radical change of heart that occurs in the new birth. His combative Buddhist wife returned utterly transformed after a hospital stay, baffling her husband, who had suddenly lost his chief opponent in life. He asked the local pastor:

> "What have you Christians done to my wife? She went to your hospital and came back completely changed. I have lived with her for 35 years, and we fought all the time. I used to curse her and she cursed me back. I used to hit her and she hit me back. Now when I curse her, she just smiles. When I hit her, she just walks away. She does better work than she ever did. Last night I woke up and heard her crying and praying for me. What have you Christians done to her?"

The Buddhist man was converted by kindness—the uncanny softening of his wife's personality—as was the son, daughter, and their grandchildren. Then the wife witnessed to neighbors and brought them to church where they were saved by Jesus, and she hugged them as they emerged from their baptismal fonts.[23]

A young Spirit-filled man named Chang led his entire family and in-laws to Christ, but only after much persecution. At mealtimes his mother would tell him "to go into the yard and ask his Jesus for food". His father was an opium addict; his mother was abusive and a rager after 25 years of managing her dysfunctional husband. The family perpetually lacked money due to the father's addiction. His sister was also miserable in her marriage to a gambler and drinker. But Chang persevered in prayer until they all turned, even his mother, who wept that she had so long "separated the Heavenly Father" from His children (her family).[24]

During the revival, little country churches were so packed that people congregated outside to listen through the windows. All had a moral awakening and came under conviction of sin. Revival spread from county to county, then throughout the Shantung province and then to other provinces: Honan, Manchuria, and Anhuei. Other denominations besides the Baptist were also affected. In some cities, people cried out in anguish over their sins before the preachers could even finish their sermons.[25]

MIRACLES

Miracles took place. Only a few examples are recounted here. An older woman from a village near Pingtu was cured of paralysis. For the first time in 28 years, she wore shoes and could walk at long last. Her sons had carried her to church so she could request prayer. No one, not even the pastor, had much faith. Yet the old woman was sure, and the congregation began to have deep confidence in her. Everyone kneeled to pray. In a few minutes, the pastor heard a noise and looked up and saw the old woman walking across the front of the church and down the aisle. Startled, he leaped to his feet and exclaimed, "Jesus has come and healed sister Chiao!" An electric shock passed through the whole congregation. The pastor's life was revolutionized. He admitted with exuberance:

> "I have been preaching for 30 years and have not been worth my salt. I was so lazy I could not walk a mile and a half to tell people about Jesus. Since the revival, I go to the prayer meeting at 5:00 o'clock in the mornings, walk 25 miles witnessing in villages and then go to a prayer meeting at night. The next morning I'm ready to go again."

His humble church of 50 members had led 1,000 to Christ in his own village and hundreds more in surrounding villages.[26]

A doctor who had joined an anti-Christian political party and had taken a public oath never to entertain that "foreign religion" swore that if two of his paralytic patients were healed, he would believe. It happened, and he did, trembling with awe. One patient had been a paralytic for 18 years; the other for 28 years. Some miracles were of strange conditions. One missionary reported that he had seen a man who had wriggled around "like a worm" because his legs were fused together, but "the flesh was separated, the man rose and walked, and he is now preaching the gospel".[27]

Some miracles were on the order of resurrections as those pining away on their deathbeds were unexpectedly revived from terminal illness. One man was dying of tuberculosis. His grave clothes and coffin were prepared, and his community was awaiting his death. An evangelist prayed for him, and he bolted up and shouted, "I am well!" He sold his coffin, and the proceeds were contributed toward the construction of a chapel.[28]

In another similar case, a woman was dressed in burial clothes. Her family stood by her side, mourning. A little blue bag of flowers, hair, and thorns was stuffed up her sleeve, according to a Chinese custom when all hope is lost. The bag was meant to ensure her passage past the "dogs of hades": the dogs would be appeased by devouring the flowers and deterred by the pricking of thorns. Just as the woman closed her eyes in death, a new convert prayed for her, and she became better immediately. Then her family sent for a missionary, and the whole family and a large number of people were saved.[29]

OUTCOMES

Rumors of these charismatic phenomena alarmed Baptists back home in America. Hence, in 1935 the Executive Secretary of the Southern Baptist Foreign Mission Board, Charles Maddry, was dispatched to China to investigate "Pentecostal excesses".[30] After hearing many missionaries testify about the miracles and personal transformations that were taking place, Maddry promised the missionaries, "I'm going back home and tell my Board that God has been walking in the midst of the North China Mission and we had better go slow in criticizing them!"[31] Indeed, the revival revived the church and society in many ways.

Here is a synopsis of outcomes:

- Witnessing became spontaneous. Old and young, male and female alike began to share Christ.

- Uneducated Chinese became more effective than missionaries at evangelizing.

- Unbelievers who had been totally indifferent to the presentation of the gospel now, under the influence of the Holy Spirit, asked how to be saved.

- Class consciousness diminished. Servants who thought the baptism in the Spirit was only for the professional classes—for teachers and preachers—received the baptism to their own astonishment.

- Detrimental and ruinous habits and customs were renounced.

- "Family idols" or "house gods" that had been worshipped for centuries were destroyed.

- Stolen goods were returned to their rightful owners.

- Breaches in relationships were repaired, and fellowship was restored.

- Chinese leaders became more conscientious in their duties and expressed gratitude for missionary work.

- Racial tensions and conflicts between missionaries and Chinese Christians disappeared.

- Church services were held regularly rather than erratically or not at all.

- Church attendance increased dramatically.

- Church auditoriums had to be enlarged to accommodate crowds of 1,000 people.

- Chinese members took ownership of their local churches and invested in them and stewarded them without foreign supervision.

- Fund raising was no longer difficult. People gave with satisfaction. Many churches became self supporting.

- Church members were disciplined.

- Pauses during church service—"Selah" moments of Holy Spirit silence and stillness—were treasured. Ministers abandoned their programmatic approach and became sensitive, yielding to the Holy Spirit.

- Prayer meetings lasted for hours. Prayers were passionate.

- Christian ordinances such as communion and baptism became meaningful and emotional.

- Christians sang continually. Those who could not sing sang well. Hymns were composed.

- Demand for Bibles and Bible study increased dramatically.

- Enrollment in Bible colleges and seminaries increased dramatically.

- National leaders were launched, whereas previously many had defected to the business world.[32]

REFLECTIONS

According to the historian J. Edwin Orr, the revival spread through every province in China from its center in the Northeast. Despite its undeniably Pentecostal features, Southern Baptists have secretly owned the Shantung Revival as "The Greatest Revival in Baptist Church History". That is quite an endorsement from a denomination known for its ambitious and sacrificial evangelism.[33] The revival lingers like a spiritual dream in missions-minded individuals who are acutely aware of the ineffectiveness and even uselessness of human effort and the need for supernatural intervention to overcome opposition to the gospel. Here is what Dr. R. Cal Guy, Professor of Missions of Southwestern Baptist Theological Seminary, said in gratitude for what had transpired, yet also in yearning to recreate it:

> "In China, a mission field well-known for its resistance to the Gospel, our Lord sent a great revival. Much of the normal mission work, so routine and unproductive as to break the hearts of the missionaries, suddenly came alive…My own reaction to the story every time I hear it is the prayer, 'O God, please do it again.'"[34]

The fact that the revival was a great surprise to Baptists and the fact that it violated their denominational norms yet produced such great results proves that the revival was of God and not of men. Dr. Baker James Cauthen, Executive Secretary of the Foreign Mission Board of the Southern Baptist Convention, discerned God's providential foresight in the revival, His lavishing of spiritual experiences needed to sustain missionaries and Chinese Christians through severe future trials:

> "We can only conclude the Lord of the harvest sent this great revival to strengthen His people in the face of the oncoming years of terrible suffering under military occupation and later communist domination."[35]

In commenting on Culpepper's treatise, Dr. Donald McGavran, Dean of the School of World Mission at Fuller Theological Seminary, said what Baptists are too polite or respectful to their own denomination to admit: apart from Holy Spirit power, missions work is generally dismal and sterile (non-reproductive). The power of God is the spiritual X factor needed in missions, in America, and around the world:

> "Dr. Culpepper has dealt with the most important aspect of Christian missions. Unless the church moves forward in the power of the Holy Spirit, there is, as a rule, not much growth and certainly not much blessing. The account of the revival in Shantung is of absorbing interest, both to Christians in America and to missionaries all around the world."[36]

Given the historic significance of the revival and its instructive value as a pattern for future revivals, one has to wonder why my Southern Baptist friend Philip had never heard of it in any of the Baptist churches or schools he attended and why I had never heard of it in any of the charismatic churches I attended or mainline denominational churches I visited over the years. Culpepper explains why:

> "Most of the things that took place in Shantung are as foreign as Chinese in American churches today, mainly because of resistance to the Holy Spirit."[37]

I agree. American churches—both denominational and non-denominational—resist the Holy Spirit. We do not experience the supernatural as much as we should because we resist God. Culpepper quotes the martyr and miracle-worker Stephen in his stinging defense before the religious council that stoned him: "You stubborn people! In your thoughts and hearing, you are like those who have no part in God's covenant! You are always actively resisting the Holy Spirit" (Acts 7:51 CEB, AMP). Culpepper concedes:

> "That charge remains true to this day. Actually this resistance is usually disguised by a professed aversion to 'pentecostalism,' but it's becoming more and more evident as nothing more than resistance to the Holy Spirit."[38]

I would add that we oppose the Holy Spirit in other ways, too, especially in matters of consecration and holiness. Many of us are compromised in ways that we do not even recognize.

In his closing remarks written in 1968—over half a century ago—Culpepper's thoughts are strangely familiar and haunting, as if he knew something about events in 2020, the violent protests juxtaposed against the silhouette of a silent church in stasis due to its acquiescence to selective governmental sequestration:

> "That [Shantung Revival] is also my prayer for America. In the midst of riots, protests, and all the dissatisfaction produced by our complex society, my heart often returns to Shantung. My soul is renewed as I recapture the aura of spiritual ecstasy which epitomized that era in my life. Then the reflective glow fades away, and I find myself in the midst of a land, my land, which needs a second touch for its impotent churches hobbled with their lack of spiritual power. Unless a great spiritual awakening overtakes our churches, there is little hope for our nation.
>
> All the revivals recorded in the Holy Writ followed a general pattern. First there was a degeneration of spiritual power among God's people. Then came the realization of desperate need. Deep conviction of sin and agonizing prayer always followed. A final action required turning aways from all wickedness and worldliness. That's the way it happened in Shantung when God kept His covenant with His people. He is waiting for us to let Him do it again in America."[39]

So we say, "God, do it again, and begin in me!"

"A MEGA PENTECOST"

Chuck Pierce prophesied that a literal Passover would take place during the feast of Passover, 2020. Indeed, a death plague passed over the land (COVID-19). After that, Tim Sheets prophesied that a literal Pentecost or outpouring of the Spirit would occur on Pentecost 2020 whose effect would become evident in days to come. Among other things, Sheets foresaw a "perpetual replenishing of outpourings" of power. Like many prophets, Sheets has sensed a mega Pentecost approaching, a mega outpouring of Holy Spirit power in days ahead, starting May 31, 2020: "Promises in the vault of your heart are going to begin to come to pass".[1]

The emergence of God's people and the release of God's power during a worldwide pandemic and panic may seem strange, but it is not. The timing mirrors the release of God's power and the emergence of God's people from the bondage of Egypt, which also occurred during a plague and panic (see Ex 11 and 12). During the quarantine in April, Sheets had a vision of angels striking the earth and proclaiming to God's people,

"Break Up, Break Out, Break Through, Pass Over and Possess!"

From this Pentecost onward, millions of angels—divisions of angel armies—will be released to assist believers in Christ and those who will come to believe in Christ through their testimony.[2]

In support of this, Sheets calls attention to the spiritual significance of a seemingly minor verse in the Old Testament that briefly reports the Israelites' exodus from Egypt in an understated, matter-of-fact way:

> Now the time the Israelites dwelt in Egypt was 430 years. At the end of the 430 years, even that very day, all the hosts of the Lord went out of Egypt.
> —Exodus 12:40-41 AMPC

Various translations of Exodus 12:40-41 highlight different shades of meaning of the word "host," including people, tribes, companies, divisions, forces, and armies:

- the LORD's people left Egypt (CEV)
- all the tribes of the LORD's people left Egypt (GNT)
- all the companies of the LORD went out from the land of Egypt (NRSV)
- all the LORD's divisions left Egypt (NIV)
- all the LORD's forces left Egypt (NLT)
- all the forces belonging to the Eternal left the land of Egypt (VOICE)
- God's entire army left Egypt (MSG)
- all the armies of the LORD went out from the land of Egypt (NKJV)

The Hebrew word "host" refers to a large mass of people. We can picture an aerial view of a large mass of people—some 2.5 million Israelites—streaming out of Egypt like a great flock of sheep. The word host also can refer to an army, a force, a campaigning company going forth in procession, organized into divisions for war. This army can be human or angelic. The word host can even refer to the "sun, moon, and stars" or the "whole creation".[3]

In the Exodus verse, "host" is in the plural form—"hosts": this indicates more than one mass of beings in battle array. Although the Israelites were numerous enough to constitute an army, they possessed no other attributes to qualify them as an army. On the contrary, they left Egypt in the humble condition of newly released slaves. They were not a military force by any stretch of the imagination. So the reference to a military force instead must apply to a mass of angels that accompanied and assisted the Israelites. These angels had been active in the judgments against Egypt, judgments inflicted on their slave drivers and task masters to force them through unbearable pressures and excruciating incentives to release a hostage nation from bondage.[4]

The Lord of angel armies orchestrated the exodus of His people through an outbreak of plagues that enabled them to break out of bondage. When the Israelites finally left, so did their angels. Their angels escorted them as a vanguard and rearguard. Later they broke into Jericho, the first city in the Promised Land. Sheets observed that the same activity is now occurring: angels are being released to assist the heirs of salvation to "Break Up, Break Out, Break Through, Pass Over and Possess!" These are angels of awakening, revival, healing, deliverance, and war.[5]

ANGELS MOBILIZED

Because angels play a major role in the impending mega Pentecost and end-time events, it would be worthwhile to briefly describe them to better appreciate the significance of the period we are entering. First and foremost, angels are servants to the heirs of salvation: they assist those who are already saved and those who are yet-to-be saved. Hebrews 1 and Psalm 104 describes angels as helpers to God's people:

> Are not all the angels ministering spirits send out [by God] to serve (accompany, protect) those who will inherit salvation? [Of course they are!]
> —Hebrews 1:14 AMP

> And concerning the angels He says:
> "WHO MAKES HIS ANGELS WINDS,
> AND HIS MINISTERING SERVANTS FLAMES OF FIRE
> [to do His bidding]."—Hebrews 1:7 AMP; Psalm 104:4

Angels are from the Father. In John's revelation, the ascended and glorified Jesus used the possessive pronoun "His" to indicate that angels belong to the Father and the

Father is the one who directs their actions: "before My Father and before *His angels*" (Rev 3:5, italics mine). The pre-resurrection Jesus also referred to the heavenly Father as the source and dispatcher of angels when He said to Peter, "Don't you realize that I am able right now to call to my Father, and twelve companies—more, if I want them—of fighting angels would be here battle-ready?" (Matt 26:53 MSG). The Father is in charge of angels. We appeal to Him for angelic assistance.

Angels are innumerable, at least by human calculation. In the book of Revelation, John reported seeing myriads of angels whose sum total he described as an indefinite and imposing product of multiplications and additions (we envision a ginormous number with lots of zeroes trailing behind it like the tail of a comet!):

> Then I looked, and I heard the voice of many angels around the throne, the living creatures, and the elders; and the number of them was ten thousand times ten thousand, and thousands of thousands.—Revelation 5:11

With so many angels on standby ready to assist, what do they all do? They specialize in different kinds of assistance. Some are warriors and executioners of judgments; some are escorts and guides; some are messengers; some are evangelists, and some are strengtheners, among other things.

Warrior angels are the "mighty ones" who "excel in strength"; they are "powerful soldiers" who fulfill or perform God's commands, who "carry out His orders," who "do His bidding," who "listen intently to the voice of his word to do it" (Ps 103:20 AMP, NKJV, ERV, TLB, NIV, TPT). The Old Testament reports that one angel on assignment slew 185,000 Assyrian soldiers in their own camp; this caused the invading king to retreat back to his country where he was assassinated by his sons while worshipping his Pagan god in a temple (2 Ki 19:35-37). If one angel can slay 185,000 men, imagine what 12 legions of angels could do?

Warrior angels constitute a military force that is organized into divisions or units. Jesus indicated that if He had wanted to escape scourging and crucifixion, He could have called on His Father to dispatch "twelve legions of angels" to rescue Him from arrest, torture, and death (Matt 26:53). How many angels is that? In ancient Rome, a legion was a military unit of approximately 6,000 soldiers (3,600 heavy infantry plus light infantry and cavalry).[6] Twelve legions at Jesus' potential disposal would have equalled 72,000 angels.

That's a lot of angels!

Warrior angels fight rebel powers of darkness or fallen angels. In the passage below, the clash of the kingdoms culminates in a war between holy angels and fallen angels and ends in a decisive defeat of fallen angels who are hurled out of heaven:

> And war broke out in heaven: Michael and his angels fought with the dragon; and the dragon and his angels fought, but they did not prevail, nor was a place found for them in heaven any longer. So the great dragon was cast out, that serpent of old, called the Devil and Satan, who deceives the whole world; he was cast to the earth, and his angels were cast out with him.
> —Revelation 12:7-9

Angels execute God's judgments. A good overview of this function can be seen in Revelation. In the final judgment, angels will dispense various kinds of "plagues," not just diseases that putrefy flesh, but other things that "plague" people: blood in fresh water, blood in salt water, scorching heat and fire, darkness, pain so severe that people gnaw their tongues, disturbing thunders and lightenings, gigantic hailstones, and an earthquake that displaces land masses and distorts the face of the earth (Rev 7:2; 15:6-8; Rev 16).

Angels are also guides and escorts. A matchmaking angel led Abraham's servant back to his home country to find a wife for Abraham's son: "The Lord God of heaven will send His angel before you, and you shall take a wife for my son from there" (Gen 24:7, 40). Angels evacuated Lot and his family out of Sodom and Gomorrah before brimstone scorched the cities: "So the angels took Lot, his wife and his two daughters by the hand and led them out of the city" (Gen 19:15-16 CEV). An angel woke Peter out of sleep in a maximum security prison cell where he was guarded by four squads of four soldiers. The angel caused the chains to drop from Peter's hands. Then he ushered Peter past two guard posts, through a locked iron gate that swung open of its own accord into the city, and down a street before he disappeared (Acts 12:4-11).

Angels are also messengers (see Rev 8:2, 6, 13). The angel Gabriel delivered a message to Mary, the mother of Jesus, and to Zacharias, the father of John the Baptist. Both messages were birth announcements under odd circumstances: in Mary's case, conception without sex while she was engaged to be married (a scandalous miracle!); in Zacharias' case, conception that eclipsed the infertility and menopausal age of the couple (Luke 1:11-

20, 26-38). Some messenger angels impart revelation of the will, purpose, counsel, and strategy of God. An angel explained to the prophet Zechariah the meaning of the visions he was having: the vision of a man riding on a red horse followed by other red, brown, and white horses (these are patrollers who bring rest and peace to the earth); the vision of the four horns (these are powers that scattered Israel); and the vision of the craftsmen (these are those who terrorize and cast down the powers) (Zech 1:7-21).

Other messenger angels evangelize or assist in evangelism, especially through preaching. How they do this, we can only guess: perhaps they goad, coax, cajole or otherwise compel or propel people to respond to an invitation to be saved by psychologically motivating and physically steering the uncertain, the doubtful, and the reluctant into agreement with the call of God on their lives:

> Then I saw another angel flying in the midst of heaven, having the everlasting gospel to preach to those who dwell on the earth—to every nation, tribe, tongue, and people.—Revelation 14:6

Angels who assist in evangelism sort, separate, divide, and order. For example, gathering angels remove from the kingdom of God all sources of offense: those who offend and that which is offensive. They remove people who hinder others in holiness and consecration to God, who mislead others into error or apostasy, who incite or seduce others to sin, and who are a source of scandal and rejection or corruption of the faith. Their work of division is analogous to reapers separating wheat from tares, weeds that look like wheat but are not:

> Weeds are gathered and burned. That's how it will be at the end of time. The Son of Man will send out his angels, and they will gather from his kingdom everyone who does wrong or causes others to sin. Then he will throw them into a flaming furnace, where people will cry and grit their teeth in pain.
> —Matthew 13:40-42 CEV

Ultimately, gathering angels will gather God's people together as an assembly of the righteous:

> And he will send his angels with a loud trumpet call, and they will gather his elect from the four winds, from one end of the heavens to the other.
> —Matthew 24:31 NIV

Angels are also strengtheners. The prophet Elijah was fed by an angel who prepared two baked cakes for him, which enabled him to trek for 40 days and 40 nights in the wilderness from a broom tree outside Beersheba all the way to Mount Horeb (1 Ki 19:5-8). Daniel was empowered by an angel to stand up on his feet after he had collapsed into a crawl position from a terrifying vision. Through the angel's repeated touches and comforting exhortations, Daniel was enabled to speak after he had become mute and breathless (Dan 10:7-19). Jesus was strengthened to endure crucifixion and hell by an angel in the Garden of Gethsemane who ministered to Him while He was in agony, sweating droplets of blood from the stress of His mission: "Then an angel appeared to Him from heaven and strengthened Him" (Matt 26:43). Jesus likely would have died from the strain *before* crucifixion had He not been supernaturally strengthened. His agony of mind was not merely due to the torture He faced, but the totality of human sin, Satanic power, and hell. Bloody sweat or hematidrosis occurs only under conditions of severe physical trauma and emotional strain. The capillaries or tiny blood vessels that supply the sweat glands burst and weep blood. So the angel strengthened Jesus to complete His mission.

GOD'S ECCLESIA MOBILIZED

With this understanding of what angels do, let's return to Tim Sheet's prophecy about a mega Pentecost, beginning in 2020, when innumerable angels will be released:

> "My people will move into a new era Pentecost. This year [2020] the ecclesia leaves its training and begins its deployment. This will be a year of deployment and change for future. The functioning ecclesia will now rise to operate in higher authority. Its advance will be rapid. The world will see the deployment of heaven's kingdom ecclesia and angel armies. This will suddenly and aggressively be revealed."[7]

The word "ecclesia" that Sheets uses to describe God's people is a Greek word that has historic political meaning. The word "ecclesia" literally means "a called out assembly or congregation".[8] Originally the term designated a ruling council in each city-state of ancient Greece. The council was a local governing body that conducted business on behalf of the citizens of a city. Periodically, the council would submit proposals—such as proposals for public works projects—to an assembly of citizens for consideration.[9] The early church applied this political term to a local assembly or congregation of God's people living in a city. For example, "Barnabas and Saul met with the church [ekklesia] at Antioch" (Acts 11:26).[10]

The word "ecclesia" has definite governmental significance. It denotes a ruling authority vested in God's people to direct the course of affairs in the city and geo-political sphere in which they live. All of God's people are His ecclesia or governing body in the earth, not just clergy but also laity, for each and every one of us has been transported out of the kingdom of darkness into the kingdom of light: "He has rescued and delivered us from the power and control, the dominion and tyrannical rule of darkness and has transferred us into the kingdom realm of His beloved Son" (Col 1:13 AMPC, AMP, NKJV, CEB, NIV, TPT, ESV). We are all citizens of another realm, a heavenly realm: "For our citizenship is in heaven" (Phil 3:20). Though we are "in the world," we are not "of it" (Jn 15:19; Jn 17:6). We are citizens of a holy nation that exists among secular nations: "You are a chosen race, a royal priesthood, *a holy nation*" (1 Pet 2:9). We are appointed to rule in the earth as a spiritual shadow government that indirectly directs the course of events and influences the public and the public forum. This governing influence will increase in magnitude:

> Of the increase of His government and peace there will be no end.
> —Isaiah 9:7

Unlike the kingdoms of this world, which will be smashed and shattered like an idol and blown away like chaff from the summer threshing floor (see Daniel 2), God's kingdom will remain and God's King will reign (see Dan 4:3, 34):

> Then to Him was given dominion and glory and a kingdom,
> That all peoples, nations, and languages should serve Him.

> His dominion is an everlasting dominion,
> Which shall not pass away,
> And His kingdom the one
> Which shall not be destroyed.—Daniel 7:14

Ultimately, God's kingdom will overtake the kingdoms of this world:

> The kingdoms of this world have become the kingdoms of our Lord and of His Christ, and He shall reign forever and ever!—Revelation 11:15

How is this takeover accomplished? In part through tongues. Tim Sheets explains: "God's Spirit language of governing authority was restored at Pentecost [after] it had been lost at the Tower of Babel". The language of the Holy Spirit is the language of divine law and government. It is the language of executive orders from heaven. Just as the Israelites received the 10 commandments and the Torah at the very first Pentecost at Mount Sinai, 50 days after many Passover lambs were slain, the disciples received the language of the Spirit and governing authority at Pentecost in the temple at Jerusalem, 50 days after Jesus—the Lamb of God— was slain.[11] This is the language of divine decrees and throne mandates. The more throne mandates we release through proper stewardship of tongues, the more we are activated in throne authority and the more the kingdom of God manifests on earth.

We are God's instrument of rule in the earth: we are the Ruler's staff, the King's scepter, the rod of God, executing His righteous judgments in a corrupt world system. Here are two Psalms that allude to this extraordinary function of God's people as regents who rule on behalf of the King:

> The LORD sends forth from Zion your mighty scepter.
> Rule in the midst of your enemies!—Psalm 110:2 ESV

As regents, we have the authority to enforce God's law, to bind and loose, to prohibit and permit, to forbid and allow. Here is a vivid example from the Old Testament:

> Let the godly exult in glory;
> let them sing for joy on their beds.

> Let the high praises of God be in their throats
> and two-edged swords in their hands,
> to execute vengeance on the nations
> and punishments on the peoples,
> to bind their kings with chains
> and their nobles with fetters of iron,
> to execute on them the judgment written!
> This is honor for all his godly ones.
> Praise the LORD!—Psalm 149:5-9 ESV

God's people who have been discreetly hidden will suddenly emerge as a ruling force in the earth, in part through their stewardship of the language of the Spirit, or tongues. Continuing with Tim Sheet's prophecy:

> "For the strongholds of hell will be broken by this deployment and the iniquitous roots will wither under superior power, authority, and administered justice. The withering of hell's kingdom will begin to be seen in indisputable ways, for the heirs of kingdom authority are being seated in their regional spheres of influence. And their angels are aligning with the assigning in their regional roles. You will now see a clear merger. Heaven and earth will merge in unified oneness of purpose to escalate the King's victory, to expand His kingdom throughout the earth and to implement His kingdom government. The merger of earth realm and spirit realm will surge in this new Pentecost era."[12]

The merger of earth realm and spirit realm is for the purpose of revealing God to more and more people so that they might choose Him. This new Pentecost era is increasing its operating speed and will culminate in a final "mega Pentecost" of mass conversions, a worldwide harvest of humanity. Revelation of God's word, strategies, and blessings will be released to facilitate this. God will deploy His ecclesia to disciple nations. The glory of God will be tangible on earth. Angel armies are being deployed with us, to partner with us, to establish God's kingdom government. The angel armies will make the difference, giving God's people the edge they need to succeed. Just as early Christians received a downpour of Holy Spirit power and supernatural gifts and from that day onward "turned the world upside down," boldly performing signs, wonders, and miracles that resulted in an explosive number of conversions until the third century of the Common Era, so too, this impending mega Pentecost will do the same (Acts 17:6). The church or body of Christ and the fivefold ministry that were born two thousand years ago will once again "turn the world upside down". This outpouring will descend on thousands of churches that are poised to receive it.

Tim Sheets continues:

> "A new apostolic age fired by new Pentecost is now at hand," says the Lord. "The second apostolic age will now rise, confirmed by My power, My miracles, My wonders, yes, miracle after miracle after miracle. Supernatural realms are opening, miraculous portals of glory are opening, and a glorious church will rise from the ashes of warfare. The forever loser will not prevail.
>
> I am building relentless faith in my radical remnant. Tenacious faith will now rise to face entrenched enemies of darkness. My remnant will run; they will pursue; they will stand, displaying a boldness that begins to startle the world. Radical remnant warriors arising to their place in the gaps. Radical warriors are accepting my challenging call. Yes, smaller in number, but all I need. Yes, unintimidated, fierce special forces warriors of My kingdom are coming to their posts, trained for such a time as this. Hell has never seen the like, the relentless ones: with the heart of the lion, the eyes of the tiger, carriers of the yoke-destroying anointing of the lion King himself, carriers of the anointing to prevail.
>
> Aggression in my remnant will now be seen demanding harvest and demanding restoration of lost harvest. Barren fields will be cleared and plowed for supernatural harvest on earth as in heaven. [This] includes fruit, fruitfulness, and copious bountiful fruit, plenteous crops in multiple yields, for the harvest of heaven's kingdom is not yearly: it is monthly. My trees produce everything monthly. My seeds produce every month. My crops produce every month. My yields cycle into supernatural multiplication times on earth as

in heaven. Multiple harvests will come in one season as I anoint for increase. Plowmen will overtake the reapers. Harvests will synergize, multiply and accelerate. Pull the combines behind the plows. Pull the fruit wagons behind the seed planters. Sink the plows. Sink the seeds, and get in harvest mode."[13]

THE OVERFLOW

"The Overflow" (June 6, 2020), Cassandra Donnelly.[14]

This mixed media painting entitled "The Overflow" was painted in alcohol inks by art therapist and prophetic artist Cassandra Donnelly after she received a vision-dream in a half-sleeping, half-waking state on June 5, 2020. Cassandra painted the painting in a quick turnaround time, which was new and unusual for her and which confirmed that she has entered into a "new Pentecost era" and that an angel has been assigned to her to remove hindrances and help her execute the visions God gives her. Cassandra had not heard of Tim Sheets' prophecy, yet she is one of many who are receiving the same or a similar message from heaven, hers through the visual language of dreams/visions, which she translates into paintings and prophecy. A quick glance at the profusion of gemstone colored droplets in the painting reveals the following prominent features: a tipped and overturned bucket in heaven pouring water into eight buckets on earth and the torn open text of what Peter preached on Pentecost when the disciples received the power of the Spirit and the gift of tongues:[15]

> In the last days, God says, I will pour out my Spirit on all people. Your sons and daughters will prophesy. Your young men will see visions. Your old men will dream dreams.—Acts 2:17 NIV; Joel 2:28

Cassandra presented the painting at a tongues activation workshop where she spoke of a "new beginning" through Pentecost, echoing Sheet's prophecy about "a new Pentecost". She spoke of the release of an angel army, echoing Sheet's prophecy about the mobilization of "millions of angels" and "divisions of angel armies". She spoke of divine grant funding and furnishing of resources for divine assignments, echoing Sheet's prophecy about plows, seeds, combines, and fruit wagons resulting in "fruit, fruitfulness, copious bountiful fruit, plenteous crops in multiple yields". She spoke of divine placement, echoing Sheet's prophecy about "trained warriors coming to their posts". She spoke of the church taking charge, echoing Sheet's prophecy about the activation of God's "kingdom ecclesia" or governing council of believers on earth. She spoke of God's people "calling the shots, not the devil," echoing Sheet's prophecy that "the forever loser will not prevail" and of "the withering of hell's kingdom". She spoke of the church releasing power and glory, echoing Sheet's prophecy about "a glorious church" operating in God's "power, miracles, and wonders":

"God has released His angel army to fight our battles for us. He's bringing a new beginning to us despite all the chaos and things in disarray right now. We're getting ready to shift into a new beginning where the church takes over, where the church is releasing its power and its glory through the Pentecost. God's bringing the Pentecost down now for us. He's equipping us. He's giving us resources. He's putting us in our positions. And when we each do our jobs, the church is going to be calling the shots, not the devil."[16]

The central image of a gushing downpour of water in "The Overflow" aptly depicts what Sheets called "perpetual replenishings of outpourings" that define the new Pentecost era we are now entering.

I share Cassandra's prophecy not to reinforce Tim Sheets' prophecy, for his prophecy needs no reinforcement. Nor do I share her prophecy to confirm it through a recognized apostle of the church, for Cassandra has the same Holy Spirit that he has. I share her prophecy because Cassandra lives where most of us live, where most ardent believers are: contending against afflictions and hardships, oppression and hindrances, and struggling to get their lives in kingdom order to move into "the upward call of God". As a survivor of Satanic ritual abuse and systematic sexual abuse involving "sadism, bondage, and exposure to snuff films" most of her childhood, Cassandra has a different kind of clout in the kingdom. She is the glorious church that is arising "from the ashes of warfare," in her case, complex PTSD. The Lord has been progressively healing and delivering her since 1995. Some of the deeper meaning of the painting is embedded in the backstory. But first, let's examine the painting itself, which has both personal and corporate meaning (find yourself in the story).[17]

On June 5, 2020, in the 50th year of her existence on earth, Cassandra saw heaven open up and an overflow of water pouring out of heaven descending into eight buckets.[18] These numbers are spiritually significant. In Biblical numerology, the number five (June 5) represents the five fingers or hand or power of God operating through the grace gifts of the Holy Spirit in the life of a believer.[19] Cassandra experienced an unprecedented ease and celerity in translating the vision into a prophetic painting and scripture verses. Usually she struggles with execution. But the smooth speed of delivery this time indicates an increase in supernatural power for her call as a prophetic artist; it indicates that the hand of God is stronger in her life. She also painted in a way that was not her customary way of working.

Usually she receives visions and messages while painting, not *before* painting, but on this occasion she received the vision and message *before* painting. This indicates an expansion of her capacity to receive and to convey in new and different ways than before. Again, this indicates that the hand of God is stronger in her life.[20]

The number eight (8 buckets) symbolizes "new beginnings, regeneration, resurrection, and new order".[21] This theme is reinforced by the timing of the vision in Cassandra's 50th year. The number 50 in the Old Testament represents the Jubilee year, a year that occurred once every fifty years or approximately once in a person's lifetime (Lev 25:8, 10). This was a year of radical restoration, debt cancellation, and slave emancipation (see Lev 25 and 27). Any Israelite who had sold his land due to hardship or misfortune or for any other reason recovered his land in the year of Jubilee and returned to his inheritance from his fathers. Any Israelite who had sold himself into servitude due to hardship or misfortune or for any other reason was set free in the year of Jubilee. So Jubilee or the number 50 signifies redemption, returning to one's God given inheritance and ultimately a state of liberty and well-being in every dimension of life (shalom).

This theme of restoration after ruin, recovery after loss, and reinstatement after displacement is illustrated in "The Overflow" by the golden liquid that is cascading down from heaven, mingling with the water, and gushing into eight buckets. The Lord showed Cassandra that the golden liquid or liquid gold represents healing and deliverance that He is pouring out. He also reminded her of a ceramic repair technique called kintsugi, or golden joinery, also known as kinsukuroi, or golden repair. Kintsugi is the Japanese art of repairing broken pottery by "pouring liquid gold"—lacquer mixed with gold powder—into the fractures between pottery fragments to seal them together with golden seams or veins.[22] The Japanese, who advocate "wabi-sabi" or "embracing the flawed or imperfect," view golden repair as enhancing the beauty and value of an object and extending its useful life. Philosophically, the Japanese treat "breakage and repair as part of the history of the object rather than something to disguise". To the Japanese, breakage does not warrant terminating the service of an object and disposing of it; it warrants golden repair. Some interpret golden repair as an expression of the Buddhist ideal of non-attachment and acceptance of change in a transient world.[23]

A higher view, however, is the celebration of restoration through God's redemptive power at work in our lives. God does not discard us when we are damaged or broken. He does not terminate our service. He does not consider our useful life over. On the contrary,

He performs something better than a golden repair; He performs a heavenly version of a golden repair, and we emerge stronger, more beautiful, and more aesthetically interesting (thought provoking!) than we ever were before. Most of us do not want to accentuate our defects or draw attention to our past shattering, but God takes pride in our redemption, and we should, too. We should show it off. Jesus retained the nail piercings in His hands and the spear piercing in His side and showed them to His disciples even though the scars could have been erased through the resurrection power that raised Him from the dead (see Jn 20:24-29). His salvaging of our lives like broken pieces of pottery is our testimony of salvation, and our testimony is the "spirit of prophecy": "The testimony of Jesus is the spirit of prophecy" (Rev 19:10).

The backstory of "The Overflow" painting makes it even more meaningful. Eight years prior (remember 8 buckets or new beginnings!), the Lord had spoken the word "restoration" to Cassandra, and He confirmed His promise of restoration to her through a sign and a wonder. She was walking outside when hurricane Sandy hit Tidewater, Virginia, and she happened to notice money on the ground. She looked more closely and saw that it was a tiny, tattered piece of a $50 bill (remember Jubilee or radical restoration!). She wondered why there was only a fragment: "Who rips up a fifty dollar bill?!" she thought. Because the wind was so blustery, she figured she would not find the rest of it, but she looked on the ground again and found another piece, and then she looked again and found another piece, and then she walked farther and found another piece, and so on. Altogether she found about 10 different pieces of the $50 bill—all in the midst of a hurricane! When she got home, she taped them together and wondered if she could use the $50 bill, if it had retained its value. So she went to her favorite art supply store, Michael's, and bought art supplies with the $50 bill. The whole time the Lord was confirming the message of restoration to her. That year God's restoration began in her life.[24] Even so, this outpouring and overflow of the new Pentecost era will facilitate radical restoration. God's golden repair or redemptive plan will become evident in the lives of individuals, this nation, and other nations.

Another backstory to the painting is a prophetic dream Cassandra had the year prior, in November of 2019. In the dream, her house was airlifted and spun in a tornado, which was both exhilarating and petrifying. She thought she would surely die, but her house was gently lowered to the ground in a different place and at a different angle, and she sensed that the world had "shifted". When she emerged, she saw there was crisis and widespread chaos. But God's people banded together to resolve the crisis. On the basis of this tornado dream, hurricane Sandy and the tattered $50 bill, and the "storm" of current events in 2020, Cassandra felt that the outpouring and overflow and redemptive golden repairs would be juxtaposed against a backdrop of worldly drama, catastrophe, and pandemonium. Certainly, the non-stop procession of evil in the U.S. since the turn of 2020 confirms the "crisis and chaos" portion of the tornado dream:[25] COVID-19 and the lockdown, the murder of George Floyd, violent demonstrations, and Luciferian marches on the summer solstice (June 21, 2020) in capitol cities of some states to release "chaos, confusion, conflict, rage, hatred, revenge, anarchy" and to usher in a "One World Government".[26] But God is turning the tables on the enemy; He is preparing a table for us in the presence of our enemies, and our cups will overflow (Est 9:1; Ps 23:5).

Along with the painting, Cassandra received several scriptures reinforcing the theme of "The Overflow". In addition to Acts 2:17—"I will pour out my Spirit"—which text is incorporated into the imagery of the painting, she received another complementary verse assuring an outpouring of God's Spirit:[27]

> For I will pour water on the thirsty land,
> and streams on the dry ground;
> I will pour my Spirit on your offspring,
> and my blessing on your descendants.—Isaiah 44:3 NIV

She also received a passage describing the simultaneous intensification of light and darkness and assurance that people will be attracted to the Lord through the glory light on His people:[28]

> Arise, shine, for your light has come,
> and the glory of the LORD rises upon you.
> See, darkness covers the earth,
> and thick darkness is over the peoples,
> but the LORD rises upon you,
> and his glory appears over you.
> Nations will come to your light,
> and kings to the brightness of your dawn.—Isaiah 60:1-3 NIV

Lastly, she received assurance that the Kinsman-Redeemer will rest upon those who repent of their rebellion, and these repentant ones will speak prophetically on His behalf:[29]

> "He will come to Zion as a Kinsman-Redeemer
> to those of Jacob's tribes who repent of their rebellion," says Yahweh.
>
> And this is my covenant promise with them," says Lord Yahweh.
> "From now on, my Holy Spirit will rest on them
> and not depart from them,
> and my prophetic words will fill their mouths
> and will not depart from them, nor from their children,
> nor from their descendants, from now on and forever,"
> says the Lord Yahweh.—Isaiah 59:20-21 TPT

SPEAKING IN TONGUES TESTIMONY

HOW I GOT THE GIFT OF TONGUES

As a newbie Christian, I was still faltering in my abstention from pot, but otherwise had just defected from eastern mysticism, the occult, recreational drug use, and sexual immorality. I wanted the gift of tongues badly. I prized it without knowing why. Beyond beautiful and fascinating, beyond the mystique of an exotic language that was compelling and commanding, a language that was made for love and war, I sensed that tongues was a gate to greater freedom and power. Judging by some of my behaviors at the time—crawling on all fours and slapping my face hard to the point of stinging—I was still in need of major deliverance, which I dutifully tried to obtain by listening to Derek Prince audio teachings and by completing self-deliverance worksheets like those of Neil Anderson. I did my part. I was reading the Bible prodigiously, worshiping at a Vineyard church in California, and praying whenever and wherever.

One day as I was unwinding from my university studies with red wine and feeling the swirl (uh oh!), I got my first sample of tongues, a different kind of wine tasting. I spoke a single sentence that sounded like this:

> "Ooorrr rahbah sheena sah hamba alah malah!"

I waited for more, but none came. Acutely aware of the irony of the moment, I mulled over the verse:

> And do not be drunk with wine, in which is dissipation, for that is debauchery, but rather be filled with the Holy Spirit.—Ephesians 5:17 NKJV, AMP

God seemed to be overlooking my inebriation and introducing another Comforter to me:

> The Father will give you another Comforter, that He may remain with you forever."—John 14:16 AMPC

Later I pondered the incongruity. Why did God do this? Why did He give me a sip of the good wine while I was nursing the inferior? Was He slack in His standards, was He being permissive with me? Or did I need grace to come to the same conclusion as the Shulamite:

> For your love is better than wine.—Song of Solomon 1:2

When I was about a year old in Christ, I attended a spiritual warfare conference in San Jose, California, to hear frontiersmen in the faith like John Dawson, Cindy Jacobs, and Ed Silvoso share about racial reconciliation, spiritual mapping, and city revival. John Dawson had settled his white family in an African-American ghetto in Los Angeles before the Rodney King riots in 1992; he discussed the divine deposits in different minorities and got everybody admiring and celebrating the manifold wisdom of God in the races. Cindy Jacobs presented a slide show of public art and architecture and demonstrated how to interpret occult symbolism and identify spirit powers holding people hostage in a locality and how to use that information to pray informed prayers. Ed Silvoso described a revival in a South American city that was preceded by fasting, repentance, and prayer and followed by a series of outreaches that canvassed a community and ministered to the felt needs and desires of individuals: many Christians prayed through to breakthrough on behalf of neighbors.

I was quieted by their field work. How did they get to be so sure and so bold in their assignments? Where did they get such revelation and strategy? How did they muster the motivation to sacrifice so much? Why did they have such largesse for people who are not their people? I knew the Holy Spirit was behind their spiritual success, but what did they do to develop a kingdom heart and mind and hands? What did they do to get all that special training and promotion? Did they have some secret beyond mere Bible study and prayer?

During one of the sessions, an altar call was given to bestow the gift of tongues. I dashed to the front. A man intercepted me and directed me to sit on the front pew beside him so that he could lay out the doctrinal basis for the gift. (I had no need of doctrine, for I had studied Corinthians and become a Corinthian in my own mind!) Just as he opened the Bible and his mouth, a woman pounced between us, grabbed my hand, jerked me into a standing position and bellowed:

"Receive the Holy Spirit!"

She blew a big blast of her breath forcefully into my face, and I keeled over like a giant tree trunk—TIMBER!—and hit the ground hard—BAM!—but was not injured. (I learned later that the woman was the man's wife!)

What happened next is difficult to describe. I found myself wallowing on the ground, laughing hysterically, sobbing convulsively, and floating in some kind of metaphysical medium: call it the womb of God. I was experiencing bi-locality of being in two places at once, both in my body lost in a cascade of emotions, endlessly tickled and panged in my soul, yet also outside my body suspended in a comforting fluid. I observed myself going through these antics, not in a detached way, but in a compassionate way; I observed myself not as an object from a remote distance, but nearby as a benevolent Presence. This out-of-body experience was different from those I had had in my B.C. days through psychedelics—LSD and psilocybin—and through eastern mystical practices like mantra chanting and non-dual meditation. Those out-of-body experiences were strangely detached and austere and alienating: I observed myself from some odd perspective, like the upper corner of a room; my body was a mere object; I myself, a stranger. The feeling was garish and queazy like a pink and green poster of a seedy Parisian nightclub. But this was different. It was good. The overall feeling was of being inside a spiritual womb and of being softly tumbled and lapped inside that womb. I became diffused and rarified and expanded beyond the borders of my skin; I seemed to be occupying a larger space around myself. What I now realize about this experience of bi-locality is that my spirit was united with the Holy Spirit. In all likelihood, I was experiencing the ubiquitous, gentle, nurturing, and brooding nature of the Holy Spirit.

While this was happening, one language after another rolled out of my mouth, clear and vigorous and unique: one sounded Middle Eastern, another Native American, another French, another African, another Asian, another Celtic, and so on. How many languages I spoke and how long this went on, the wallowing and laughing and sobbing and vocalizing, I don't know. The whole thing was surreal, a tangible dream. Since then, I have had many spiritual experiences, including radical deliverances involving dramatic demonic manifestations, but nothing has ever surpassed this experience in grandeur and splendor. This is what Jesus described as the living water of the Spirit:

> On the last day, that great day of the feast, Jesus stood and cried out, saying, "If anyone thirsts, let him come to Me and drink. He who believes in Me, as the Scripture has said, out of his heart will flow rivers of living water." But this He spoke concerning the Spirit, whom those believing in Him would receive; for the Holy Spirit was not yet given, because Jesus was not yet glorified.—John 7:37-39

This is mind boggling. It's marvelous enough that the Spirit who resurrected Jesus out of hell and putrefaction would be given to us through the new birth; that God's own nature would be deposited inside our nature when we say yes to God; that God would make His home in us and room with us and keep us company (we can be such bad company!); and that we would have God as a constant source within us (God at our disposal?!). But this is the kicker! that we would become outlets for His Spirit, like a fountain, to others.

Jesus said that the baptism in the Spirit empowers us to evangelize. The Greek word for baptize refers to a capsized vessel fully submerged in water; it implies that a person is overwhelmed and fully immersed in the Spirit:[1]

> And being assembled together with them, He commanded them not to depart from Jerusalem, but to wait for the Promise of the Father, "which," He said, "you have heard from Me; for John truly baptized with water, but you shall be baptized with the Holy Spirit not many days from now. [And] you shall receive power when the Holy Spirit has come upon you; and you shall be witnesses to Me in Jerusalem, and in all Judea and Samaria, and to the end of the earth".—Acts 1:4-5, 8

By ordering His disciples to be capsized in the Spirit before going anywhere, Jesus implied that we cannot evangelize properly without this submersion experience. That's why He said wait: don't leave home without the Spirit; don't try to evangelize the nations apart from the Spirit's power.

For me, the baptism in the Spirit with the manifestation of tongues was a landmark experience. It sustained me through many lackluster years when nothing special was happening and God seemed scarce. Apart from the crazy love of righteousness and turmoil over sin that are indelible marks of the new birth, there were many times when I would have been tempted to doubt or renege my faith because of the torturous daily grind of self denial, the low returns for relentless sacrifice, and the war of attrition on dreams. But the gift of tongues has been a perennial reminder of the supernatural nature of the faith and incontrovertible proof that the faith is not a figment of my imagination. Tongues are a distinguishing mark of God on a believer.

I find that tongues are a very practical and versatile gift, one that comes in handy in a blasé or violent mood, in a routine or in an emergency. Tongues are a gift that can make you adaptable when you're not and resilient when you're not. Tongues function when you don't have all of the facts or are misinformed or downright deceived, when you have bog brain or a firestorm in your head, when the trail or trial is tricky and the problem is gargantuan or byzantine, when you have compassion fatigue and battle fatigue, when your virtues vacate and you want to cuss a blue streak or spray bullets, when you feel hopeless, jaded or cynical, when witchcraft is afoot, and when a shortcut to heaven looks like the Premiere Plan. As long as your mouth works, tongues work; nothing else about you has to work, and that's a huge relief. Actually, you don't even need your mouth for tongues; you can talk in tongues in your mind the same way that you can think in English. You can lie down and cover your head with a towel and silently rehearse tongues.

My baptism in the Spirit was sensational, to say the least. In comparing notes with other Christians over the years, I have met only two others who had a radical power encounter like mine. One woman was catapulted backward through the air, and the other spoke in tongues for four days straight and could not speak in English at all. Yet most Christians have a much more subdued, even mundane initiation into the gift. (I would like to see that change!) So to balance the scales, let me share how my friend Sveta Spear got the gift. But first, her conversion story…

MY RUSSIAN FRIEND SVETA: HOW SHE GOT THE GIFT OF TONGUES

My friend Sveta grew up in communist, atheist Russia. Sveta considered Christianity a preposterous myth and Christian apologetics as pathetically illogical. Her conversion story is eerie, the stuff of a psychological thriller with a redemptive twist (I tell only a fraction of it here). Her tongues testimony is almost anti-climactic. But her story is an important counterpoint to my story. Most people do not get tongues as easily and dramatically and supernaturally as I did. Most people get tongues by puzzling over the gift and practicing it to the point of exasperation and wondering whether it is their own zany forgery. Sveta never doubted the source, but divine utterances only emerged from her mouth after she had exhausted her own efforts. Then the gift of tongues accrued gradually through an incremental process of language building.

Around the time the Berlin wall fell and the iron curtain tore, Sveta began having misgivings about certain Pagan practices and superstitions that were the cultural norm in Russia and about a newly introduced parlor game of contacting spirits through a homemade Ouija Board (also known as the spirit board or talking board). One night Sveta had a nightmare in which she and a number of guests were crowded around a table in her home playing the Ouija Board. During one of the board manipulations, an ominous voice announced, "I am here!" and suddenly all of her guests disappeared. The room was plunged into darkness. The temperature dropped to icy cold. A violent wind blew the curtains horizontally into the house. The house quaked and rattled with tremors, and Sveta dove under the table in dread. The disembodied voice said, "I am your master!" Intuitively Sveta knew the voice was the Devil and that he had come to claim her soul. But Jesus came to her rescue and said, "I will come anytime you call my name. But do not do this again." When Sveta awoke, she realized that the source of all the occult parlor games she had routinely played for entertainment was sinister, and she pledged to never again play the Ouija Board or consult Tarot cards or otherwise engage in the occult. After the scare of that nightmare, Sveta started seeking God, but she was still mixed-up.

Many ministries flooded into Eastern Europe and Russia, some legitimate, some not. Among the legitimate ones, Billy Graham and Gideon's Society partnered in a crusade to bring the gospel as far north as the Arctic Circle where Sveta was living. Many locals attended the crusade, not because they were remotely interested in Jesus but because they wanted the freebies that the Americans would hand out. Sveta watched the Jesus film with a certain skepticism and revulsion and was weirded-out by a scene featuring the Gadarene demoniac buck naked (she may have had a demonic hallucination, for the Graham ministry is too reputable to show an actor fully nude, and the Jesus film is certainly not rated R!). When the altar call was given for salvation and stuff, Sveta refused to go forward on principle because she considered it demeaning to choose God on the basis of material goods.

Sveta's friend did go forward, and she returned with a New Testament in hand and offered it to Sveta because she had already received one at a previous crusade. Sveta took the book with the objective to learn more about God. She began to incorporate Bible reading into her elaborate ritual of preparing for bed at night, faintly hoping that it might help her insomnia, either by boring her into a deep slumber or as a potential antidote to the night terrors she was having. Until then, she had been delving into eastern mysticism and had fasted and meditated herself into an unstable state of angst and insomnia. Every time she was on the brink of sleep, an overwhelming oppression and dread seized her. Her health had become dangerously precarious. She feared she was going insane. To her great surprise and relief, the New Testament elevated her and gave her a peace that enabled her to sleep unmolested for two hour blocks of time, which was her rope back to recovery. The strange thing, however, was that she could not understand a word of what she read—the letters were squirming hieroglyphics; the meaning was cryptic—even though she could comprehend any other text in English. (After her conversion, she realized this mental block was demonic.)

Some time later, Sveta had another nightmare. She found herself dangling over an abyss, hanging on by a toehold to the edge of a precipice. Below her was a long fall into hell. She woke up terrorized and heard Jesus say, "Choose". Immediately Sveta understood the alternative and decided to follow Jesus. After this nightmare, she stopped investigating other religious alternatives—especially eastern mysticism—and concentrated on Christianity alone. She sampled the Russian Orthodox church where a minister offered to sprinkle her with holy water, but the rituals of the Orthodox church could not satisfy her spiritual longing. Eventually she found a charismatic church and was introduced to a more authentic and vibrant form of Christianity.

After Sveta accepted Christ, she needed a rocket booster to live in a country where almost everybody is a functional alcoholic, friends and relatives prove untrustworthy, and every detail of your life is government dictated, controlled, and mismanaged: from the subject you are permitted to study at the university (if any), to the entertainment you get at the Cultural Palace, to the apartment you are assigned, to the inadequate and unappealing rationed goods you are allotted that you wait for hours in long lines to buy—your black or white bread and your bulky drab dresses (sandals galore in Siberia, but never enough coats…).

The Lord told Sveta that her future was in the English language, so she did everything in her power to study, practice, and apply English. Eventually Sveta gained enough proficiency to translate for American missionaries. One of those missionaries offered to pray for her to receive the gift of tongues. There was one slight but monumental barrier, and that was mistrust. Receiving the gift required Sveta to surrender a good measure of control, but she had never voluntarily relinquished control for anything or anybody in her life, and she was not about to start now (ironic, given her dedication to Christ). The missionary got so frustrated with her stonewalling that he shouted at her, "You will NEVER EVER EVER get the gift of tongues!" But flat denial was exactly what steely Sveta needed to hear. She thought to herself, "Oh yes I will!"

After she and the missionary parted company in a huff (they got engaged later), she went home and plunked herself down on the couch and said to the Lord, "I am not getting up off of this couch until You give me the gift of tongues!" With that ultimatum, she prayed half the night in her native language of Russian for something to happen, and nothing happened. Exhausted, she fell asleep. While in a deep sleep, the Holy Spirit woke her and impelled her to utter a sound while she was still half asleep and her mind was logged off. She felt an upward-bound pressure in her throat and sensed that tongues were emerging. The sound "k" bubbled up. She knew that the sound did not come from a decision of her will and her own conscious effort to form it but from another source of power within her. Sveta was thrilled beyond measure and spent the rest of the night yielding her mouth to that one sound. All she had to do was open her mouth and the "k" sound would manifest. She was excited by her newfound trust and surrender and the gentleness of her "coach" to help her learn to speak as a child.

The next night Sveta found herself uttering a different sound all night long, the consonant "s". After that, progress came faster, but a couple weeks elapsed before she and the Holy Spirit had eked out all the basic sound units—vowel sounds and consonant sounds—that are the building blocks of words. These sound units are known as phonemes: they are what children parse when they are learning to read simple sentences like "Run Rover, run!":

> Rrrr—uuu—nnn
> RRRR—oooh—vvvv—ehhh—rrrr,
> rrrr—uuu—nnn!

After rehearsing these basic sound units effortlessly through the power source of the Holy Spirit inside her, Sveta found herself cobbling together phonemes into syllables, syllables into words, words into phrases, phrases into simple sentences, and then she was off and running in the Spirit, gargling and gurgling under living water! Soon she spontaneously sang in tongues liberating tunes.

Sveta got her breakthrough when she learned how to yield control of her mouth, first in a half-sleeping semi-conscious state, then in a fully conscious waking state. Now Sveta is comfortable with the gift and adept at it; it feels natural to her. In Russia, she spoke in tongues, sang in tongues, and warred in tongues together with other Christians in great assemblies. When she moved to the United States, she was perplexed that Christians did not speak and sing in tongues together more often, much less in great assemblies (as they once did at Maria Woodworth-Etter healing revival meetings). But Sveta understands the value of the gift and speaks in the Spirit whenever she can: while doing chores, running errands, and so forth. She also rallies with friends who understand the significance of the gift.

For Sveta, tongues have been a gateway to revelation and other dimensions of the Holy Spirit's ministry, especially through music. Sveta wanted to learn how to play the piano, but she could not afford music lessons and no musician was willing to tutor her. So she asked the Holy Spirit to tutor her, and in one month she supernaturally acquired several musical skills: the skill of playing the keyboard, the skill of reading and notating chord progressions, and the skill of taking divine music dictation and recreating on the keyboard heavenly melodies of angelic choirs she sometimes hears in the middle of the night. Sveta also receives lyrics by inspiration and later discovers how perfectly they fit together with heavenly melodies she hears on separate occasions.

The reader may be interested to know that Sveta had learned to play the accordion in Russia, but the accordion is a very different instrument from the piano. She also had learned to read the classical music notation system in Russia, but the American chord notation system is quite different. Classical music is represented by notes on a music staff, whereas guitar chords are represented by letters of the alphabet. Because there are thousands of chords and variations on chords, learning the American chord system felt to her "like learning Chinese". But she learned the foreign notation system and how to play a new instrument in one month of Holy Spirit tutorials facilitated by tongues.

Sveta appears to be a budding impresario, and it all began with tongues. Just so, the Holy Spirit can train us to do things beyond our imagination, capability, opportunity, and budget. So let's begin!

Sveta Spear at the keyboard (2019).[2]

SPEAKING IN TONGUES: IMPARTATION AND ACTIVATION

This chapter is organized into two main sections: impartation and activation. Impartation is about receiving or giving the gift of tongues, including multiple, diverse tongues. Activation is about stewarding and developing the gift in different ways on your own or with others. The impartation section explains how a person can receive the gift of tongues directly from God without a human intermediary. It also explains how tongues speakers can impart the gift to others through immersion prayer, demonstration, and interactive exercises using baby babble and scat as verbal jump starters for actual tongues. The individual activation section offers practical applications for everyday use, a time length challenge, and a Book of Life incentive, while the group activation section offers prayer topics for corporate intercession.

For an introductory teaching video on the baptism in the Spirit and the primary functions of tongues as prayer, prophecy, and spiritual warfare, please see, "Pentecost: the Gift of Tongues for Power Evangelism, Prayer, Prophecy and Spiritual Warfare," posted May 23, 2021, on The River Room YouTube channel.[1]

RECEIVE THE GIFT OF TONGUES BY YOURSELF

A good way to prepare yourself to receive the baptism in the Holy Spirit and the gift of tongues is by reading scriptures to boost your faith about God's good intentions for you. Tongues are a gift from the heavenly Father that He promised to give you:

> Every good gift and every perfect gift is from above, and comes down from the Father of lights with whom there is no variation or shadow of turning.
> —James 1:17

> "Behold, I [Jesus] send the Promise of My Father upon you; but tarry [wait] until you are endued [endowed] with power from on high."
> —John 24:49 (abridged; interpolations mine)

> Jesus commanded them [the disciples] to wait for the Promise of the Father, "which," He said, "you have heard from Me; for John truly baptized with water, but you shall be baptized with the Holy Spirit not many days from now."
> —Acts 1:4-5 (abridged)

The gift of tongues is an aspect of God's kingdom or the King's domain. Our heavenly Father takes pleasure in giving you this instrument of dominion so that you can extend His kingdom on earth and especially so that you can be a more effective witness for Christ to others:

> "Do not fear, little flock, for it is your Father's good pleasure to give you the kingdom."—Luke 12:32

> "But you shall receive power when the Holy Spirit has come upon you; and you shall be witnesses to Me to the end of the earth."—Acts 1:8 (abridged)

The gift of tongues is yours for the asking. When you ask for the gift of tongues, God will give it to you, for He is a good Father who loves to give more of His Holy Spirit. When you ask for the gift, you will not get a "serpent" or "scorpion" (symbols for demonic agents); you will not get a stealth bomb, a counterfeit, a booby prize, or nothing. God will not give you anything contrary to His own nature, for you are asking HIM for the gift.

> "So I say to you, ask, and it will be given to you; seek, and you will find; knock, and it will be opened to you. For everyone who asks receives, and he who seeks finds, and to him who knocks it will be opened. If a son asks for bread from any father among you, will he give him a stone? Or if he asks for a fish, will he give him a serpent instead of a fish? Or if he asks for an egg, will he offer him a scorpion? If you then, being evil, know how to give good gifts to your children, how much more will your heavenly Father give [good things and] the Holy Spirit to those who ask Him!"—Luke 11:9-13 and Matthew 7:7-11 combined

The gift of tongues is often imparted through human contact, particularly the laying on of hands, as Paul indicated:

> I long to see you so that I may impart to you some spiritual gift to make you strong.—Romans 1:11

> For this reason I remind you to fan into flame the gift of God, which is in you through the laying on of hands.—2 Timothy 1:6 NIV

> Do not neglect your gift, which was given to you through prophecy when the body of elders laid their hands on you.—1 Timothy 4:14 NIV

Nevertheless, the disciples received the gift of tongues directly from God apart from any human intermediary (see Acts 2). You can receive directly from God without anyone ministering to you:

> No more shall every man teach his neighbor, and every man his brother, saying, "Know the LORD," for they all shall know Me, from the least of them to the greatest of them.—Jeremiah 31:34

As a believer in Christ, you already have the best teacher in the whole wide world: the Holy Spirit. He will teach you whatever you need to know about tongues as you inquire of Him:

> But the Helper (Comforter, Advocate, Intercessor—Counselor, Strengthener, Standby), the Holy Spirit, whom the Father will send in My name [in My place, to represent Me and act on My behalf], He will teach you all things.—John 14:26 AMP

As a follower of Christ, you can minister to yourself in the absence of another Christian to minister to you, for you also are called to be a priest; the priesthood is by appointment from God, not man, and you are appointed:

> But you are a chosen generation, a royal priesthood, a holy nation, His own special people that you may proclaim the praises of Him who called you out of darkness into His marvelous light.—1 Peter 2:9 (abridged)

Decide in your heart to receive what Jesus died to give you:

> When He ascended on high, He led captivity captive, and gave gifts to men.—Ephesians 4:8

Insist upon the best for yourself:

> The kingdom of heaven suffers violence, and the violent take it by force.—Matthew 11:12

Set your hope on Him, put your trust and confidence in Him:

> Whoever believes on Him will not be put to shame.
> —Romans 9:33; 10:11

Release yourself from any performance anxiety or pressure; be playful and child-like about this impartation; and have fun:

> Jesus called a little child to Him, set him in the midst of them, and said, "Assuredly, I say to you, unless you are converted and become as little children, you will by no means enter the kingdom of heaven. Therefore whoever humbles himself as this little child is the greatest in the kingdom of heaven."
> —Matthew 18:2-4

PRAYER FOR THE GIFT OF TONGUES

Say your own prayer out loud or this one:

> Dear heavenly Father, I earnestly desire the gift of tongues! I thank You for Jesus who made the gift of tongues available to all believers after His ascension. I thank You that this gift of divine communication is an heirloom from my Bridegroom that He has held in reserve for me. I recognize it as a special, supernatural work that Jesus left for me to do.
>
> I ask You now to pour out Your Holy Spirit upon me in a great cascade and to baptize me and submerge me under the power of Your Spirit so that I may experience Your liquid love and receive Your power to be an effective witness of Your truth, power, and love to others. Please accept my humble offerings of sounds and use them to release articulate languages of Your choosing. I ask for a variety of tongues! Thank You for using me as Your spokesperson and Your mouthpiece!

SENSATIONS AND FEELINGS YOU MIGHT HAVE

It's probably best not to rely on sensations and feelings as a guide to receive the gift of tongues because all aspects of the Christian faith are appropriated by faith. Nevertheless, Jesus did say that "rivers of living water" would flow "out of your belly"; "out of your gut"; "out of your side"; "out of your heart"; "from your innermost being"; "from deep inside you" (Jn 7:38 NKJV, KJV, EXB, GNT, ESV, AMP, CEV). So you might feel a flowing sensation or current or an upward bound movement or spring issuing from the abdominal region, cuing you that tongues are emerging and that you need to yield and cooperate.

Marcus Rogers offers a helpful pointer about receiving. He notes that many Christians mistakenly assume that the baptism in the Holy Spirit is a totally involuntary experience that requires no motor control on their part. It was for me, but for most people it is not. Most people receive it as a voluntary experience that requires some effort on their part to vocalize, to make sounds, to utter words. The tongue does not just "jump around inside your mouth out of control". Instead, you might feel "an unction to utter words"; you might feel "a stirring in your belly" rising toward your chest and throat, but you will have to "surrender your tongue" and "speak those words in faith". And you may have to dismiss negative internal talk that belittles, ridicules, criticizes or otherwise negates your efforts or invalidates the sounds that are emerging. Such talk could come from your mind or the enemy of your soul. Don't "overthink it"; just go with the flow of the Holy Spirit.[2] If you don't feel an internal spring, don't worry. Just as drawing water from an underground source sometimes requires vigorous pumping, you might have to put forth some effort to "prime the pump" before you get anything. That is what the vocalization exercises are for.

PRACTICE EXERCISES TO RECEIVE THE GIFT OF TONGUES

Start with praise and worship to get into a receiving mode.

1. Language Building Blocks

    Begin to yield your vocal capacity to the Lord. There are several ways you can prime the pump. Choose one or try them all! Start by making rudimentary sounds. A good way to initiate tongues is to choose a vowel sound—a, e, i, o, u—and add consonants in front of it or behind it to build syllables, the basic sound units of language. What you are doing is giving the Holy Spirit a vocal offering to transform. The goal is not to fabricate a make-believe language; the goal is to move your mouth and make utterances until the Holy Spirit takes over, until you begin to speak a Holy Spirit language. It's easier to ride a bike that is moving than one that is standing still. So give the Holy Spirit some material and momentum to work with.

For example, make long or short "a" sounds:

ayy, may, ray, pay, lay, kay, day, say, tay, hay, way, jay…
ah, mah, rah, pa, la, kah, dah, sah, tah, fah, nah, hah…

Then make long or short "e" sounds:

ee, kee, wee, tee, bee, nee, hee, lee, ree, zee, fee, dee…
eh, teh, heh, leh, feh, keh, neh, meh, beh, peh, weh, veh…

Then make long or short "i" sounds:

i, my, sigh, guy, rye, why, jiy, vie, nigh, tie, shy, pie…
il, til, kil, pil, nil, wil, shil, fil, mil, ril, hil, sil, dil, bil…

Then make long or short "o" sounds:

oh, no, bow, so, row, tow, ho, voh, mow, yo, go, cho, ko…
bot, tot, sot, kot, mot, wot, dot, rot, lot, fot, yot, not, zot…

Then make long or short "u" sounds:

yoo, hoo, foo, goo, boo, zoo, koo, woo, doo, joo, shoo…
uh, puh, ruh, wuh, vuh, guh, buh, fuh, huh, nuh, tuh, suh…

2. Baby Babble or Pet Talk

This next one is for baby lovers and pet lovers. Talk baby babble to a baby or pet talk to a pet (if you don't have a baby or pet handy, talk to a doll or stuffed animal or pillow or thin air). Comfort with babble. Praise with babble. Console with babble. Babble on! All of these exercises are designed to activate your mouth apart from your mind. These are ways to cooperate with the Holy Spirit and actively yield to Him. (Passivity does not produce results.)

3. Scat

You can also scat. Scat is a type of jazz vocalization that is done by improvising nonsense syllables to instrumental musical accompaniment or by mimicking the sound of musical instruments. For those who remember Walt Disney's animated film, *The Jungle Book* (1967), the orangutan character King Louie who had scaled the ranks of monkeys to become the "king of the jungle," sang a song entitled, "I Wan'na Be Like You," that contains a healthy dose of scat on the theme of becoming a "man cub" and learning the secret of man's red fire; Baloo the Bear joins in the scat, intoxicated by rhythms. I recommend listening to a recording of this song to get into a playful, carefree mood.[3] The gift of tongues comes easier when you are relaxed and having fun.

Ella Fitzgerald is another jazz vocalist you can listen to for an example of scat. Fitzgerald was a proficient and prolific scat vocalist. Many historic videos, including video montages, of Fitzgerald's performances are available on YouTube, but one particularly stellar one is "How High The Moon/Epic scat LIVE 1966 [RITY archives]," by Reelin' In the Years Productions.[4] Fitzgerald's performance seems almost superhuman, except for her profuse sweating (her vocal acrobatics and stamina make you wonder whether she spoke in tongues behind the scenes!). Bottom line, play music that you can scat to! Your scat can become God's scat, and before too long you may be doing Special Combat Assault Team (SCAT) missions in the Spirit!

4. Zany Nonsense Dialogue with Yourself

This last one is for the bold and zany. You can carry on a nonsense dialogue with yourself. Stand in front of a mirror and ask a question in nonsense with an upward inflection at the end. Answer yourself with a few matter-of-fact nonsense statements. Then give a command in nonsense with an emphatic tone of voice and an exclamation at the end. Answer with a few conciliatory nonsense statements, as if you were going to comply. Then crack a joke in nonsense, and respond hilariously in nonsense. Then tell a sob story in nonsense and respond with condolences in nonsense. Keep on!

TROUBLESHOOTING BLOCKAGE

If for some reason you feel blocked, ask the Holy Spirit to reveal what is blocking you. It could be a wrong perspective and attitude about yourself or God such as "Nothing good ever happens to me," or "God doesn't really want to bless me". It could be a religious idea such as "My parents and grandparents never spoke in tongues, and they were good Christians," or "My denomination doesn't endorse this," or "I need a minister to officiate; I can't receive this on my own". It could be pride or intellectualism: "How embarrassing. This is silly. This makes no sense. This is nonsense". It could be offense toward someone, which can hinder prayers as the Apostle Peter pointed out: "Husbands, likewise, dwell with them with understanding, giving honor to the wife, that your prayers may not be hindered" (1 Pet 3:7). It could be lack of sanctification, habitual sin in thought, word or deed. Whatever the case, when you recognize your responsibility, do your part to get free: forgive, repent (change your mind! make a U-turn), affirm the truth, and return to God with a mustard seed of faith. Then ask the Lord again for the gift of tongues.

Occult involvement can block the gift of tongues since occult knowledge and power are substitutes for God that displace God. Occult involvement is a violation of the first and second commandments and must be repented of as idolatry. The spirit realm regards participation in occult arts or practices (how ever long ago and how ever seemingly innocuous or tenuous) as a personal preference for and commitment to spirits other than the Holy Spirit. In fact, such participation is contractual in nature: you partner with the spirit realm, and the spirit realm has a partnership agreement or contract out on you. Ultimately, occult sources of knowledge and power derive from the Devil, whether or not practitioners and recipients realize this. While there may be some up-front benefit, there is always a back-end liability. The Devil gives with the right hand but takes with the left: he gives a Trojan horse—a gift containing an enemy alien—that diminishes or destroys physical or mental health, safety or freedom, kingdom relationships and success, spiritual potential and sacred purpose in life. By contrast, the Lord's gifts contain no embedded curse: "The blessing of the Lord makes rich [or] brings [true] riches, and He adds no sorrow with it" (Prov 10:22 NKJV/AMP).

If you have entertained occult sources of knowledge (from horoscopes to the Enneagram); if you have conjured occult sources of power (from Feng shui to fantasy role playing games); if you have conferred with or retained occult practitioners (fortune tellers, psychics, channelers, mediums, spiritists, shamans, sorcerers, Wiccans, etc.) or consulted their works, no matter what the reason, whether out of curiosity, as a joke, to have fun, to please somebody, to avoid offending somebody, to be socially relevant, to experiment, to develop your potential, out of desperation, etc.:

- forgive whoever introduced you to the occult art and whoever practiced the occult art,
- break any soul bond with those people,
- repent heartily for resorting to sources of supernatural knowledge and power other than the living God,
- renounce the occult art and all of its benefits (your reasons for entertaining it),

- destroy any instructional material such as books, manuals, audio/visual training sources (palmistry hand map, astrological natal chart, Zodiac signs chart, numerology chart, I Ching oracles, spells and hexes),
- destroy any paraphernalia and accessories used in the practice (Tarot cards, runes, pendulum, crystal ball, tea leaf cup, coins, sticks, ring, cloak, mask, wand, chalice, dagger),
- destroy any amulets, talismans, sigils of ritual magic (dream catcher, evil eye, four leaf clover, rabbit's foot, horse shoe, lucky dice, witch's wheel),
- destroy any symbols of false religions (Hindu OM symbol, Taoist Tai Chi/Yin Yang symbol, Egyptian Ankh, Wiccan pentagram),

- command any spirits empowered by the occult art to release you and go swiftly to judgment in Christ.

You may also have to repent on behalf of your generational line—family members, living or deceased, particularly those in relational authority or whose influence misguided you—who were involved in occult arts. Then ask the Lord again for the gift of tongues.

There are countless occult arts, but I want to highlight one that has become popular among Evangelical Christians in recent years: the Enneagram personality typing system. The Enneagram is not a product of the science of personality or Christian thought; it is a product of divination and sorcery practiced by modern New Age and occult practitioners who contributed to its development. These authors gave the Enneagram a myth of origin (one secular, another Christian) to provide credibility to audiences who take their claims at face value without researching provenance. Please read the Appendix and renounce it. There is no scientific validation for this instrument, and its origin and design make it a carrier of spirit power.

A passage from Acts may provide some inspiration for renunciation. After the Ephesians discovered the superior power of Jesus through a Jewish exorcism that backfired, many were thunderstruck and made a big bonfire of their occult arts, which they had been practicing:

> Also, many of those who had practiced magic [sorcery, witchcraft] brought their books [scrolls] together and burned them [publicly] in the sight of all. And they counted up the value of them, and it totaled fifty thousand pieces of silver. So the word of the Lord grew mightily and prevailed.—Acts 19:19-20 NKJV, NIV, CEV

> Many of those who believed came out of the closet and made a clean break with their secret sorceries. All kinds of witches and warlocks came out of the woodwork with their books of spells and incantations and made a huge bonfire of them.—Acts 19:17-20 (excerpt) MSG

> Many of the believers who had been practicing black magic confessed their deeds and brought their incantation books and charms and burned them in a public bonfire.—Acts 19:18-19 TLB

PARTNER IMPARTATION OF THE GIFT OF TONGUES

The impartations in this section feature partner ministry between a tongues speaker and a non-tongues speaker.

1. The Tongues Speaker Speaks in Tongues over the Recipient

The tongues speaker asks permission to lay a hand on the recipient's shoulder. Most recipients will gladly receive a light touch; some may not. Do not take it personally if the recipient declines. You never know someone's personal history or reason. Although spiritual gifts are often bestowed through the laying on of hands, human touch is not necessary. On the day of Pentecost, the disciples received directly from God with no human agency whatsoever (see Acts 2). Likewise, God-fearing Gentiles received directly from God apart from ministry of Jewish believers in Jesus (see Acts 10).

Ask the heavenly Father to baptize the recipient in the power of the Holy Spirit and to bestow the gift of tongues. Then "cascade" and "saturate" and "immerse" the recipient in tongues by speaking in tongues, praying in tongues, proclaiming in tongues, praising in tongues, and singing in tongues out loud over the person. You can also interpret tongues for the recipient as the Holy Spirit gives impressions, but tongues should be emphasized Do not lapse into conversation, prayer, counseling, or any other form of ministry (unless to remove blocks). This is about the baptism in the Spirit.

Encourage the recipient to participate in the heavenly downpour with language building blocks, baby babble, pet talk or scat. Cheerlead the recipient to make rudimentary sounds. At some point, the recipient may start to feel sensations of language emerging. If so, he or she should cooperate with that and invest in that by vocalizing the sounds. Even if the recipient has no feeling of language emerging, language building blocks, baby babble, pet talk, and scat are a great way to give God an offering that He can use and transform. Lean into joy and uplift. Laughter is often a byproduct of the baptism in the Holy Spirit.

Some recipients may get weak and wobbly and unsteady under the power of the Holy Spirit; some may even fall. Do whatever is needed to facilitate a smooth transition while continuing to saturate the recipient in tongues: direct the recipient to a chair or bring a chair to the recipient; enlist the help of someone to catch the recipient in case he or she falls; catch the person yourself if you can do so without straining. While you want to ensure safety as much as possible, do not be overly concerned about this aspect of ministry. God is in charge, and He can buffer a fall. God does not hurt people. When I received the baptism, I fell to the floor unexpectedly and was totally uninjured. I had a great time on the floor. Do not encourage a "courtesy drop," for that is not of God.

2. The Recipient Mimics the Tongues Speaker

This exercise adds to the immersion method described above. Sometimes tongues speakers need to persevere with impartation while recipients overcome inhibitions. The tongues speaker pronounces a word in an unknown tongue slowly and clearly and the recipient repeats what is heard, mimicking as best as s/he can. The tongues speaker pronounces another word, and the recipient mimics that. Continue with a series of words for a while. Then progress to a series of phrases, then to a series of sentences.

To promote diversity of tongues in the recipient, the tongues speaker switches from one unknown language to another unknown language and articulates words, phrases, and sentences in that other language, which the recipient mimics. Repeat with more languages.

3. The Tongues Speaker and Recipient Engage in a Pretend Dialogue

The tongues speaker initiates a pretend dialogue with the recipient by asking a question or making a statement in an unknown tongue (use the proper inflection for a question or statement). The recipient responds accordingly in baby babble or scat. Be animated: express interest, enthusiasm, concern, surprise, perplexity, etc. Talk over one another, too (both talk at once). The goal is not to be profound but to be human and available for God. Being silly kills religiosity and the pressure to perform. It can be very helpful for gaining traction in the Holy Spirit. (Become as a little child to inherit the kingdom!)

GROUP IMPARTATION OF THE GIFT OF TONGUES

In a fellowship of believers, some may not have the gift of tongues; some may speak in one tongue; and some may speak in more than one tongue. The facilitator should ask for a show of hands: who does not yet have the gift; who speaks in one tongue; who speaks in more than one tongue? The first priority is to impart the gift of tongues to those who want it. If the group is small, direct tongues speakers to surround recipients and "saturate" them with Spirit languages. If the group is large, direct any tongues speakers who are sitting or standing near someone who wants to receive to surround and "saturate" the recipient with Spirit languages. If the physical structure of the meeting place or the seating arrangement (permanent pews or other fixtures) prohibits the formation of small groups or if altering the structure would pose too much of a disruption (relocating chairs), then simply direct all tongues speakers wherever they are to speak vigorously in tongues in a sustained manner for a period of time (ten minutes or longer) while recipients concentrate on yielding their mouths to the Holy Spirit and vocalizing.

A final option is to assign partner exercises for mimicking words, phrases, and sentences in one or more unknown tongues or assign the mock dialogue in tongues and baby babble or scat. Partner exercises can be more challenging for some participants, even the initial step of volunteering to partner or being assigned a partner. Partner exercises require freedom and playfulness, especially in the tongues speaker who leads, but also the recipient who follows. If some recipients find themselves without a partner, the facilitator can call forward those who do not have a partner and recruit other tongues speakers to minister to them as a small group, or as a last resort, the facilitator can minister to them. Ideally, the facilitator would assign others to do the work of the ministry to train everyone to impart the baptism in the Spirit. We want to promote the royal priesthood of believers as much as possible (laity become clergy)!

GROUP ACTIVATION OF MORE THAN ONE TONGUE

There are several ways to organize a group to activate multiple, diverse tongues in those who speak in only one tongue. Some arrangements may be easier logistically or psychologically, but the Holy Spirit can minister in any arrangement. One option is to "surround" the recipients: direct those who speak in several tongues to gather around those who speak in a single tongue and to stretch out their hands toward the recipients or to lay hands on the recipients (with permission) and to "saturate" the recipients with diverse tongues. Recipients should listen and bask in the input of diverse tongues for a time before attempting to articulate a new language.

Another option is to instruct everyone to remain wherever he or she is in the room. This may be more convenient and practical for a larger group. Direct those who speak in many tongues to speak vigorously in a sustained fashion for a length of time, alternating from one tongue to another while recipients concentrate on listening and basking and later articulating a tongue that is different from their dominant tongue.

A final option for the bold and free is to direct those who speak in diverse tongues to pair up with those who speak in one tongue and to do the partner exercises for mimicking words, phrases, and sentences in tongues that sound substantially different from the one the recipient has. In case of an odd number of participants or someone left without a partner, the facilitator can recruit someone else to activate, or she can do the honor of activating the recipient/s herself.

INDIVIDUAL ACTIVATION: STEWARDING TONGUES SOLO

The following practice exercises are for tongues speakers who want to steward the gift better for themselves, for others, and for God.

For Rest and Refreshing: When you feel fatigued or muzzy headed, instead of taking a nap or drinking coffee or eating a candy bar, do a light activity or engage in light recreation and talk in tongues: walk or bike in nature and talk in tongues; sit in a hot tub and talk in tongues; gaze at fire or water, art or photography and talk in tongues; knit, crochet, whittle, fish, play Corn Hole (beanbag toss) and talk in tongues.

To Counteract Negativity and Endure Trials: When you feel anxious, frightened, worried or mad, instead of yielding your mouth to the negative emotion and saying something you will regret, channel the negative emotion into tongues until you feel the harassing or oppressive feelings dissipate or disperse. When you are going through a trial, talk in tongues for an extended period every day (an hour or more).

For Spiritual Self Care (Mental Health and Emotional Stability): Talk or sing in tongues while you shower, bathe, and groom. Record yourself and others speaking and singing in tongues; play the recording while you rest, stretch, work out, do arts or crafts, cook, etc. Talk in tongues while you pet your cat or dog.

For Social Situations: Before an important or stressful conversation or meeting, talk in tongues. During a tense interaction, talk in tongues under your breath or excuse yourself and take a break somewhere (lobby, restroom) and talk in tongues. After a conflict, talk in tongues until you feel release or peace. When someone acts in an inappropriate or a menacing way around you, take charge of the situation and talk in tongues, even out loud if necessary.

Recently I was at a trail head early in the morning pulling on my boots for a hike when a rough looking couple approached. The woman swaggered and cussed like a locomotive. I decided to signal jam her profanity and disrupt the spirit behind it, so I launched into loud, militant, machine gun fire tongues. Instantly the woman shut up and tip toed gingerly by me, glancing furtively at her partner. A ranger observed the whole thing. Afterward, I explained to him what I was doing, and it turned out he was raised Pentecostal. But even if he had had no grid for that startling display, it was a good teaching moment and a shoehorn into the gospel.

To Redeem the Time: Speak in tongues while driving a car or riding public transit or waiting in line or doing chores or other light duty. You might lapse into silence as your mind wanders or fixates on something else; if so, just return to tongues as soon as you realize you stopped. Getting into the habit of speaking in tongues when your mind is not engaged will help you be ready in season and out of season to testify: "Always be ready to give a defense to everyone who asks you a reason for the hope that is in you" (1 Pet 3:15).

Tongues can also abort the adversary's plans. On one occasion, I spoke in tongues before grocery shopping and miraculously escaped a serious injury when I slipped on a cluster of crushed grapes. My body flipped backward horizontal to the floor but inexplicably righted itself. On another occasion, I spoke in tongues on the way to a fellowship meeting and miraculously escaped a head-on collision with a reckless driver who sped around a tight curve, lost control, lurched into a ditch and rebounded, bouncing right in front of me at an angle. The car righted itself against the laws of physics with a square jerk.

For Discernment, Understanding, Revelation: Write down a question you need answered; a problem you need solved; an issue you need resolved; a mystery you need revealed. Speak in tongues over this. Journal any words or impressions or counsel you get from the Holy Spirit. Also pay attention to other ways the Spirit may communicate in days to come: through dreams, people, objects, circumstances.

To Activate Divine Destiny: Write down what you believe is your sacred purpose or divine destiny (this often relates to heartfelt desires, spiritual gifting, and a redemptive reversal of misfortune). Or write down a divine commission or assignment as best as you understand it. Submit this to God. Speak in tongues over this. Journal any words, impressions, counsel or directives you get from the Holy Spirit.

As Prayer: Think of a need or desire (yours or someone else's) and submit your request to God in English (or your native language). Follow with tongues. Use a humble and earnest tone of voice, a meek mood, and submissive body language. After you feel a release (lightness, peace or victory), follow with thanks in English and in tongues, using a grateful tone of voice, uplifted mood, and appreciative or reverential body language.

As Spiritual Warfare: Think of a wrong that you want rectified or a person who needs to be redeemed. Bind the adversary and command him in English (or your native language) to loose the hostages or to make restitution and pay punitive damages. Follow with warring tongues. Chanting is well suited for this purpose. Use a confrontational, militant or combative tone of voice, a heroic or fierce mood, forceful and aggressive body language and prophetic acts to prosecute war. God's justice is the heart of spiritual warfare.

As Prophetic Proclamation: Think of two or three things that you want to see become a reality that you know are God's will for you or someone else or for a ministry or a state or nation. Begin by proclaiming these in English (or your native language). Use a command form like, "Let there be!" or "There will be!" or "I command this to manifest in Jesus' name!" Then follow with proclamation in tongues. Use an authoritative and magisterial tone of voice, a royal mood, and emphatic body language to issue divine decrees, executive orders, and throne mandates. Sovereignty is the heart of prophetic proclamation.

As Praise: Think of at least two or three things you want to praise God about. Begin by extolling Him in English (or your native language) for those things; then follow with tongues. Use a joyful tone of voice, a celebratory mood, and exuberant body language to convey praise. Rejoicing is the heart of praise.

TAKE THE 90 DAY CHALLENGE!

In mid January, 2020, Jennifer LeClaire was hosting her live morning broadcast featuring praise, prayer, and prophecy when suddenly she felt prompted by the Holy Spirit to challenge her listening audience to speak in tongues for one hour every day for 90 days to "remove the bottleneck" from your life. The 90 Day Challenge is not so much Jennifer LeClaire's challenge as the Holy Spirit's challenge to you. Ideally, you would allocate one hour to fully invest yourself in nothing but praying in tongues, but this may not be feasible. LeClaire noted that you can pray in short installments throughout the day while multitasking, while running errands and doing chores; in this way, you can accumulate a total of one hour.[5] Profuse use of the gift of tongues will help you overcome inveterate habits and demonic opposition and other things that may be hindering or blocking you from walking in your sacred purpose in life. Once you have completed the challenge, you are likely to incorporate praying in tongues as a lifestyle, which is an important key to fulfilling your divine destiny.

Television show host Sid Roth testified that a friend of his who is a Jewish believer in Jesus and an evangelist got a major breakthrough when he incorporated tongues as a daily discipline into his life. The adversary was assaulting him right and left; he was going through a divorce and other hardships and was even entertaining skewed, non-Biblical ideas. Roth encouraged him to speak in tongues every day and to start modestly with five minutes per day. After his friend got into a routine, Roth encouraged him to work up to ten minutes; then fifteen, and so on, until he could do an hour. When Roth checked again on his friend, his friend was praying in tongues two hours every day and provoking Roth to jealousy! All of his problems had been resolved or disappeared, and he was experiencing a tremendous level of revelation and supernatural power.[6] May this testimony motivate you to undertake what seems like a hard discipline at first. What begins as discipline eventually turns into freedom and pleasure (think of world class performers who start with neophyte grunt work but end with finalé finesse!).

TAKE FIRE FROM THE ALTAR EVERY DAY: SAY "YES!" TO YOUR BOOK OF LIFE!

Kevin Zadai offers a similar challenge, but for a lifetime! Let's frame this for motivation: one of the most important applications of prophecy in tongues is your own future. You can prophesy in tongues and alternate with prophecy in English. Prophesy that your life will unfold each and every day according to God's good will for you and that you will walk in your sacred purpose and fulfill your divine destiny, as recorded in the Book of Life for you. The Book of Life is a divine register of the names of those who have been redeemed by the blood of the Lamb (Jesus), those who labor in the gospel and who overcome the evil of this age (see Ex 32:32; Phil 4:3; Rev 3:5; 13:8; 17:8). The Book of Life is like a charter: a charter is a grant by a sovereign power that confers certain rights and privileges on a person and authorizes that person to undertake some stated official purpose. In a similar way, the Almighty has charged you with a divine purpose and conferred every right and privilege upon you to enable you to function in your calling and complete your purpose, and all of this is recorded in the Book of Life.

Kevin Zadai, who died on an operating table during a dental procedure, got a glimpse of his own book, God's charter for his life. Jesus showed him that "everything was already written down before any of my days came into being". This is what the psalmist describes in the book of Psalms:

> Your eyes saw my substance, being yet unformed. And in Your book they all were written, the days fashioned for me, when as yet there were none of them.—Psalm 139:16

God's plan for us is written in this book. Even better, the book authorizes us to do the great things God has planned: it gives us full permission and prohibits the Devil from interfering. After glimpsing his own book, Zadai realized that "nothing is random" and "everything is rigged in your favor," and he returned from death to share with our generation that "the limitations have been taken off" and "it's open heaven now": it's your turn to do great exploits. You only need to cooperate with God. One powerful way to cooperate with God's plan is to prophesy over yourself in tongues and in English.[7]

To put the Book of Life into action every day, Zadai does what the Lord directed him to do: "take fire from the altar". He recommends that we do this, too. The split second Zadai wakes up, he yells, "Yes!" to his entry in the Book of Life, "Yes!" to God's plan. This wakes up his wife, and then she yells, "Yes!" to her entry in the Book of Life, "Yes!" to God's plan. Then they launch into warfare tongues and prophesy about all the great exploits they are going to do; they prophesy "the Devil's doom"; they prophesy that the hearts of people will be enlightened to God, per Paul's prayer in Ephesians:

> that the Father of glory, may give to you the spirit of wisdom and revelation in the knowledge of Him, the eyes of your understanding being enlightened; that you may know what is the hope of His calling, what are the riches of the glory of His inheritance in the saints, and what is the exceeding greatness of His power toward us who believe.—Ephesians 1:18 (abridged)

They end the day the same way that they started it: they go to bed saying, "Yes!" to God's Book of Life for themselves and for others.[8]

Zadai advises us to do this; to never look at circumstances; to never entertain any thought of limitation or of chance because all of heaven is for us: the cloud of witnesses, the angels, the Holy Spirit, Jesus, and the Father. If you say "Yes!" to God's plan and war in tongues, it will help you align with heaven's agenda. It will move you out of the endless obstacle course of needing one breakthrough after another. It will establish you in the continual "overthrow" of the enemy. When you prophesy liberally in tongues over yourself and others, you will be reciting out of your Book of Life; you will be "repeating your book verbally". Angels assigned to assist you will "harken to the voice of the Lord" out of your mouth and will facilitate any necessary transformation and even "escort you" into your next assignment. Zadai says, "The number one way to participate in this supernatural is to pray in tongues".[9]

I would like to add that we will be rewarded and judged by the Book of Life, which logs the deeds we have done in comparison to God's intended purpose for us:

> And I saw the dead, small and great, standing before God, and the books were opened. And another book was opened, which is the Book of Life. And the dead were judged according to their works, by the things which were written in the books.—Revelation 20:12

Let's make sure our daily deeds match God's plan! Let's track with God! Live your life as if you cannot fail. All of heaven is for you![10]

CORPORATE PRACTICE: STEWARDING TONGUES AS A GROUP

Corporate tongues are a powerful form of intercession and proclamation; they are a governmental function of the church. If you have never participated in corporate intercession in tongues and do not have access to a Spirit filled group of believers, I recommend watching and participating in the first episode of Sid Roth's "God Talk: The Key to Unlocking Your Destiny," which he debuted on his television program *It's Supernatural!* in March of 2017. In this special episode, the television studio audience prayed in tongues for almost 30 minutes, and various audience members shared their impressions afterward. Since the first taping of "God Talk," the show has become a regularly featured program on It's Supernatural! Network (ISN) every Wednesday at 5:30 a.m., 1:30 p.m., and 10 p.m. Eastern Standard Time.[11]

Another online resource is the monthly activation workshops I teach at The River Room. These workshops are archived on the church's YouTube channel, The River Room. Since January, 2020, the videos have included group activation in tongues, sometimes followed by participants sharing their impressions afterward. You can listen to the teaching and then participate in tongues. Below is a list of workshops that explain the Biblical basis for the corporate expression of tongues and that demonstrate group intercession in tongues, followed by a time of sharing impressions:[12]

"Speaking in Tongues Workshop: For the Common Good or Profit of All," Ray Boetcher/The River Room YouTube channel, January 17, 2020.

"Speaking in Tongues Workshop: Praise, Worship, and Prophecy," The River Room YouTube channel, February 21, 2020.

"Speaking in Tongues Workshop: Unity in the Holy Spirit and the Royal Priesthood," The River Room YouTube channel, March 20, 2020.

"Speaking in Tongues Workshop: The Royal Priesthood of All Believers, the Laity as Clergy," The River Room YouTube channel, April 17, 2020.

In these activation workshops, group intercession in tongues focused on current events, most of which evolved in complexity. The burden of concerns about the state of the nation, the spiritual dynamics at work, and the causal agents behind the scenes escalated throughout the year 2020. In one workshop we prayed to neutralize witchcraft during the 2020 election cycle, and we prayed for the United States to fulfill its God given destiny.[13] In two other workshops, we prayed against the corona virus (COVID-19) and its social, religious, legal, and economic ramifications.[14]

Cassandra Donnelly, an art therapist and prophetic artist who attended the workshops, painted a prophetic painting about the corona virus to release, through imagery, a divine decree that life will overtake death. Cassandra superimposed vibrant sherbet colors and collage elements over the bleak scene of masked figures under quarantine. Her digital mixed media painting and comments on the symbolism are for your reflection.

"Door of Hope" (April 6, 2020), Cassandra Donnelly.[15]

Artist's Comments

I felt a sense of urgency with this painting as we enter into the darkest, bleakest hour of the corona virus pandemic within the next few weeks, depending on where you live. We need hope. We need encouragement. God has been stirring me heavily with this artwork and prompting me to get it out to you.

I wanted the artwork to speak for itself, but there are several symbolic images within. First off, of course, is God opening the door to the dawn of a new day: the Door of Hope. We are entering a new beginning. The flowers are blooming, the birds are singing. God has heard our prayers and He is coming to the rescue! His grace (symbolized by the number 5) is being poured out. Corona means crown, and the enemy is trying to bring glory to himself through mass destruction and devastation with this virus, but guess who gets the last word? God! He is King of Kings and Lord of Lords. Every knee shall bow to Him! He says, "Enough is enough!" The corona virus must bow to God. The artwork serves as a prophetic decree that the corona virus shall come to an end. It's time is up (clock)! God is sovereign and in control. It's time for His plans and will to unfold. He is bringing us healing and deliverance. He wants us to dream and hope again (hot air balloon). We are entering a season for his promises to come into fruition. It is time for our circumstances to be transformed (butterflies). Our dark day is ending. God is opening the Door of Hope!

Supporting verses [abridged]:

There I will give her back her vineyards, and will make the Valley of Achor [trouble] a door of hope. There she will respond as in the days of her youth, as in the day she came up out of Egypt.—Hosea 2:15 NIV

See, darkness covers the earth and thick darkness is over the peoples, but the LORD rises upon you and his glory appears over you.—Isaiah 60:2 NIV

God is within her, she will not fall; God will help her at break of day. —Psalm 46:5 NIV

—Cassandra Donnelly, April 6, 2020, Creative Passages, FaceBook

Activation: The facilitator presents topics of concern for the group to address in their prayer languages. Topics may be inspired by current events. Encourage participants to stand and move around for the activation. Standing is more authoritative than sitting and is more conducive to motivation, energy, and voice projection. Direct those who speak in more than one tongue to cycle through all of their tongues during the activation. Instruct participants to monitor themselves for any impressions they get while speaking in tongues and to make a mental note of these impressions or to write them down: any perceptions, sensations, emotions, visions, scriptures, allusions to Bible stories or other literature, the voice of God, memories, cultural experiences or phenomena that may be relevant to the topic at hand. These impressions can be shared on a voluntary basis after the activation.

Recruit several volunteers to "lead the charge" of speaking in tongues at the microphone, each for a short shift of one to five minutes, depending on the total length of time allotted and the number of volunteers. The allotted time should be at least 10 or 15 minutes, if not longer. (Divide the time by the number of volunteers, for example: 10 minutes ÷ by 5 volunteers = 2 minutes each. 15 minutes ÷ by 5 volunteers = 3 minutes each.) Direct volunteers to line up at the side of the microphone and speak in tongues while awaiting their turn to "lead the charge". After they have finished their turn, they may return to their seats and stand or walk around and continue speaking in tongues with the group until the allotted time is up.

At the end, observe silence for one or two minutes before calling volunteers to share their impressions at the microphone. This will give participants time to recall their impressions and formulate their thoughts. Ask volunteers one by one to come to the microphone (or to the front) to share their impressions. Sharing impressions is great practice for interpreting tongues. In fact, impressions are a basic form of interpretation. Participants may share themes from their own tongues and/or the tongues of others who spoke at the microphone. The time of voluntary sharing can be very enlightening. The manifold wisdom of God is revealed through the different understanding of His people.

Here are some suggestions for general topics:

1. Prophesy in tongues over the house or church or ministry that is hosting the tongues activation, for it to thrive and flourish and prosper and for the adversary's work to be thwarted and his influence to be removed.

2. Prophesy in tongues over your nation (city, state or province) to establish God's will, for:

    - God to orchestrate whatever needs to happen behind the scenes,
    - angels to be released on assignment,
    - God's people to excel and prosper in their unique ministries,
    - truth, righteousness, and justice (as God defines it) to prevail,
    - unbelievers to experience a moral awakening and spiritual realignment,
    - the nation to fulfill its God given purpose.

3. Prophesy in tongues for every believer in Christ to discover and express his or her kingdom identity and for the royal priesthood of all believers to emerge and be established worldwide:

    - for individual believers to discover their unique call to ministry,
    - to consecrate themselves to holiness and their calling,
    - to function in their priestly role of representing people to God,
    - to function in their kingly role of representing God to people,
    - to complete their spiritual assignments,
    - for women and minorities who have been suppressed or censored to be released into ministry,
    - for youth to escape schemes of seduction to destruction and pursue God's vision for their lives,
    - for children to minister to each other and to adults.

SINGING IN TONGUES TESTIMONY

A prophetic woman at a church I attended had a dream about the congregation singing underwater. I thought, "That's it! In over our heads in the river of life!" The pastor had just seen the movie *Mary Poppins Returns* (2018), a musical about a magical nanny who restores joy and wonder to a distressed family. He jokingly commented that singing underwater is natural (as depicted in the scene where the children and their nanny dive through the drain hole of a bathtub into a watery wonderland to sing underwater). Of course, he was referring to Holy Spirit inspired songs, especially singing in tongues. God is restoring this profound vocal and musical gift right at a time when the secular world is showing early signs of its readiness to receive in movies such as *Mary Poppins Returns*.[1] The rivers of living waters are flowing out of our hearts, and as they do, a great multitude of fish—the saved and as-yet-to-be saved—will frolic in the river on a glee spree (Jn 7:38; Ez 47:9).

A STAIRWELL OF THE SPIRIT

For me, singing or chanting in tongues is more passionate, intimate, and powerful than speaking in tongues. Depending on the kind of song, it is more forceful and commanding or more adoring and winsome than speaking in tongues. Singing or chanting in tongues shifts the atmosphere quickly. Though it requires more effort to initiate and sustain, I enjoy it more and get faster and greater relief. Ray Hughes, a musician who speaks about "Presence music" (spontaneous melodies that host the Holy Spirit) describes singing as impassioned speech. I agree. Singing is a more robust form of communication and more heart-felt than speaking: singing in the Spirit feels like a bi-directional flow from my heart to God's heart and from God's heart to mine. It is a passionate way to host the presence of the Holy Spirit.

When singing in tongues, I often feel an exhilaration or exultance that I do not feel when speaking in tongues or extolling God in English. Likewise, when chanting in tongues to prosecute justice through the Spirit, I feel a jackhammering, blowtorching power that is greater than what I feel when speaking in tongues or proclaiming scriptures to prosecute justice. On one occasion when I was singing in tongues with two other believers, we got to a place where we were harmonizing in the Spirit, and I felt something like a cylindrical shaft of light opening between heaven and earth and a draft spiraling upward to heaven. It seemed to be a stairwell in the Holy Spirit, like Jacob's ladder or staircase, only rotating like a spiraling double helix. This kinesthetic experience confirmed what I have always suspected, that singing in tongues can open a gate and a tube lift to heaven:

> Then he [Jacob] dreamed, and behold, a ladder was set up on the earth, and its top reached to heaven; and there the angels of God were ascending and descending on it. The Jacob awoke from his sleep and said, "Surely the LORD is in this place, and I did not know it." And he was afraid and said, "How awesome is this place! This is none other than the house of God, and this is the gate of heaven!"—Genesis 28:12, 16-17

Jacob's Ladder, Nicolas Dipre (c. 1495-1532).[2]

Corporate worship in tongues with twenty or more people participating can be very powerful. Sometimes it crescendoes into a festal shout that makes you feel swallowed in surround sound:

> Happy are the people who know the joyful sound, who know the festal shout, who walk, O LORD, in the light of Your countenance.
> —Psalm 89:15 NKJV; NRSV

SERENADING OTHERS IN THE SPIRIT THROUGH TONGUES

I believe that tongues are a lost tool of power evangelism. I first became aware of the full potential of tongues at New Age expos. One of the churches I attended booth rents and offers free healing prayer and prophecy inside a venue of pay-for-services by astrologers, aura readers, palm readers, Tarot card readers, mediums, psychics, Reiki healers, Qigong practitioners, and merchants who peddle New Age paraphernalia.

    I had long known that tongues oppose occult spirit power. On one occasion, for example, I had a conversation with an astrologer in the booth next to ours, and I was talking in tongues under my breath. I was looking for an opportunity to minister to her, but the spirit in her also wanted to minister to me. When she tried to do an astrological reading on me, which I did not ask for, her mind blanked out and she commented on her confusion. I am certain that my tongues were signal jamming her demonic intelligence feed. She also said that when I gave "spiritual readings to clients," she could feel enormous energy waves mounting from our booth and crashing into her booth, which distracted and disconcerted her. She assumed that this was because I was a rookie, an overzealous newbie who needed to learn to "chill out". She did not realize that I was operating in a different Spirit that scrambled and scattered hers. In a mentoring and professionally competitive way, she advised me to calm down. I took it as a backhanded compliment that the spirit of astrology in her was disturbed and overwhelmed by the Holy Spirit in me.

    I soon began to realize, however, that tongues might serve a bigger purpose than counter resistance to occult power. I began to realize that tongues might actually serve an evangelistic purpose of hosting the presence of the Holy Spirit in a non-threatening way to

New Agers without directly challenging their ideology: seed planting, if you will. I stumbled upon this when I felt prompted to serenade those who came to receive a "spiritual reading". Some of the responses have been promising.

On one occasion, a channeler was heading toward the men's restroom when his path intersected mine. He looked at me intently and said, "Don't I know you?" I had never met him before in my life, so I suspected that this was a Holy Spirit set-up. I offered to give him a brief word, but having none at that moment, I serenaded him in the Spirit instead. While singing in tongues over him, he looked intrigued and bemused and puzzled as if listening for the first time to a form of infotainment that he could not figure out. He raised his eyebrows, bobbed his head, looked quizzically at me and smiled. I could see his mental wheels were spinning to understand a phenomenon that was totally outside of his grid. Perhaps he wondered which spirit I was channeling and why it sang in a byzantine language?

Then I got an impression from the Holy Spirit and said, "You have become very proficient at speaking on behalf of others. You have spoken on behalf of many others, but now God wants you to develop your own voice. Invest in your own voice." He looked a bit surprised, thanked me, and invited me to sample his services at his booth (which I politely declined). The Holy Spirit had just graciously pinpointed a major flaw in his occult trade—the subordination and submergence of his humanity and identity to other entities that take over and express themselves through him as if he were no more than an empty gourd. I did not have the wisdom, boldness or tact to challenge him, but the Spirit did through tongues and interpretation. I also discovered that singing can be very disarming to the wary, for what harm can a song do? (Plenty to the Devil!)

On another occasion, a woman who needed emotional healing let me serenade her in the Holy Spirit.

> "How beautiful!" she said. "That reminds me of the lost language of Atlantis."
> "Oh really?" I said. "What exactly do you mean?"
> "You know, the people of Atlantis were reputed to be very wise," she said.
> "Tell me more," I said.
> "They chanted. I imagine their chanting sounded something like what you're singing."
> "Ah," I said.

Then I explained to her that tongues are a gift of the Holy Spirit. This redirected the conversation. She confided that she had gotten hurt in the church. (Unfortunately, many who attend New Age expos have been hurt by Christians.) My ministry partner and I were then able to provide a measure of reconciliation and comfort for her.

Another time the Holy Spirit alerted me through tongues and interpretation that an older woman with long gray hair would approach our booth and that the Indian philosophy of detachment and Universal Oneness had not been working for her and that what she wanted most in life was spiritual freedom. Sure enough, an older woman with long gray hair approached the booth. Her ancestors were from Riga, a Latvian city she proudly identified as "the occult capitol of the world" (whether this is true, I do not know). She had been a life-long consumer of the occult and New Age, though surprisingly she had had some exposure to charismatic Christianity as a teenager. Some Christians had tried in vain to impart their gift of tongues to her. She concluded that the gift wasn't for everybody. I concluded privately that generational demons of psychic phenomena and witchcraft had blocked the gift and that her heart was not fully turned to God as the one and only source of life (a pre-condition). She wanted spiritual freedom, but she confused spiritual freedom with free-for-all spirituality, which she had had plenty of and which had done her no good.

When we asked about her prayer needs, her personality changed. Hostility distorted her face as she recounted the misdeeds of a family interloper, an in-law who had disrupted her relationships and encroached on her inheritance. Prayer for this concern yielded negligible relief, if only to validate her feelings (I sensed there was more to the story). On the other hand, singing in tongues had an almost magical effect on her! She got immediate relief from malice and rage. She wept and felt uplifted and transported. Hearing songs in tongues repositioned her in her better nature, her true nature, the one God gave her. By serenading her in tongues and hosting the Presence of the Spirit, she got a taste of the spiritual freedom she really wanted: "Now the Lord is the Spirit and where the Spirit of the Lord is, there is liberty" (2 Cor 3:17).

On yet another occasion, a college-aged woman who was enrolled in a nursing program and interested in holistic medicine asked me about the gift of tongues, and I shared the entire Book of Acts story with her. Sometimes I explain the gift; sometimes I don't; it just depends on the person's receptivity and how the Holy Spirit prompts me. But many can experience God's goodness through the gift, whether or not they ask for an explanation, and the gift releases divine decrees over a person, to which angels hearken:

> Bless the LORD, you His angels, who do His word and His pleasure. Are not the angels all ministering spirits (servants) sent out [by God] to serve those who will inherit salvation?—Psalm 103:20-21; Hebrews 1:14 AMP

SIGNAL JAMMING ENEMY INTELLIGENCE

Besides serenading a person in the Spirit, singing or chanting in tongues disrupts demonic power and signal jams enemy intelligence in the same way that speaking in tongues does. The added advantage of the musicality of this gift is that singing or chanting in an unknown language is less suspect and more readily accepted—even welcomed!—than speaking in an unknown language. The ability to sing or chant in tongues is especially crucial in outreach missions. I give a couple examples below.

On one occasion I attended a New Age church to support a friend who had been invited as a guest speaker to give her Jesus message. The founder of this church was an ordained Christian minister who had deviated from Christian orthodoxy during the 1970s. While participating in hypnosis experiments, another voice spoke through him, and the entity behind the voice propounded some doctrines that fascinated him and his colleagues. Unfortunately, the minister and his colleagues lacked discernment; none had any inkling of the possibility that the voice could be demonic and that the teaching could be demonic propaganda advancing a demonic agenda. They welcomed the entity as a divine messenger, and the minister dedicated the rest of his life, which was cut short, to transcribing and propagating the teachings of this entity.

The church was universalist and entertained the latitudinarian notion that God has no definite identity; that there is no correct doctrine and no single way to God; that the only absolute is that there is no absolute (a self-contradictory tenet). They believed as Hindus do, that God inhabits everything and everybody and that creation is co-equal and co-extensive with the Creator: that all is One Being or God. Portraits of Jesus were displayed side-by-side with human masters of other religions, suggesting that Jesus is merely human or that Hindu, Buddhist, and Taoist masters are also divine. The teachings of Jesus were shuffled and compounded with other religions into strange spiritual cocktails that contradicted Jesus and the Bible.

The service opened with a period of eastern style meditation that ushered in a heavy, narcotizing atmosphere. I refused to drift down that current, so I sang softly in tongues while studying a picture of a rainbow landscape that symbolized an ascent through the chakras, the psychic energy centers of Hinduism. During the greeting time, two ladies who sat in front of me turned around and welcomed me warmly and commented approvingly,

"Your chanting is lovely. We chant, too!"

"Ah, if only you knew what I was doing!" I thought, "Then you would get mad at me or adore the Holy Spirit, too!"

Throughout the service, I spoke in tongues under my breath, doubling up when the announcer distorted the meaning of Bible verses and when the bereaved were invited to light candles and offer prayers for the dead and to the dead, a sentimental ritual of necromancy that does not recognize the finality of death the way the Bible does and that seeks the counsel of spirits who impersonate the dead.

At the close of service everyone was obliged to stand in a circle and hold hands and recite a universalist creed and chant OM—the acoustic spell of Brahman, the supreme reality of Hinduism. The man who had officiated during the service stood beside me and held my hand. I chanted loudly and beautifully in tongues to dispel the spell, patterning my chant in the same register as their monotone drone. The man squeezed my hand during the incantation and afterward turned to me and smiled warmly. I smiled back and thought, "Ah, if only you knew what I was doing! Then you would get mad at me or adore the Holy Spirit, too!"

On another occasion at a New Age expo, the booth next to ours was conducting vibrational attunements. The practitioners directed recipients to stand inside a large brass bowl (which reminded me of a witch's cauldron) around which symbols of occult power were displayed. The attuner walked in a circle around the brass bowl and repeatedly struck the bowl with a mallet to release a loud resonant sound. It was apparent to me that the ritual was an initiation of sorts that dedicated the recipients to the spirit power that was conjured through the ritual, but the recipients thought they were being vibrationally aligned with the Universe and its oscillations. It was an alignment, all right, but with the wrong spirit. After I arrived for my shift, this activity mounted to a frenzy, which was very disruptive and distracting to the low-key interactions at our booth. I felt war in my spirit, so I spoke and sang in tongues at every opportunity in between English interactions with the spiritual seekers at our booth. By the end of the day, the line of paying customers for vibrational attunement had dissolved. A young man who worked our booth reported that the following day the activity was low to nill.

Singing or chanting in tongues is an engaging and appealing way to love people and a diplomatic way to sabotage spirit powers. When you are invited to participate in an occult activity or are forced to observe it, tongues are polite way to refrain from the wrong metaphysical practice and participate at a higher level to the satisfaction of all. Singing in tongues hands a rose to a New Ager while stabbing the enemy in his ear, right through to his head. Love and war: what a great combo! Only God could arrange that.

MORE SERENADING IN THE SPIRIT

Some friends and I recorded a singing in tongues music CD to hand out for free at outreaches to those who respond favorably to being serenaded in tongues and who have CD players. Realizing that CDs are "old school" technology, we also arranged for the songs to be available through free audio streaming services like Spotify. We want people to experience the presence of the Holy Spirit without wrangling over world views just yet. God can answer their questions and resolve their difficulties later after they fall in love with His goodness. We want to introduce the gift to an open and unguarded audience, so we omit all direct references to Christianity, including the word "tongues". Instead, the musical vocalizations are described as "multilingual polyphonic plainsong" and "spontaneous melodies sung a cappella in languages unknown": just the naked voice, the original instrument closest to the heart.[3]

The CD, which is entitled *Spirit Stairwell: A Cappella Voices Hosting the Presence*, is categorized as New Age Spiritual and World Chant. This categorization is not a sorry mistake, but deliberate, not only because the broad definitions of those music genres can accommodate Christian sacred music, but because we want to reach those who listen to those genres, primarily practitioners of eastern mysticism and/or western metaphysics.[4]

We hope to intrigue. The CD jacket says,

> Join us as we host the Presence and ascend the secret stairway in the sky!

The secret stairway in the sky is Jesus, but they don't need to know that while they are being courted in a way that circumvents their prejudices: "Most assuredly, I say to you, hereafter you shall see heaven open and angels of God ascending and descending upon the Son of Man" (Jn 1:51).

We have been test driving the CD on unbelievers and Christian friends and getting feedback. An Aikido instructor (not yet saved) listened to the CD while receiving a massage. At first he tried to figure it out: "Is that Native American? Is it Aramaic? It sounds like improvisational chanting". Usually he is very talkative during his sessions, but he became unusually quiet, which is uncharacteristic of him. He reported afterward that the CD "droned on" like "background music," and he could not do his martial arts breathing to it, for it was too "irregular". I was thrilled to hear this because martial arts breath-work is a form of eastern meditation that cultivates the skill of detachment and releases Taoist and Buddhist spirit power. His feedback told me that listening to singing in tongues subdues a person and disrupts eastern metaphysical practices. A Christian pastor fell asleep to the CD, confirming that tongues aid rest. A Christian who had been upset and was venting relaxed on a couch, and another Christian who always got provoked in traffic remained unruffled while listening on her car stereo, confirming that tongues are conducive to peace and repose. Such anecdotal reports suggest that singing in tongues can be a balm for the soul and has the potential to compose, pacify, and aid sleep, among other things.

The potential for singing and chanting in tongues far outruns my current experience. I foresee drum circles with chanting in tongues; choral performances; and sound ministry over unbelievers who stand in a cascade of sound as several believers sing in tongues over them and interpret. I foresee a series of music CDs fostering different moods for different purposes, lullabies and blowouts. Let's sing underwater and see what the Lord will do!

POST SCRIPT: UNSEEN SINGERS IN THE SANCTUARY

One evening at a church that had been built about a century ago, many of us lingered in the afterglow of a special prayer and worship service that included singing in tongues. I found myself praying ad hoc for the United States with other intercessors. As I was deeply absorbed in prayer, I heard behind me the exquisite, sublime harmonies of three or four voices in the back of the sanctuary. The singing was in no discernible language but was so beautiful and compelling that I finally turned around to see who on earth was singing. Nobody was. Some random people were chatting.

I asked my prayer partners if the sound booth operator had been playing a cappella music. They said no. Then I asked if they had heard the singing, and they said, "No. You probably heard angels." But the voices sounded human. I began to wonder. Had I tuned into a living memory in the sanctuary of bygone Christians who had sung songs a hundred years ago? Was I hearing the past? Were the songs embedded in the walls and the ceiling of the sanctuary? Later I told a friend about it, and she thought that I was hearing prophetic voices singing—an earshot of the future, the voice of the future. On the other hand, perhaps I was hearing a heavenly choir like those heard at the tent revival meetings of the healing evangelist Maria Woodworth-Etter during the late nineteenth and early twentieth centuries. Such mysteries occur when you sing in tongues.

SINGING IN TONGUES PRACTICE

While you are getting started and comfortable singing in tongues, experiment in private to minimize inhibitions and performance anxiety. Once you get more confident with your own voice and more adept at melodies, venture out and sing over others in increasing order of difficulty and challenge: for most that will be family and friends first, then sympathetic Christians next, and finally the public.

SOLO: SING IN TONGUES TO A FAMILIAR SONG

If flowing in a Spirit inspired melody seems mystifying to you, try singing in tongues to a familiar praise song or worship song that you really enjoy; follow the melody or harmonize. Practice singing in tongues to several different songs you know by heart. Then ask the heavenly Father to give you custom designed melodies from His limitless repertoire to suit your voice and express your unique personality. Do not critically appraise the melody, lyrics or your voice; just be a child at play and have fun!

SOLO: SING OVER YOURSELF

Identify your top three needs and desires. Write down your needs on one piece of paper and your desires on another piece of paper. Lay your hands on the papers and sing and chant in tongues. Then wave the papers around, one in each hand, like a banner or streamer and sing and chant some more. Finally, put the paper with needs under your feet and lift the paper with desires to heaven and sing and chant some more.

You might wonder about the meaning of the symbolic actions suggested: laying hands on your recorded desires and needs and waving them; placing your feet on top of your needs; lifting your desires to heaven. In all of these actions, you are ministering to yourself by the power of the Holy Spirit: you are both the minister and the recipient of ministry. In the New Testament, the laying on of hands is a basic doctrine and practice (see Hebrews 6:1-2); this may be done to impart the Holy Spirit (Acts 8:17-18; Acts 19:6), to impart gifts of the Holy Spirit (1 Tim 4:14; 2 Tim 1:6), to bless by the Holy Spirit, to heal through the Holy Spirit (Acts 9:17), and to ordain into ministry (Acts 6:3-6; Acts 13:2-3). Here are two examples from the life of Jesus:

> And He took them [the children] up in His arms, laid His hands on them, and blessed them.—Mark 10:16

> When the sun was setting, all those who had any that were sick with various diseases brought them to Him; and He laid His hands on every one of them and healed them.—Luke 4:40

You can certainly lay hands on yourself, but you can also lay hands on your documented requests: these requests represent you, your desires, and your needs. Essentially you are releasing the power of the Holy Spirit in you for the fulfillment of your desires and needs through a prophetic act of faith.

Waving an offering and lifting an offering are acts of consecration to God in the Old Testament. The priests partook of offerings that were waved and lifted (see Lev 7:34; 10:14-15). Here is an example:

> And from the ram of the consecration you shall consecrate the breast of the wave offering which is waved, and the thigh of the heave offering which is raised, of that which is for Aaron and of that which if for his sons.
> —Exodus 29:27

In the same way, you consecrate your desires as offerings to God and partake of them (enjoy them as God's blessings).

Placing your foot or feet on top of something is a prophetic act of taking dominion, of ruling or asserting ownership. God directed the Israelites to walk on or around territory to stake an ownership claim to that territory. The Israelites also placed their feet on the necks of their enemies as a sign of their subjugation and defeat. Placing your foot on something is taking dominion or subjugating a foe. Here are examples from scripture:

> Every place on which the sole of your foot treads shall be yours.
> —Deuteronomy 11:24

> Every place that the sole of your foot will tread upon I have given you.
> —Joshua 1:3

> So it was, when they brought out those kings to Joshua, that Joshua called for all the men of Israel, and said to the captains of the men of war who went with him, "Come near, put your feet on the necks of these kings." And they drew near and put their feet on their necks.—Joshua 10:24

In a similar way, you subjugate the "enemy" of lack in any area of your life (lack of provision, protection, health, well being, peace, joy, favor, grace, opportunity, success, etc.), for that is contrary to God's best for you: "The Lord is my Shepherd; I shall not want" (Ps 23:1). You take dominion of your rightful inheritance in God. Through these prophetic acts, you engage your will with God's will and demonstrate by faith what will be.

SOLO: SING OVER A FAMILY MEMBER OR FRIEND

Invite a family member or friend to sit in a comfortable chair in a place where there is enough room for you to move around the chair. Ask your friend whether s/he prefers a non-disclosed or disclosed session. In a non-disclosed session, your friend says nothing, and you have no information about his or her condition. This is a purely Spirit led session. In a disclosed session, your friend shares burdens and/or aspirations, and you have information to sing or chant with these things in your mind and heart. This is a collaborative venture between you and the Spirit.

Feel free to walk a full circle around your friend clockwise or counterclockwise or both; or station yourself at the four corners of the chair at different intervals to sing and chant, either facing your friend inward or facing the four cardinal directions outward. Walking in a circle is a symbolic act that has prophetic significance. In scripture, encircling or encompassing a person can refer to different aspects of God's care for that person. Encircling can signify protection, as in the examples below.

> [The LORD] found [Jacob, His people] in a desert land
> And in the wasteland, a howling wilderness;
> He *encircled* him, He instructed him,
> He kept him as the apple of His eye.
> —Deuteronomy 32:10 (italics mine)

> As the mountains surround Jerusalem,
> So the LORD *surrounds* His people
> From this time forth and forever.
> —Psalm 125:2 (italics mine)

> The angel of the LORD *encamps all around* those who fear Him,
> and delivers them.
> —Psalm 34:7 (italics mine)

> You are my hiding place;
> You shall preserve me from trouble;
> You shall *surround* me with songs of deliverance. Selah.
> —Psalm 32:7 (italics mine)

As you walk around your friend and sing, you are surrounding your friend "with songs of deliverance".

Compassing a person can also signify God's provision, as indicated in several translations of the same psalm that are combined below:

> Then the righteous shall *gather about* me
> [and] *surround* me [in triumph]
> because of your goodness to me,
> for You will look after me;
> You shall deal bountifully with me.
> —Psalm 142:7 NIV, NKJV, AMP (italics mine)

Encircling a person can also express God's mercy, compassion, and loving kindness, as in the two translations of the same psalm combined below:

> But he who trusts in the LORD, mercy shall surround him;
> loving kindness and compassion shall surround him.
> —Psalm 32:10 NKJV, AMP

Finally, circumambulation can represent God's favor and goodwill as in these two translations of the same psalm:

> For You, O LORD, will bless the righteous;
> With favor You will surround him as with a shield.
> —Psalm 5:12

> For You, LORD, will bless the [uncompromisingly] righteous;
> as with a shield You will surround him with goodwill (pleasure and favor).
> —Psalm 5:12 AMPC

Walking or stationing yourself around your friend as you sing or chant is a great way to affirm and enact God's protection, provision, mercy, and favor.

After you are done, share any impressions, thoughts, feelings, sensations, and scriptures that came to your mind. Get feedback from your friend on any impressions, thoughts, feelings, sensations, and scriptures that were evoked by the song or chant. This can lead to more ministry or to closure.

SING OVER YOUR NEIGHBORHOOD, CITY, STATE OR NATION

Sing and chant over your street, neighborhood, city, state or nation from your own home or in public. From home, stand and raise your hands, palms outward, and turn in the four cardinal directions facing your neighborhood as you sing and chant. This is especially powerful if you have access to an aerial view such as a balcony, fire escape or rooftop. Another option is to place a map, satellite photo or other emblem (a city or state seal) of the geographical area over which you are singing and chanting on the floor and walk and dance around it and lunge, jump or stand over it as a prophetic act of taking dominion for God and extending His kingdom in the earth realm. Ask God about His purpose and redemptive plan for your street, neighborhood, city, state or nation and keep that purpose and redemptive plan in mind as you sing and chant and move around.

Where is this in the Bible—raising the hands, walking around something or standing over something as a sign of dominion? Raising the hands can be an appeal to God for intervention, but it is also a victory stance that releases supernatural power into a situation. Moses lifted and held his hands in the air over a battle until sunset, and Israel defeated Amalek (Ex 17:11-13). Aaron stretched out the rod in his hand over the waters of Egypt, and the waters turned into blood (Ex 7:19). Some time later, Aaron repeated this action of stretching out his hand that held the rod, and frogs emerged in droves and overran the land (Ex 8:5). Moses lifted up and stretched out his rod-bearing hand over the sea, and the sea parted, leaving a dry channel for the Israelites to pass through on foot (Ex 14:16).

In Biblical times, standing or walking on land implied the right of possession, ownership, and rule. In fact, real estate transactions were ratified by the land owner giving his shoe to the buyer in the presence of witnesses, signifying that the right to tread on and use and enjoy the land had been transferred (Ruth 4:1-9). Middle Easterners were (and still are) particularly sensitive to land claims: the Edomites refused to grant the Israelites passage through their land on the King's Highway (Num 20:14-21). The Israelites' conquest of Canaan began with a march around the city of Jericho once a day for six days and seven times on the seventh day, after which the walls collapsed: "By faith the walls of Jericho fell down after they were encircled for seven days" (Josh 6:1-5; Heb 11:30).

Similarly, standing over something (or someone) is a sign of dominion. In Joshua's raids of Canaan, he ordered his military men to place their feet on the necks of the defeated kings of five city-states as a sign of dominion over their territory. Let's read this passage again:

> Joshua called for all the men of Israel, and said to the captains of the men of war who went with him, "Come near, put your feet on the necks of these kings." And they drew near and put their feet on their necks.—Joshua 10:24

Likewise David said, "You have given me the necks of my enemies," and "they have fallen under my feet" (Ps 18:40, 38). When we raise our hands and walk around or stand over emblems of a region, we are claiming the land and its inhabitants for God. We are also subduing and overthrowing rebel powers of darkness that have staked a claim to the land and its inhabitants.

Go for a walk, bike ride or drive and sing and chant as you travel and cover ground. Extend your hand, palm outward, to houses and buildings and parks to release God's purposes as you feel led. All of these structures represent people who need God.

SING OVER SOMEONE OR ABOUT SOMETHING

Picture a specific person or situation in your mind's eye and sing or chant in tongues over that person or situation. Songs or chants in tongues can be sung or chanted remotely when you live elsewhere, are on a business trip, vacation, deployment or are interceding or doing spiritual warfare for unbelievers. The Holy Spirit in you is not limited by distance; nor are angels. Remember that Jesus healed a centurion's bedridden, paralyzed servant from a distance, and He delivered a Canaanite woman's severely tormented, demonized daughter from a distance (Matt 8:5-13; Lk 7:1-10; Matt 15:21-28; Mk 7:24-30). Here are some suggestions (some may be difficult):

- Sing a lullaby to a baby in your arms (cradle a pillow and sway or dance around).
- Sing a love song to your sweetheart (pretend to slow dance or swing dance with your sweetie).
- Sing a song of comfort over pets or well-being and productivity over farm animals.
- Sing a song of flourishing over house plants, a garden or farm.
- Sing a song of healing, health, and life over a hospital patient.
- Sing a song of wholeness and sound mind over an overwrought or mentally ill person.
- Sing a song of salvation over a neighbor or co-worker.

- Chant to expose and prosecute waste, fraud, abuse, sabotage, treason, violations of just laws, and human rights crimes.
- Chant to rescue victims of natural disaster, facilitate emergency response personnel and humanitarian relief operations, and to integrate displaced refugees.
- Chant to release hostages, victims of slave trafficking, or falsely imprisoned political prisoners.
- Chant to empower a special operations team.
- Chant to unwind a tornado or dissipate a hurricane and deflect it out to sea.
- Chant to end a drought, abate a flood, extinguish a fire.
- Chant to end a pestilence or plague or the malicious creation of one.
- Chant to avert a nuclear attack, an electromagnetic pulse or a power grid collapse.

Address any specific concern elicited by current events, the state of the union, national or foreign policies, international relations, through songs or chants in tongues. This is an alternate way of praying.

A CAPPELLA DUET, TRIO, QUARTET OR CHOIR

Duet (two). Alternate between singing and chanting. The person who is most comfortable or adept at leading starts a melody and the other person harmonizes. If both can lead, alternate who leads the melody and who harmonizes.

Trio or quartet (three or four). Appoint a leader or takes turns leading. Span the spectrum of singing softly, loudly, smoothly, rhythmically.

Choir (five or more people.) Appoint a leader or takes turns leading. Span the spectrum of singing softly, loudly, smoothly, rhythmically.

INSTRUMENTAL ACCOMPANIMENT

Here is a general proviso about instruments: Musicians must curb their zeal for volume and defer to tongues singers because instruments can easily overpower voices. It might be best to play acoustically (unplugged) at first. When amplification is used on instruments, singers should be amplified on microphones. Here are some possible arrangements:

One instrument plays softly as background accompaniment for the singer/s who lead. The musician should be adept at improvisation and sensitive to follow the lead of the singers: "The singers went before, the players on instruments followed after" (Psalm 68:25).

Two or more musicians play instruments at a low to moderate volume as accompaniment for the singers. Again, the singers lead and the musicians to follow (unless the musicians can lead without dominating).

String, wind, and percussion instruments accompany the singers. Singers and musicians take turns leading. Incorporate call and response or a lively repartee between singers and musicians. Let every person be featured and fore-fronted at different intervals during a jam session.

Drum circle (percussion instruments only). Singers chant. Chanters and drummers take turns leading. Incorporate call and response between chanters and drummers.

Let solo drummers and chanters be featured and fore-fronted at different intervals during the jam session.

CORPORATE WORSHIP AT CHURCH

Corporate singing in tongues can occur spontaneously during worship service, though it can be purposefully initiated, too. The worship leader or pastor can prompt the congregation to sing in tongues. This is a special ministry to God. Vocalists on the worship team should stop singing through their microphones and let the congregation lead (vocalists can join off microphone). All musicians should play soft accompaniment or stop playing their instruments and join singing off the microphone.

This bears repeating: no singer should sing through a microphone; no musician should play an amplified instrument loudly during this special offering to God. Those who do so monopolize musically and spotlight themselves and spoil the corporate song in tongues. Amplified voices and amplified instruments prevent members of the congregation from discovering their own voices and melodies because amplified sound drowns them out. Worship leaders must resist the temptation to lead. Let the Holy Spirit lead and create an oceanic sound through His people. This supernatural phenomenon cannot be orchestrated or engineered by people. Let's reserve a time for this special kind of worship that can only be done by the corporate assembly and that cannot be reproduced by a single individual or even a small group. This beautiful manifestation of the Holy Spirit through hundreds of people should be carefully cultivated and jealously guarded as the rare treasure it is.

IN THE PUBLIC FORUM

Here are some possible applications in the public forum:

- Sing or chant in tongues softly as you shop or wait in line or wait to complete a transaction or ride the metro.

- Rent a booth at a New Age expo, occult event, holiday festival or other public pow wow. Offer free healing prayer, peace of mind prayer, and prophecy, and supplement these spiritual services with songs in tongues. Explain what you want to do. For example, "I speak in a heavenly language and would like to sing over you prophetically and let God serenade you through me. I often get impressions while I sing, and I'll let you know afterward what I got. Would you be interested?" When you are done serenading the recipient, share any impressions you got while singing. Often the novelty of this experience and the presence of the Holy Spirit emboldens the recipient to share prayer requests.

- Two or more people sing in tongues simultaneously over a person. (You should practice harmonizing together before you do this.)

- Worship band with singing in tongues and dancing.

- Drum circle with chanting in tongues and dancing.

- Record a singing in tongues CD and give it away for free at a public event to those who listen to CDs and/or make the music available for free streaming on a digital music service like Spotify.

- Post a YouTube video of singing in tongues.

Singing in Tongues Videos: Teachings and Activations

For a live teaching on the subject of singing in tongues as spontaneous praise of an unpremeditated, unrehearsed nature with melody and lyrics composed by the Holy Spirit, see "Singing in Tongues Part 1: Spiritual Songs," posted January 15, 2021, on The River Room YouTube channel.[1]

For a live teaching on the different purposes of songs in tongues, including love, personal transformation, protection, and warfare, see "Singing in Tongues Part 2: Love, Transformation, Protection, Warfare," posted February 16, 2021, on The River Room YouTube channel.[2]

For a live teaching on singing in tongues for power evangelism in the public forum, see "Singing in Tongues Part 3: Power Evangelism," posted March 12, 2021, on The River Room YouTube channel.[3]

For a live teaching on the Old Testament "new song," the instrumental and vocal forerunner to a song in tongues, see "Singing in Tongues Part 4: A New Song," posted April 9, 2021, on The River Room YouTube channel.[4]

For a live teaching on the tonal quality and mood of different kinds of songs in tongues, see "Singing in Tongues Part 5: Tonal Quality and Mood of Different Themes," posted May 14, 2021, on The River Room YouTube channel.[5]

INTERPRETING TONGUES TESTIMONY

I first became interested in systematic training or practice interpreting tongues thanks to a church service in which I and another woman delivered interpretations of the same tongue that were different but not incompatible. I got Micah 6:8, and she got Jeremiah 29:11:

> The Lord has shown you, O man, what is good and what He requires of you: to do justly, to love mercy, and to walk humbly with your God.—Micah 6:8

> For I know the plans that I have for you, says the Lord, plans for peace and not for evil, plans to prosper you and not to harm you, plans to give you a hope and a future.—Jeremiah 29:11 (NKJV/NIV)

Interestingly, my interpretation of the tongue happened to be the other woman's life verse, and her interpretation happened to be personally relevant for me at the time. It seemed that the Holy Spirit was delivering individually tailored words to each of us (and we trust also to others who were present).

After pondering these verses, I discovered the logical connection between them. The Jeremiah verse that my friend got presented God's blessing, whereas the Micah verse that I got presented the conditions for blessing. Together the two verses explained that God's good will for our lives comes to pass when we live according to His ways. In other words, holiness is a prerequisite to the good life in God. I also noticed a structural similarity in the three-part form of the verses that followed the tripartite pattern and cadence of the tongue: "1) do justly; 2) love mercy; 3) walk humbly"; "1) for peace and not evil; 2) to prosper you and not harm you; 3) for a hope and a future".

Perhaps the most fascinating connection between the messages was our individual identities as messengers. My friend has a mercy temperament and is always ready to extend mercy and an abundance of grace. I have a justice temperament and am always ready to prosecute war to establish justice. The verses we received were in accord with our different temperament types: she got the "God wants to bless you" verse, and I got the "you better straighten up and fly right" verse. We represented different aspects of the nature and character of God, and together our two interpretations gave a more complete picture of the ways of God. So different interpretations may look dissimilar at first glance but be deeply complementary on further analysis. Different interpretations of the same tongues are often like jigsaw puzzle pieces that fit together to make a complete picture or like working parts that fit together to make a machine run.

The difference in our interpretations really got me pondering the difference between a translation and an interpretation. A translation is a more literal and exact word-for-word rendering, whereas an interpretation conveys impressions of meaning. I have since realized that interpretations of tongues are more akin to impressions of meaning than verbatim translations. This means there is room for more than one interpretation! Often different interpretations are compatible in thought provoking ways.

By far the most exciting experience interpreting tongues has been in the public forum. I had an opportunity to participate in a creative and clever Christian outreach at a Mischief and Magic event (formerly a Harry Potter event, but the name had been changed due to licensing issues). The event was founded by a Tarot card reader and had become an opportunity for psychic readers to ply their trades, but a Christian couple rented an office downtown to do ministry. They hand-built staging to divide the larger office space into many private antique parlors to accommodate a maximum number of visitors. Outside the building they hung medieval banners that invited folks to enter for "Free Dream Interpretation," "Free Prophecy," and "Free Curse Removal". An A-frame sign on the sidewalk near the entrance announced, "The Real Magic Starts Here". In preparing for the event, local Christians prayed that God would give visitors vivid and even disturbing dreams to compel them to inquire within. The previous year some visitors had responded to the offer for free curse removal in jest or in all sincerity with reports such as "I'm seeing apparitions in my room at night".

Mischief and Magic event, downtown Staunton, Virginia, 2019.

A-frame sign outside office building.

Interpreting Tongues Testimony   111

Staged parlor inside building.

Because the people attracted to the event enjoy supernatural entertainment, I broached the subject of speaking in tongues with the coordinator of the Christian outreach. As I saw it, the acceptance of magic formulas and incantations was an open invitation to offer the general public an authentic demonstration of a supernatural language. (Recently I had seen T-shirts displaying magic spells for sale at Walmart.) I suggested that they could add another banner announcing, "Free Revelation through Mystery Languages!" or "Free Spirit Serenades!" To my surprise, the coordinator was thrilled. The Lord had been coaxing her to go public with tongues earlier that year, and her husband was totally on board with what some might consider a dangerous idea or an inane idea, except that "the foolishness of God is wiser than men and the weakness of God is stronger than men" (1 Cor 1:25). The goal of the event was to give people a word to move them further along in their journey toward Jesus. The great thing about tongues is that it is an attraction in its own right; it piques curiosity while the tongues speakers sing songs of deliverance and allurement to God, songs of sacred purpose and divine destiny.

"Free Prophecy" banner.

"Free Dream Interpretation" banner.

"Free Curse Removal" banner.

The coordinator and I partnered together to interpret messages in tongues. Our partnership felt dynamic, thanks to the Holy Spirit. Sometimes our interpretations were the same or similar; sometimes they were different but complementary. The interpretations could be categorized as confirming, redemptive or directive: a word of knowledge about a person's most stellar attributes or about a life theme; a prophecy about God's plan or a person's sacred purpose; a word of wisdom to guide or counsel a person about a concern. We reminded people of the best about themselves or about things that were significant to them and that had been impactful; we told them about their call or about God's redemptive reversal of misfortune; and we recommended re-calibrations for the course.

To give a few examples, I serenaded in tongues a young lady who was a software developer, and I received verses from the Song of Solomon as the interpretation. At first this seemed unusual, but then she told us that her dream was to found a wedding company. I explained to her that the Song of Solomon is a poetic, historically celebrated book about romance and the marriage sacrament. She got excited, and so did I, and then my partner gave her a QR code for a free Bible application program, and I recommended *The Passion Translation* of the Song of Solomon, including the footnotes, which are so eye opening. I told her, for example, that the word "ravished" in the sentence "you have ravished my heart with one look of your eyes" means "to rip the bark off a tree". Likely this was her first exposure to the Bible, and it was presented in an appealing, personal way.

I serenaded in the Spirit another young lady who was studying to become neonatologist at a prestigious university, and my partner and I got several interpretations about her future in this field, about research and development, wisdom, revelations in the night, and medical breakthroughs. I sensed that doubt and skepticism were her chief enemies and that she would have to ward them off to free her imagination for creative solutions. She responded visibly to the warning about doubt and skepticism; she looked startled, recognizing these as familiar occupants of her mind, but she had not yet considered them obstructions to her best interest and progress.

I serenaded another lady, fixing my gaze on her steadily, and as I sang, her eyes wandered and became downcast and swollen with tears. The song got her in touch with her heart, and her heart was quite sad. In fact, she was steeped in sorrow. I mentioned this to her, and she confided in me that she and her husband had had a terrible argument and that she was very concerned about his emotional health. This turned into an opportunity to pray for him, for her, and for their marriage, which was beautifully constructive.

I serenaded another woman, a crisis counselor, who was enjoying a bachelorette party before her wedding. While serenading her, I had the distinct impression that she had been through the very trial that her clients were going through and that she had found meaning and purpose in rescuing people from suicide. I told her from the Holy Spirit, "You have done well in your journey. You are to be commended for turning back to help those who are in the place you left behind. You know the worth of a human being, and you are a hero for telling others their worth." She became very tearful.

During the event, one woman accepted Christ (her conversion brought me to tears); another re-dedicated her life to Christ (this was equally moving); some nominal Christians were beckoned into deeper realms of their own faith; and some secular humanists were introduced to the presence of the Holy Spirit, the Bible, and non-religious Christianity. A Buddhist Vietnamese family accepted our ministry under their universalist assumption that all religions are the same, but a distinction was made when the spokeswoman for the family offered us money for our services and we declined, much to her astonishment; we explained that we were doing it out of gratitude for all that Jesus had done for us. Being a civic minded worker on Capitol Hill in Washington D.C., she kept raving on and on about the incredible community service we were providing, attracting business and generating revenue and good will for the city. I wanted to send her as a good will ambassador to the founder of the event, the Tarot card reader, who was disturbed by our activities. Two witches in full costume, one of whom wore prosthetic elf ears, left weeping, something you don't expect witches to do. All we can say is, the Holy Spirit moved!

You might wonder how we broached the subject of speaking in tongues or singing in tongues. Here are some examples of permission questions we asked or statements we made:

> "May I sing over you in a heavenly language?"
> "May I serenade you with a heavenly song?"
> "This is a heavenly language. I am proclaiming over you the mysteries of God. I am prophesying into your future, your sacred purpose in life."

We first explain to people that we want to invest in their sacred purpose and divine destiny. Then we tell them that we have a gift of heavenly languages that we want to share, with their permission, and that as we speak or sing over them we may get impressions about them. Depending on a person's worldview, we might explain the gift of tongues later. Those with Christian backgrounds (such as Catholics) often get an explanation that the gift of tongues is a ministry of the Holy Spirit as described in the Bible. We point them to Acts 2 and 1 Corinthians 12 and 14 for further study.

Generally I do not explain the gift to recipients from a non-Christian background unless they ask. I prefer to leave them intrigued and allured by a direct experience of God's goodness and more subtle indications of the source, including scriptures I get and other gifts of the Holy Spirit. My partner, however, felt a duty to inform recipients about our Christian orientation by the end of each session because she did not want them mistaking tongues and interpretation for psychic readings or divination. By and large, this went well. However, she once made the mistake of disclosing her Christian identity to Pagans at the start, and they scornfully rejected ministry and left disgusted. I was not present at this session, but we discussed it later.

As a former Pagan, I understand this. Pagans have been ideologically indoctrinated and socially conditioned to mock Christianity and despise Christians. They have been trained to hate (in fulfillment of prophecy): "They hated Me without a cause. They hated Me without reason" (Jn 15:25 NKJV, NIV). In my B.C. days before Christ, I never thought critically about what was presented to me in mainstream American culture. I never read the Bible or visited a church or exposed myself to any intelligent discourse about Christianity. I never addressed the Christian God in prayer, challenging Him to make Himself known to me. My view of Christianity was formed by Monty Python films, by scenes of monks smashing Bibles against their foreheads with metronome regularity and a Catholic woman ejecting a gushing baby from between her legs while washing dishes. Sorry to say, such representations made me conclude that all Christians were robotic, self-abusive idiots or silly, pathetic, socially backward subhumans.

My partner discovered that it is best not to mention Christianity to certain people, especially Pagans, because their minds are poisoned with irrational prejudice. For these people, seed planting is best. We want them to experience God without wrangling about the nature of truth and reality. God can order their minds later. Tongues and interpretation are a back door to the heart when the front door of the mind is locked and bolted. For me, the main objective was to make the recipients feel special and significant and to let them experience the presence of the Holy Spirit.

While speaking or singing, I maintain steady eye contact with the recipient so that the light of the Holy Spirit can shine from my eyes into their eyes:

> No one, when he has lit a lamp, puts it in a secret place or under a basket, but on a lampstand, that those who come in may see the light. The lamp of the body is the eye. Therefore, when your eye is good, your whole body also is full of light.—Luke 11:34 (see also Matthew 6:22)

> You are the light of the world. A city that is set on a hill cannot be hidden. Nor do they light a lamp and put it under a basket, but on a lampstand, and it gives light to all who are in the house. Let your light so shine before men, that they may see your good works and glorify your Father in heaven.
> —Matthew 5:14-16

Eye contact is extremely powerful. I often find that I am transported by the Holy Spirit into a euphoric state and experience something like a light trance. Recipients may be similarly affected.

You might wonder how we handled tricky cases. Regarding the wariness of some recipients, we had the grace to navigate those occasional situations, and they were only occasional. In one case, three university students came together, one of whom did not want to receive anything, but after we ministered to her two friends and she saw how accurate and uplifting the encounters were and how they affirmed one friend's call in life and the other friend's disposition, she let us minister to her, too. My partner immediately spoke to her temperament type, for she was a person of discernment and discriminating judgment, one who analyzed and evaluated before engaging and committing. Our ministry proved reassuring because it validated her way of navigating through life as the unique way God had made her.

In a similar case, the chaperone of a youth group on a field trip at Mischief and Magic looked alarmed when we first spoke in tongues, but she relaxed when she heard the interpretations, and she had all the youth repeat the words they got. I had a strong impression that John 10 was relevant for her: "I am the good shepherd. The good shepherd gives His life for the sheep. But a hireling who does not care for the sheep sees the wolf coming and flees" (Jn 10:11-13). I shared with her that she was a good shepherdess and that she was conscientious in her duty to guard the sheep against wolves; she was not like a mere hireling who would abandon them. Her job was not just a job to her, but a ministry. She resonated with that word and left feeling gratified.

Ministering at this event was intense and challenging, but I felt extraordinarily alive. There is nothing more fulfilling than partnering with the Holy Spirit. To be a vehicle of courtship for God and humanity is amazing.

The author, Corinna Craft (left), and her ministry partner, Louisa Priore (right).[1]

INTERPRETING TONGUES PRACTICE

The exercises and drills in this chapter are organized from individual to partner to small group to large group activities. All of them help prepare a person to deliver a tongue and an interpretation in church and in public. There are several unique and engaging activities: my favorite uses prophetic art as a springboard to prophecy through the gift combination of tongues and interpretation. Others are designed for public outreach, including fishbowl and booth prophecies and fishing for men prophecies, per Jesus' instructions: "Follow Me, and I will make you fishers of men" (Matt 4:19; Mk 1:17). Along the way to vocal spiritual fitness are interesting teachings and discussions: how God communicates by word or by picture; the difference between Biblical casting of lots by divine design and so-called chance drawings of secular or Pagan philosophy; and artful ways to tailor your ministry to people of different ideological persuasions at New Age and occult fairs.

On a practical note, certain tools of the scribe trade may be helpful, especially writing and research tools. Here is a list:

HELPFUL TOOLS

- paper and pen;
- a smart phone, tablet or laptop with Internet access, a stop watch function, and an audio recording function;
- an online Bible application program such as Bible Gateway or Bible Hub;
- an online concordance such as Blue Letter Bible;
- an online dictionary such as Merriam-Webster;
- an online encyclopedia such as the Free Dictionary's Encyclopedia, Wikipedia or Encyclopaedia Britannica;
- in the absence of electronic telecommunication devices, a Bible, a concordance, a dictionary, an encyclopedia set, a stop watch or clock, and audio recorder or note pad and pen.

OPEN-ENDED OR CLOSED COMMUNICATION

All practice exercises can be pursued as open-ended or closed. Open-ended practice of tongues and interpretation is an unqualified invitation for the Holy Spirit to communicate anything He pleases without any conditions. An open-ended invitation forgoes personal concerns and sets no parameters on the communication received. This gives the Holy Spirit total freedom to determine the content of the message.

Closed practice of tongues and interpretation limits the communication to the inquirer's specific question or concern and sets parameters for content. The inquirer determines the subject matter. Nevertheless, the Holy Spirit is sovereign and can override the request or give an answer that is deeper than the question or concern, or give an answer that addresses an unidentified issue of the heart, just as Jesus did with the woman at the well (see Jn 4:1-26).

Those who are new to practice or who are still developing proficiency and ease in the gifts should choose open-ended communication with the Holy Spirit, which allows Him to determine the subject matter. This way the participants will not be encumbered with any preconceived ideas or expectations that could potentially limit the ministry of the Holy Spirit.

More experienced practitioners may ask closed questions of the Holy Spirit: these could include requests for understanding, wisdom, counsel, direction, and guidance on particular issues. When doing closed practice, recipients should choose partners with whom they feel comfortable sharing personal concerns and the Holy Spirit's response to them (which could include discipline, correction, and warning, right?!).

CAUTION: DO NOT APPROACH OR PRESENT PROPHECY AS DIVINATION

Here is a word of caution that the Holy Spirit gave me that I now pass on to you: Do not approach tongues and interpretation as a form of divination or fortune telling, and do not present them to others this way. God is not your answer boy (or anybody else's!). We cannot interrogate Him and force Him to answer a particular line of questions. The Holy Spirit is not at our beck and call. Any spirit that is at our beck and call is not the Holy Spirit, for no one summons and orders the Spirit of God. Tongues plus interpretation should not be treated mechanically as a standardized process or ritual by which you (or another inquirer) secure the information you want so that you can forge ahead on your own. Tongues and interpretation are gifts from God, and God is a person. God's gifts are not more valuable than He is. God's gifts are aspects of His person. God's gifts are not a way to manipulate Him to perform. God does not do command performances. The vocal gifts, in particular, are a way to communicate with Him and to others on His behalf. They are a relational activity, a way to get to know Him better. They are not merely an information exchange or a religious transaction. Since He is personally involved, they are holy and consecrated (reserved for His honor) and a sacred trust to be handled reverentially.

With that in mind, let's begin!

SOLO (1)

This solo practice exercise can be done at home or any inspiring devotional site. It also can be done as warm-up to more challenging partner or group exercises in a workshop setting. When done as a warm-up in a group, the facilitator can use a stop watch to mark the time. Speak in a tongue to yourself for about 20 to 30 seconds (do not speak too short or you might not have enough material to work with; do not speak too long or you might have too much material). Stop and wait for an interpretation. Here are some possible ways the Holy Spirit could communicate with you:

- a vision or visual impression;
- a Bible verse or passage; a Bible story or character;
- a key word, phrase or statement;
- a memory;
- a mood or feeling;
- an intuition;
- a sensation;
- something from any field of human enterprise: literature, art, sports, entertainment, media, education, business, law, government, science, industry, service trades, history.

Go with your first impression. Write it down. Repeat speaking in tongues and interpreting for a total of three rounds. Now ask yourself: Is there a theme? Do you feel encouraged? strengthened? motivated? uplifted? Did you receive understanding about something or guidance?

Please watch my teaching video, "Interpreting Tongues (Part 1): Impressions of Meaning," on The River Room YouTube channel. In it, I explain that interpretation is more like an impression of meaning than a literal, verbatim translation of a message in tongues. There is latitude in interpreting a tongue just as there is latitude in interpreting the symbolism in a painting. The reason is threefold: the conversion of a message from one language to another often defies a neat one-to-one correspondence (especially the conversion of a heavenly language into an earthly language); God's messages are multi-dimensional; and God's people are unique in their perspectives, life experiences, and styles of expression. The prophet Daniel who interpreted "the writing on the wall"—a divine judgment in a celestial language—took the liberty of substituting one word in the cryptic script for another in his interpretation; he also took the liberty of converting the mystery message, which came as a brief bullet point list, into lengthier explanatory prose. He did this to clarify meaning. The point is well taken that to a certain extent interpretations are processed by and for human understanding. Knowing this may encourage you to embrace the impressions you get as valid interpretations.[1]

PARTNERS (2)

This partner exercise can be done with a friend at home or in any comfortable setting conducive to receiving from the Holy Spirit. For most people, this will be a relatively quiet place free of distractions and disruptions. Partner exercises also can be done in a workshop setting. The best time to introduce partner exercises in a workshop is after a group exercise. Group exercises tend to be ice-breakers and community bonders; they can be deeply engaging and compelling. After that, pairing off for partner exercises is not awkward or intimidating.

One partner speaks in a tongue for 20 to 30 seconds, and both interpret. Take at least one minute but no more than five minutes to develop your interpretations. During this time of formulating interpretations, remain quiet and do not consult one another so that you do not influence or disturb each other. Write down the first impression you receive. Do a key word or key phrase search on the Internet or in a Bible application or concordance to develop what you have. Consult an online dictionary or encyclopedia or other resource as necessary.

After sharing your interpretations, compare them, looking for likenesses or equivalencies. Is there a common subject or theme? Are there common elements? Are there other similarities: the type of audience addressed, the tone of the message, the structure of the message?

<u>Similar Interpretations</u>
same or similar subject or theme (general concept);
same or similar elements, features or qualities (constituent parts, attributes);
same or similar audience (persons addressed);
same or similar tone or quality of message (mood, impact);
same or similar structure.

If there is no obvious similarity at first glance, are the interpretations compatible or complementary in some deeper way after further analysis? For example, does one interpretation offer a promise while the other specifies the conditions for its fulfillment? Does one present causes and the other effects? behaviors and consequences? Does one interpretation portray the inner life, the hidden person of the heart or character, while the other describes the outer life and circumstances? Do the interpretations use different metaphors (symbols) to illustrate the same principle or process? Do the messages (and the messengers) demonstrate different aspects of the nature or character of God? Do the interpretations fit together like jigsaw puzzle pieces, providing a more complete picture?

> Different Interpretations
> compatible or complementary in some way;
> may use different metaphors to illustrate the same principle or process;
> one offers a promise, the other specifies conditions for fulfillment;
> one deals with causes, the other with effects;
> one portrays the inner life, the other the outer life or circumstances;
> both demonstrate different aspects of the nature or character of God;
> both fit together like jigsaw puzzle for a more complete picture.

Now evaluate each other's messages for congruence with scripture, resonance with your own spirit, and rapport with the Holy Spirit (you can inquire directly: "Holy Spirit, what do you say?"). Most evaluations consist of nothing more than quick approval because the message can be supported by scripture, your inner being affirms the truth of the message and the spirit of the message, and you sense that the Holy Spirit approves.

> Evaluate Interpretations
> Can the content of the message be corroborated by scripture?
> Are you at peace or reconciled with the message, even if it is challenging?
> Do you feel a doubt, an internal caution or misgiving?
> Does the Holy Spirit approve or object?

On rare occasions, you may have a concern about your partner's interpretation or a suggestion for improvement on content or delivery. If so, tactfully explain why. Describe how the message impacted you and offer scripture as a standard, especially for a discrepancy. Carefully consider the interpreter's rationale or justification. Sometimes an explanation will resolve any issue and clear any doubt; an explanation could correct a misperception on your part or a miscommunication on the speaker's part, and you will be able to endorse the message. If not, you might need to mull it over further or confer with other mature believers or pray for your partner if you sense error. Don't preclude the possibility that you might be mistaken and that God might be adjusting your understanding about something:

> As iron sharpens iron, so a man sharpens the countenance of his friend.
> —Proverbs 27:17

Conversely, if you receive constructive criticism about your own interpretation, take it under advisement, search the scripture, and ask the Holy Spirit and other mature believers, especially those in leadership, about the validity of the feedback you got. If the concern is significant enough, both partners should discuss this with the facilitator after the workshop.

This completes round one. Now do another round. For round two, switch who speaks in tongues: the second person speaks, and both of you interpret the tongue and discuss. If you have more time, do two more rounds and continue to alternate who speaks in tongues. For an extra challenge, those who speak in more than one tongue can use a different tongue each time they speak.

At a later time you might want to watch my teaching video, "Interpreting Tongues (Part 2): Comparing Multiple Messages," on The River Room YouTube channel. In it, I discuss how to compare multiple interpretations. Interpretations that are similar are relatively easy to compare because they share common elements or themes that can be quickly identified. Interpretations that are different are harder to compare because their connections are not obvious at a first glance and require thoughtful reflection. With deeper analysis, you may discover that different interpretations are not only compatible, but complementary and mutually reinforcing. They may present the same message using different metaphors; they may present different parts of a whole; or they may have some other working relationship such as sowing and reaping, rights and duties, mercy and justice.[2]

You also might find it helpful to watch the teaching video, "Interpreting Tongues (Part 3): Judging and Delivering an Interpretation," on The River Room YouTube channel. I delve into greater detail about the nuances of evaluating interpretations, particularly monitoring your own responses and reactions to an interpretation. A positive response is always welcome, but a negative reaction could indicate that you are discerning that something is wrong with the interpretation—the content, the delivery, or the spirit. On the other hand, a negative reaction could indicate that you are being challenged and convicted by the Holy Spirit in some way. Evaluation is part of the stewardship responsibility of the gift of interpretation. It is a sacred trust.[3]

SMALL GROUP (3 TO 5)

Only one person speaks; all, including the speaker, interpret and share. Take turns until everyone has spoken in tongues once and all have interpreted (three to five rounds total). If everyone gets the same or similar interpretation or complementary interpretations, this would be worth sharing with all in a workshop context. A recurring theme among interpretations is good; among a majority is excellent; by all is unusual and worth sharing as an encouraging example of how the Holy Spirit connects God's people in interdependent ministry and how God's multi-faceted wisdom is displayed through His people (Eph 3:10).

THE WHOLE CLASS: ART AS A SPRINGBOARD TO PROPHECY THROUGH TONGUES AND INTERPRETATION

This series of exercises uses Holy Spirit inspired art as a springboard to prophecy through the gifts of tongues and interpretation. The paintings in this section were painted by charismatic Christian artists during extemporaneous worship at church or at home. The manifest Presence or inspiration of the Holy Spirit was felt as they painted.

Before we look at the first painting, let's review the Biblical basis for this exercise. One of the most common forms of prophecy is a picture; another is a word. 1 Samuel 3 sums up these two major ways of receiving a message from the Lord: "And *the word of the LORD* was rare in those days; there was no widespread *vision*" (1 Sam 3:1, italics mine). Word prophesies are a matter of hearing the voice of God and repeating what He says. A beautiful illustration of this is narrated in 1 Samuel 3. The young boy Samuel who had been dedicated to priestly service as a baby was lying down and resting in the tabernacle when he unexpectedly heard the voice of the Lord. Because Samuel was unfamiliar with the Lord's voice, he mistakenly assumed that the high priest Eli was calling him. After three rounds of the Lord calling Samuel and Samuel reporting to Eli, Eli realized that Samuel was actually hearing God's voice. Eli instructed him to lie down again, wait for the Voice, and respond with, "Speak, for your servant hears" (1 Sam 3:10). Then the Lord gave Samuel an ear-tingling prophecy, a dire judgment against the house of Eli for the sacrilegious behavior of his sons that he did not restrain, including their fornications with women who served in the temple and their forcible confiscation the people's offerings to God. This "word" or hearing the voice of the Lord was a radical induction into prophecy.

The other form of prophecy is visual. Picture prophesies, visual impressions, visions, trances, and dreams are so common that a prophet was referred to as "a seer" in ancient Israel:

> Formerly in Israel, when a man went to inquire of God, he spoke thus: "Come, let us go to the seer"; for he who is now called a prophet was formerly called a seer.—1 Samuel 9:9

Visual impressions can range from simple to complex, from still life picture or vignette to documentary drama to a live tour in the Spirit. Among the simpler visions, Amos saw a plumb line and a basket of summer fruit on different occasions (Amos 7:8; 8:2). Among the more complex, Ezekiel was airlifted by a lock of his hair between heaven and earth and transported from captivity in Babylon all the way to Jerusalem (some 500 miles away as the crow flies or 1,500 miles as caravans travel) where he witnessed a series of abominations in the temple, one of which required him to dig a hole in the wall to spy on the elders who were offering incense to creature deities; he also saw women weeping over the mythological death and rebirth of an Adonis-like fertility god, and the elders performing a salutation of obeisance to the sun (Ez 8).[4]

Picture prophecies can be described in detail, but they require an explanation to make sense of them and to understand their application. Scripture records several occasions where the Lord showed a picture to a prophet and then asked the prophet, "What do you see?" Consider the following brief dialogue between the prophet Jeremiah and the Lord:

> The LORD showed me something in a vision. Then he asked, "What do you see, Jeremiah?"
>
> I answered, "A branch of almonds that ripen early."
>
> "That's right," the LORD replied, "and I always rise early to keep a promise."
>
> Then the LORD showed me something else and asked, "What do you see now?"
>
> I answered, "I see a boiling pot in the north, and it's about to spill out toward us."—Jeremiah 1:11-13 CEV

After the Lord showed Jeremiah the boiling pot tipping toward his land, He explained that it represented impending judgment coming against Israel through an invading army from a northern country. A similar dialogue of "What do you see?" and "I see" is recorded in Amos (Amos 7:8; 8:2). The Lord explained the meaning of these pictures right away without the prophet inquiring. This is a divine show-and-tell sequence.

    On other occasions the meaning of a prophetic picture was not volunteered right away or automatically given; the prophet had to ask for an explanation of its significance. Consider the following dialogue between the prophet Zechariah and a divine messenger:

> The angel who explained the visions woke me from what seemed like sleep. Then he asked, "What do you see?"
>
> "A solid gold lampstand with an oil container above it," I answered. "On the stand are seven lamps, each with seven flames. One olive tree is on the right side and another on the left of the oil container. But, sir, what do these mean?"
>
> Then he asked, "Don't you know?"
>
> "No sir," I replied.

So the angel explained that it was the following message of the LORD to Zerubbabel:

> I am the LORD All-Powerful. So don't depend on your own power or strength, but on my Spirit. Zerubbabel, that mountain in front of you will be leveled to the ground. Then you will bring out the temple's most important stone and shout, "God has been very kind."

The LORD spoke to me again and said:

> Zerubbabel laid the foundation of the temple, and he will complete it. Then everyone will know that you were sent by me, the LORD All-Powerful. Those who have made fun of this day of small beginnings will celebrate when they see Zerubbabel holding this important stone.
>
> Those seven lamps represent my eyes—the eyes of the LORD—and they see everything on this earth.

Then I asked the angel, "What about the olive trees on each side of the lampstand? What do they represent? And what is the meaning of the two branches from which golden olive oil flows through the two gold pipes?"

"Don't you know?" he asked.

"No sir, I don't," was my answer.

Then he told me, "These branches are the two chosen leaders who stand beside the Lord of all the earth."—Zechariah 4:1-14 CEV

Through the prophet's inquiry about the vision, we learn that the seven lamps represent the eyes of the Lord that see everything on earth, the two branches represent two spiritual leaders who are close to the Lord, and that oil is a symbol for the mountain-leveling power of the Holy Spirit, in direct contrast to the strength of man: "'Not by might, nor by power, but by My Spirit,' says the LORD of hosts"; by this power God will empower His people to rebuild His temple (Zech 4:6-7 NKJV).

The takeaway point from this passage is that you can ask the Holy Spirit, the Spirit of truth and revelation, to explain the meaning of a picture that you see in your mind's eye. You can also inquire through the wonderful gift combination of tongues plus interpretation, which reveals divine mysteries. Tongues are divine mysteries: "He who speaks in a tongue does not speak to men but to God; in the spirit, he speaks mysteries" (1 Cor 14:2). Interpretation reveals those mysteries; it is a revelatory gift (1 Cor 14:5; 1 Cor 2:9-13). The combination of these two vocal gifts equals prophecy (1 Cor 14:5). Prophecy makes the will, purpose, and counsel of God known to man.

We will use tongues plus interpretation to receive a message from the Lord through prophetic art. This next exercise integrates two forms of prophecy, visual and auditory, a picture and a word: art (a picture) and tongues plus interpretation (a word). We will look at a painting, which contains a visual message from God much like a vision, trance or dream. We will speak in tongues, which contains an auditory message from God, and we will receive an interpretation to make the message plain.

Activation: Ask workshop participants to look at the artwork featured on the next page, or any other Holy Spirit inspired work of art. (The title of the painting is omitted to avoid influencing interpretation. Please see the chapter endnotes for the title.) Describe the following hypothetical scenario:

> Suppose the Lord flashes this picture in your mind's eye as a visual prophecy while you are interceding in tongues for someone or for a situation.
>
> How would you interpret it?
>
> One way you could get an interpretation from the Holy Spirit is by continuing to speak in tongues until you get an impression of meaning.

Interpreting Tongues Practice 133

(2019), Eddy Cutrera.[5]

Direct participants to speak in tongues for a few minutes as they gaze steadily at the painting. Remind them to make mental notes of their impressions or to write them down, especially if they get an abundance of impressions or think they might forget the details. Afterward, allot several minutes of silence for everyone to develop an interpretation. When the time is up, instruct participants to pay close attention to any common elements and themes as individuals share their interpretations. Ask volunteers to stand at the front one at a time to share their interpretations. At the end of the collective time of sharing, ask for more volunteers to identify common elements and themes that were presented during the individual interpretations. Ideally, workshop participants will discover a spiritual leitmotif—a dominant and recurring theme—in all the prophecies.

More Holy Spirit inspired art is presented below to practice the gift combination of tongues and interpretation. Follow the same procedure as above: speak in tongues for a few minutes while gazing at a painting. Take a few more minutes of silence to formulate your impressions into an interpretation based on the image. In a workshop setting, the facilitator recruits volunteers to share their interpretations for all to ponder, then recruits more volunteers to identify common elements and themes in the interpretations.

The titles of the paintings are omitted to avoid influencing interpretations. Titles are provided in the chapter endnotes.

(2019), Eddy Cutrera.[6]

(2016), Alison Webster.[7]

(2017), Alison Webster.[8]

Interpreting Tongues Practice 137

(2017), Alison Webster.[9]

(2017), Alison Webster.[10]

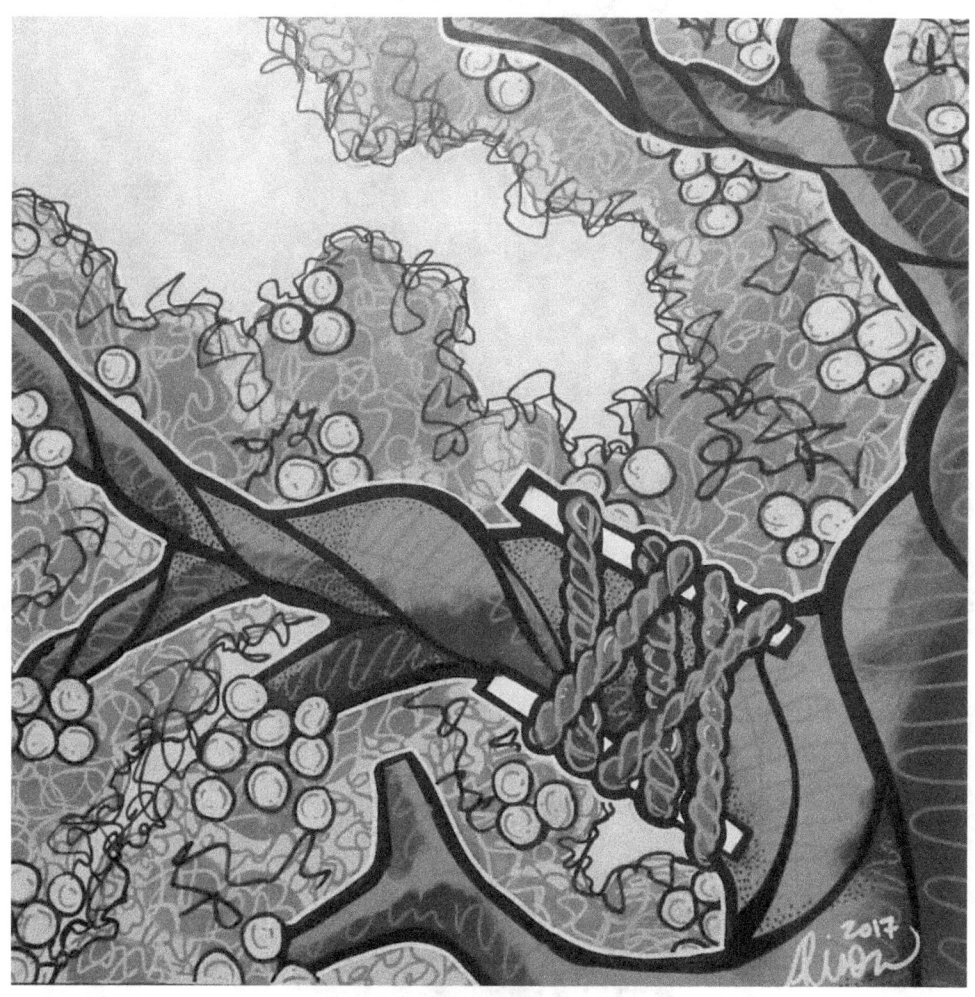

(2017), Alison Webster.[11]

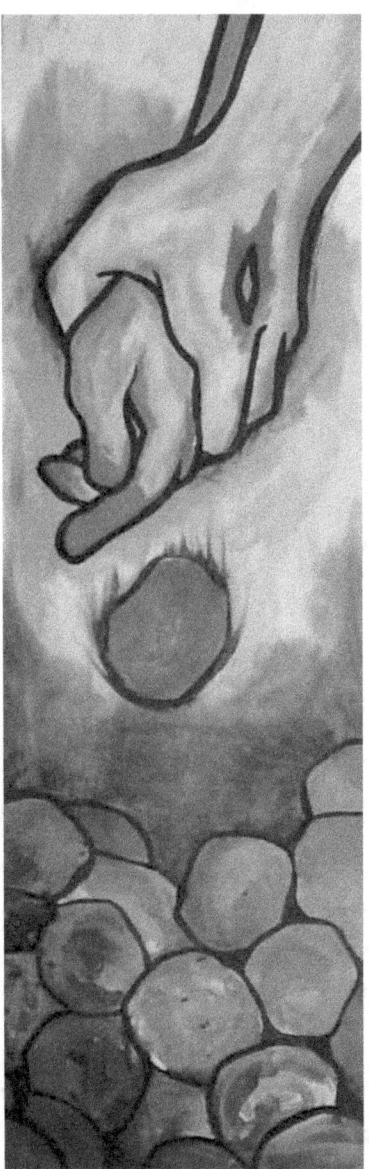

(2017), Alison Webster.[12]

(2017), Alison Webster.[13]

(2017), Alison Webster.[14]

(4.17.2020), Cassandra Donnelly.[15]

(4.03.2020), Cassandra Donnelly.[16]

Interpreting Tongues Practice 145

(4.17.2020), Cassandra Donnelly.[17]

(2.21.2020), Cassandra Donnelly.[18]

(4.06.2020), Cassandra Donnelly.[19]

(2019), Jill Eulo.[20]

Interpreting Tongues Practice 149

(detail, 2016), Andre Dial.[21]

THE WHOLE GROUP: SOLO PRESENTATION OF TONGUES AND INTERPRETATION

This drill prepares participants to deliver a tongue and an interpretation in a more formal setting such as a church service or other assembly of believers. In a formal setting such as a church service, three solo tongues plus three interpretations is the maximum number advised by Paul (see 1 Cor 14:27). This limit does not apply to an activation workshop. The purpose of a workshop is to practice drills so that everyone can develop proficiency and gain confidence. Because training is the purpose, we exceed the limit of three tongues and three interpretations to give everyone an opportunity to practice and grow in these vocal and revelatory gifts.

Let's begin with some pointers about effective delivery. When speaking in a tongue before a group, speak loudly, clearly, and distinctly: enunciate your words as if you were an artist sculpting art with your mouth. Form matters because form affects function, the effectiveness of a message. Your tongue should sound articulate and robust. Do not mumble, slur, garble or whisper your words. A deformed message is a dysfunctional one because it does not inspire confidence and a good response. Here is what Paul said about a deformed, dysfunctional message:

> Whether flute or harp, when they make a sound, unless they make a distinction in the sounds, how will it be known what is piped or played? For if the trumpet makes an uncertain sound, who will prepare for battle?
> —1 Corinthians 14:7-8

So deliver your heavenly language as if you were delivering the oracles of God, because you are!

> If anyone speaks, let him speak as the oracles of God.—1 Peter 4:11

Here are some more pointers on good form:

- make eye contact;
- project your voice to fill the room;
- speak with a specific emotion or no emotion as the Spirit leads;
- add gestures and dramatize through body language as the Spirit leads. In most cases, the focus will be on speech, not action, though action can reinforce or embellish speech.

Now let's embark on instructions for the drill. The facilitator asks a volunteer to speak in tongues or assigns someone the task. The volunteer walks to the front and faces the group, speaks loudly and clearly in a tongue for 20 to 30 seconds, and then returns to his or her seat. Everyone waits in silence for one minute and mentally prepares or writes down impressions of the meaning of the tongue.

The first person who is ready to interpret stands up, walks to the front, faces the group, and delivers the interpretation loudly and clearly, then returns to his or her seat. If there are no concerns (no objections to the interpretation that warrant discussion), the next person who is ready to interpret does the same until all who want to interpret have interpreted. The pace should be brisk and continuous to train people to receive and deliver a message quickly.

Repeat this drill with a different tongues speaker and different interpreters until everyone who wants to participate has had a chance to participate in both capacities. The formality of standing up, walking to the front, facing the group, and using good diction gets people accustomed to delivering a tongue and an interpretation in a formal assembly. Everyone should practice interpreting each and every time, whether or not they present at the front during a particular round.

THE WHOLE GROUP: COMPARING AND CONTRASTING INTERPRETATIONS

This comparison and contrast exercise trains participants to process interpretations. This provides an opportunity to admire the manifold wisdom of God in His people:

> to the intent that now the manifold wisdom of God might be made known by the church to the principalities and powers in the heavenlies.
> —Ephesians 3:10

When comparing and contrasting interpretations, look for similarities that confirm the messages and differences that expand the messages. An interpretation that is different from others yet Biblically sound and spiritually resonant (does not contradict scripture and is not unsettling to the human spirit or disapproved by the Holy Spirit) can be quite enlightening.

After a volunteer presents the first interpretation of a tongue, the facilitator asks if there are any other interpretations that are similar. Every interpretation that is similar is shared, as many as there are, and common elements or themes are identified. After similar interpretations have been shared, the facilitator asks if there are any interpretations that are different. These are also shared, and the group discusses how they are compatible with or complementary to the others given (often this requires thought).

If there is no discernible connection between those interpretations that are similar and those that are different, this would be a great opportunity for the facilitator to explain the validity of diverse interpretations. (Again, the assumption is that all interpretations are Biblically sound and spiritually resonant: they neither contradict scripture nor are spiritually unsettling.) An example of diverse interpretations of the same divine message is the sound from heaven recorded in John 12. The bystanders who heard the sound perceived it differently: some identified the sound as thunder; others identified the sound as an angel speaking; Jesus identified the sound as the Father's voice (Jn 12:27-30). Although Jesus had perfect understanding, the others were not incorrect; they were reporting their subjective perceptions of an objective phenomenon. Indeed, at times the Lord's voice does sound like thunder as reported in Psalms and the book of Job: "The God of glory thunders," and "God thunders marvelously with His voice" (Ps 29:3; Job 37:5). At times the Lord's voice does sound like an angel speaking: "So it was, when the Angel of the LORD spoke these words to all the children of Israel, that the people lifted up their voices and wept" (Judg 2:4; see also Judg 13:6). From the sound from heaven incident, we see that different interpretations are admissible and acceptable.

The principle of diversity in divine communication is also supported by many scriptures that refer to the Lord's voice and the voice of God's people as the sound of "many waters" (Rev 1:12-15; Rev 19:6). The phrase "many waters" suggests the potential for multiple messages. Remember that Jesus referred to the baptism in the Spirit or the gift of tongues as "rivers" (plural) of living water flowing from a person's innermost being (Jn 7:38-39). Some who hear tongues may experience one river that flows from the Spirit within a person, while others may experience another river that flows from the Spirit within a person. Each may receive a different message, for the Spirit can minister simultaneously to many individuals, just as the Lord can speak simultaneously to millions of people and millions of angels. As the language of the Spirit of God, tongues have multi-layered meaning.

DELIVERING TONGUES AND INTERPRETATION BEFORE AN ASSEMBLY

Here are some considerations for a formal delivery of tongues and interpretation. In an actual church service, local protocol must be honored when delivering a tongue and an interpretation. Usually a tongues speaker stands up wherever he or she is in the sanctuary at an appropriate time and delivers a tongue in a way that commands the attention of the whole congregation. The best time is during a pause in the service such as the pause between worship songs or the transition between worship and teaching or preaching. An inappropriate time is whenever someone is already addressing the congregation, and especially when a pastor or guest speaker is speaking. Such a delivery is disruptive and may be ignored as a form of correction.

Following a tongue, there is a narrow window of opportunity to deliver an interpretation, usually only a minute to two, because leadership feels responsible to maintain the flow of service. If you are willing or feel compelled by the Holy Spirit to interpret, move toward the platform as quickly as possible as an act of faith, even while you are still receiving the interpretation. This reduces wait time for the congregation. Sometimes the Holy Spirit will brood over a person in a telltale way to propel a person forward. A friend of mine who is a good public speaker but who dislikes public speaking feels butterflies in her belly and her skin flushes every time the Lord impresses her to speak. I sometimes feel elevated in my spirit and my heart races when the Lord impresses me to speak. You may experience other signs of stirring.

Some leaders may require an interpreter to submit an interpretation to someone in leadership before releasing it to the congregation. Once you have permission (someone hands you the microphone), face the congregation, speak to command the attention of all, and deliver the interpretation boldly, looking members of the congregation in the eye. Generally, the absence of any feedback from leadership means no objection and acceptance of the message (though there may be exceptions). Be prepared to receive feedback at a later time. The most frequent form of feedback is encouragement and curiosity from other members of the congregation.

PERSONAL PROPHECY WITH TWO, THREE OR MORE

This section covers personal prophecy. Personal prophecy through tongues and interpretation should be audio recorded or at least transcribed as completely and accurately as possible, preferably by someone other than the giver and receiver so that giver and receiver are not burdened with that secretarial task and can give themselves fully to their respective duties; otherwise, writing can be encumbering, especially when the presence of the Holy Spirit is strong and emotions are touched.

Both the giver and receiver benefit from a recording. The receiver does not have to rely on memory to retain the details and totality of the message but can refer to the recording and invest in the message later with prayer and proclamation, personal preparation, and an action plan. This is good stewardship of the gift. Recording also holds the giver accountable and protects the giver in case of a misunderstanding or disagreement about the message. Sometimes what is said is not what is meant, and sometimes what is said is not what is heard. Disconnects can occur when the giver miscommunicates or the receiver misperceives or misinterprets the message.

Paul observes that we do not always see face to face, but we see through a glass darkly; we see a dim or blurred reflection of reality in a mirror (1 Cor 13:12). For example, the receiver may process the message through the distortion of soul wounding or even demonic interference, or the giver may judge according to the flesh and not according to the Spirit (Jn 8:15; 2 Cor 5:16). A recorded message can be consulted to correct any misunderstanding or mistake. Fortunately, such mishaps are rare. Generally, recordings are celebrated and treasured, especially by the receiver who gets a God's eye view of his or her life.

PARTNERS

The recipient records the tongue and its interpretation on an audio recording device. The tongues speaker/interpreter may give the entire message in a tongue followed by an interpretation or may alternate back and forth between tongues and interpretation until he or she feels satisfied. Alternating back and forth may be easier for many, especially intercessors; it could result in a more developed, robust prophecy. After the tongue and its interpretation are complete, the recipient may offer feedback of any immediate impressions. Then switch roles.

THREE OR FOUR

The recipient records tongues and interpretations given by all members of the group. Every member gives a tongue and its interpretation, each one in turn, until the recipient has received from everyone in the group. Rotate the role of recipient until every person in the group has received from all members of the group. In the end, every individual will have received three or four personal prophecies and will have given three or four personal prophecies. Feedback is optional, time permitting. The priority is giving and receiving tongues plus interpretation.

THE WHOLE GROUP

Collect on small folded pieces of paper the full names (first and last) of those who want to volunteer to receive a personal prophecy; deposit the names into a drawing bowl, shuffle them and draw a name. The designated person sits in the center of the group and records on an audio recording device or a volunteer takes notes. Group members surround the recipient. Different members of the group step forward one by by one (in no particular order) as they feel prompted and give a tongue and its interpretation for no more than one minute until everyone who wants to participate has participated. Repeat until all the names are drawn (or time runs out).

PERSONAL PROPHECIES BY DIVINE DESIGN

This practice section incorporates drawing lots, what the world would characterize as "random" or "chance" drawings but what the Bible characterizes as divine design. There are many examples in the Old Testament of decisions made by casting lots that demonstrate divine design rather than the arbitrariness or inequity and injustice we tend to associate with "random" or "chance" drawings. The Israelites cast lots to obtain their parcels of land by tribe and by family, and the lots fell in proportion to the size of the tribe and family; in other words, by rational and intelligent design, by just and equitable distribution, conferring more land on the larger clan and less land on the smaller clan:

> But the land shall be divided by lot. They shall receive their inheritance according to the names of the tribes of their fathers.
> —Numbers 26:55 NASB

> You shall inherit the land by lot according to your families; to the larger you shall give more inheritance, and to the smaller you shall give less inheritance. Wherever the lot falls to anyone, that shall be his.
> —Numbers 33:54 NASB (abridged)

> And Joshua cast lots for them in Shiloh before the LORD, and there Joshua divided the land to the sons of Israel according to their divisions.
> —Joshua 18:10 NASB

The priests also cast special lots to receive guidance from God, and especially His judgment in a particular matter (Ex 28:30): for example, to identify who was at fault for alienating God or for a defeat in war; whether or not to go to war, whether or not to pursue a raiding band, and so on (see 1 Sam 14:18-19, 37-42; 1 Sam 30:7-8; Josh 7). These special lots were stored in the priest's vest ("breastplate") and were called Urim and

Thummim, Hebrew words that could mean "the Curses and the Perfections". They were cast "in times of crisis to determine the will of God" and may have functioned like "yes" or "no" answers.[22]

King David used lots to organize the priests into 24 divisions of service:

> With the help of Zadok, David separated them into divisions for their appointed order of ministering. They divided them impartially by drawing lots, for they were officials of the sanctuary and officials of God.
> —1 Chronicles 24:3, 5 NIV (abridged)

An intriguing form of lots is found in Numbers: when certain disgruntled and ambitious Israelites challenged God's appointment of Moses and Aaron as priests, the tribal leaders brought their rods—cast their lot, as it were—to see whose rod would be distinguished for leadership, and God confirmed His prior appointment by making Aaron's rod, which was a dead stick, sprout and bud and blossom and produce ripe almonds (Nu 17:5, 8). Incredible! In the New Testament, the disciples cast lots to determine who would replace the traitor Judas as a disciple, and the lot fell to Mathias (Acts 1:26).

The Biblical drawing of lots takes for granted God's sovereignty in orchestrating human events. God is like a universal project manager and universal event coordinator. Whether you call this synchronicity, serendipity, convergence, divine alignment, divine intersection, providential oversight, a kairos (opportune) moment, or something else, the principle is this:

> The lot is cast into the lap,
>   but its every decision is from the LORD.—Proverbs 16:33 NASB

In the Bible (and in reality), there is no such thing as chance. The concept of chance—random occurrence, accident, fortune, misfortune, good luck, bad luck—denies cause or agency. Think about that. Chance attributes outcomes to sheer accident. When the accident is favorable in outcome, the world calls it good luck or good fortune; when the accident is detrimental in outcome, the world calls it bad luck or misfortune. The concept of chance presupposes that there is no reason for something happening, that there is no accounting for anything, and that there is no rational being who is responsible or in control. Years ago auto collisions were called "accidents," not collisions. They were framed as random occurrences happening by chance. Why was that? The purpose was to deny human agency and responsibility and fault. Obviously, this is untrue.

Chance frames the world as haphazard. This view suggests that life is governed by irrational forces and is therefore meaningless and purposeless. The concept of chance negates the very existence, nature, and character of God. It suggests that God doesn't exist, or if He does exist:

- that He doesn't know something (and is therefore not omniscient as God should be);
- that He can't do something (and is therefore not omnipotent as God should be);
- that He is unavailable or absent (and is therefore not omnipresent as God should be);
- that He is indifferent to human need and desire (and is therefore not loving as God should be);
- and that He condones evil (and is therefore not holy as God should be).

The Bible presents the opposite view. We learn that everything occurs by intelligent design. Intelligent design includes God's divine design, which is good, the Devil's evil design, and humanity's mixed designs, which are good or evil. Ultimately, God's design prevails precisely because He is God: all-knowing, all-powerful, ever present, loving, and holy.

For something to be truly chance, it must be lawless. But can anything be totally lawless? This implies that God's laws do not govern the universe or that there are things outside of God's control or that God cannot anticipate everything, which contradicts the nature of God and what we know of Him from scripture, the inner witness of the Holy Spirit, and personal experience.

In the field of science, randomness has certain useful applications, but randomness is different from chance. Chance is chaotic, but randomness works within design. Randomness is about unpredictability and uncertainty: it is the surprise element in design. We see this unpredictability and surprise element in nature, in ourselves, and in God. In the field of science, randomness is used in security encryption, stock market simulation, and the unbiased selection of experimental research subjects. But random is not as random as we imagine it. For example, randomly generated numbers are generated according to intricate, "astonishingly long patterns":[23]

> Researchers typically use random numbers supplied by a computer, but these are generated by mathematical formulas—and so by definition cannot be truly random.[24]—*BBC Science Focus*

Modern scientists now grope to find uncertainty in the subatomic world, which so far, satisfies a certain need for the haphazard.[25] But we must ask ourselves, is the subatomic world really that uncertain to God, or is it only uncertain to humans at this juncture in time? Colossians says,

> In Him [Christ], all things consist, cohere, hold together. [His is the controlling, cohesive force of the universe.]—Colossians 1:17 AMP, AMPC

In God all things consist and cohere: He holds the universe together. He is the mystery glue. I believe that Albert Einstein's quest for the "Unified Field Theory"—a single theoretical framework that unifies all fundamental forces of physics and relationships between elementary particles—was really a quest for God.[26] The one common denominator in all creation is the Creator. Since all things are created by Him and for Him "in the heavens and on earth, visible and invisible," it stands to reason that nothing is random or chance (Col 1:16 NASB).

Now let's consider a startling passage of scripture, which frames an archer's chance or "random" shot as occurring by divine design:

> Now a certain man drew a bow at random [at a venture], and struck the king of Israel between the joints of his armor. So he said to the driver of his chariot, "Turn around and take me out of the battle, for I am wounded." The battle increased that day; and the king was propped up in his chariot, facing the Syrians, and died at evening. The blood ran out from the wound onto the floor of the chariot. Then, as the sun was going down, a shout went throughout the army, saying, "Every man to his city, and every man to his own country!"

So the king died. Then someone washed the chariot at a pool in Samaria, and the dogs licked up his blood while the harlots bathed, according to the word of the LORD which He had spoken.—1 Kings 22:34-37; 2 Chronicles 18:33-34; KJ in brackets

The archer's chance or "random" shot strikes King Ahab right between the chinks of his armor in fulfillment of a prophecy of divine judgment! This grim example of divine design is packaged in a seemingly random occurrence. The takeaway point is that we are not victims of accident, chance, luck, hazard, fortune or fate. These are humanistic or Pagan notions, and most of them have a demigod and demon presiding over them, especially when they are personified as a benevolent, malevolent or capricious being.

To reinforce this teaching, I encourage you to watch the video on personal prophecies by divine design on The River Room YouTube channel, which was posted November 25, 2020: "Casting Lots: Prophecies by Divine Design".[27] The following exercises incorporate the drawing of lots. Tongues and interpretation are used to develop a personal prophecy, but no one knows who the recipient will be until the drawing is done. We leave the assigning of prophecies to God, not chance.

Exercise #1: All for One: all prophesy over one

Collect on small folded pieces of paper the full names (first and last) of everyone present; drop all the names into a drawing bowl and scramble them. Set a stop watch for 2 minutes. Direct the whole group to speak in tongues vigorously for 2 minutes. After this, reset the stopwatch for 3-5 minutes and observe silence as everyone interprets his or her own tongue and writes impressions of meaning and any scriptures that come to mind on a piece of paper. The facilitator collects the papers, draws a name from the bowl, and gives all the paper prophecies to the recipient, who refrains from reading them immediately. Repeat this process until everyone has received a pile of paper prophecies and there are no more names to draw (or as many times as feasible under time constraints).

Time permitting, everyone reads their paper prophecies. Afterward, the facilitator asks volunteers to read aloud their favorite or most impactful paper prophecies and comment on them. If time is short, the facilitator can postpone sharing until the next meeting or allow some sharing now and finish the rest later. Participants take their paper prophecies home to read and ponder and formulate feedback. Before the next meeting, the facilitator reminds everyone to bring their paper prophecies for sharing.

Exercise #2: One on One: each one prophesies over another

Collect on small folded pieces of paper everyone's full name; drop the names into a drawing bowl and scramble them. Set a stop watch and direct everyone to speak in tongues vigorously for 2 minutes. Reset the stop watch for another 3-5 minutes while everyone writes the interpretation of his or her own tongue and scriptures on a piece of paper. When everyone is finished, the facilitator holds the bowl in front of a participant, who draws a name; the participant presents his prophecy to the person whose name he just drew. The facilitator holds the bowl in front of the next participant, who draws another name and presents her prophecy to the person whose name she just drew, and so on, until everyone in the group receives a paper prophecy. The facilitator invites volunteers to read aloud their paper prophecy and comment.

Suppose a participant draws her own name and receives her own interpretation of tongues as a personal prophecy? What then? This is not a dilemma, for God can speak to us through ourselves. However, most of us want to hear God speak to us through someone else. Unless there is a compelling reason (the participant is suddenly thunderstruck by the profundity and relevance of her own prophecy!), the default action is to invite that participant to draw another name from the bowl and afterward return her own name to the bowl.

Exercise #3: Divine Design Personal Prophecies (drawings from a pot)

This exercise is similar to the preceding ones except for the method of distribution and feedback: each participant draws a personal prophecy from a collection of shuffled prophecies in a pot; feedback is given later in private through personal contact rather than in front of the entire group.

Instruct the group to speak vigorously in tongues for 2 minutes. Observe 3-5 minutes of silence to formulate interpretations. Write down any impressions of meaning and any scripture references on a piece of paper. Write down your name and contact information—a cell phone number or email address—on the paper so that the recipient can give you feedback in the days ahead. Fold the paper prophecy in half three times and write your initials on the outside. Place the prophecy in bowl #1.

Repeat the activation. Speak vigorously in tongues for 2 minutes. Take 3-5 minutes to write down impressions of the meaning of the tongue and any related scriptures and personal contact information. Fold the paper prophecy in half three times and write your initials on the outside. Drop the prophecy in bowl #2.

Everyone removes one prophecy from bowl #1 and one prophecy from bowl #2 without looking into the bowl. If a participant draws her own name, she can keep it or draw another prophecy and then return her own prophecy to the bowl. God can certainly speak to us through ourselves, but most of us want to hear from God through someone else.

The homework assignment is for each recipient to contact the person who wrote the personal prophecy and give feedback.

FISHING FOR MEN PERSONAL PROPHECIES

This exercise should be reserved for when everyone has grown in the gifts of tongues and interpretation. The instructions are similar to those in the previous section of drawings of personal prophecies by divine design with one notable exception: unbelievers are the recipients.

Collect on small folded pieces of paper the full names of unbelievers who have a relationship with someone in the group as a friend, relative, neighbor, co-worker, client, etc., and the full name of the group member who is submitting the unbeliever's name. (Be aware that some professional codes of ethics prohibit fraternizing between a client and a practitioner. Follow the Holy Spirit: see Acts 4:18-20.)

Direct everyone to speak vigorously in tongues for 30 seconds and to write the interpretation on a piece of paper within three minutes. Collect the interpretations or paper prophecies; draw a name; give all the paper prophecies to the person who knows the name-bearer. The person who knows the name-bearer reviews the interpretations later in private and gives those that have merit to the recipient and asks the recipient for feedback.

Repeat the process of tongues, interpretation, collection, and name drawing until time runs out or there are no more names to draw.

Follow up: At the next meeting, the facilitator asks volunteers for feedback about the prophecies that the unbelievers received.

Further follow up: If the unbelievers are favorably impacted by the paper prophecies, invite them to come in person to receive more personal prophecies through tongues and interpretation from the whole group or as many as are willing to participate (the rest can observe).

FISH BOWL AND BOOTH PROPHECIES

There are many ways to minister a prophecy through tongues and interpretation. Here are two possibilities that can be done at a home party or at a rented booth at a New Age conference or occult fair or similar event.

FISH BOWL PROPHECIES

Fast, pray, and ask the Lord to give you tongues and interpretations that are customized for individuals who will draw them from a fish bowl. Ask for words that will touch hearts and enlighten minds. Speak in tongues and write the interpretations on paper (the interpretations can be typed and printed for a professional look). Put the prophecies in a fish bowl or other attractive receptacle. Repeat this process for the anticipated number of guests or projected number of visitors.

BOOTH PROPHESIES

This ministry takes unabashed courage and faith! Tongues and interpretation go public! To embolden yourself, watch these two teaching and activation videos, which explain the Biblical basis and validity of the public expression of tongues:

> "Speaking in Tongues Workshop: Public Purposes of Tongues, Part 1," The River Room YouTube channel, May 22, 2020.[28]

"Speaking in Tongues Workshop: Public Purposes of Tongues, Part 2," The River Room YouTube channel, June 19, 2020.[29]

Remember also that participants in New Age conferences and occult fairs are very open and seek all kinds of voices and spirits, so tongues and interpretation are no more bizarre than any other psychic service offered. Nonetheless, because of the daring and novel nature of this outreach, it is best to have a ministry partner present who is directly involved or available on standby.

Before the event, fast and pray and ask the Lord to send (or assign angels to escort) specific people to your booth who are open and to block others who are not open or who would syphon or otherwise spoil or sabotage ministry efforts. Forbid the enemy to send anyone to subvert your outreach. Ask the Lord to reveal Himself in a demonstrative way to recipients. Ask to host His presence so that recipients can sense or feel Him tangibly. Ask that they would feel known by God and special to God. Ask for a revelatory message to direct them to Himself.

At the event, be friendly and invite a recipient to receive a free prophecy. Introduce yourself and your ministry partner before you begin. Explain that you have a vocal gift and that you will speak (or sing) in a heavenly language and share any impressions you get about the message. Invite the person to look into your eyes as you speak or sing. Many people find looking directly into a stranger's eyes challenging, but this can be extremely powerful because the Holy Spirit in you transmits the light of Jesus directly to their spirit:

> The lamp of the body is the eye. Therefore, when your eye is good, your whole body also is full of light. But when your eye is bad, your whole body also is full of darkness. Therefore take heed that the light which is in you is not darkness. If then your whole body is full of light, having no part dark, the whole body will be full of light, as when the bright shining of a lamp gives you light!—Luke 11:34-36 (see also Matthew 6:22-24)

> You are the light of the world. A city that is set on a hill cannot be hidden. Nor do they light a lamp and put it under a basket, but on a lampstand, and it gives light to all who are in the house. Let your light so shine before men,

> that they may see your good works and glorify your Father in heaven.
> —Matthew 5:14-16

Speak in tongues or serenade the recipient with a song in tongues and then interpret. Observe the recipient's non-verbal responses. If the recipient is having a good experience and wants more, invite him or her to express a need, desire or concern that you can lift up to God through tongues and interpretation. If the recipient is not having a good experience, stop and inquire or stop and redirect.

Provide follow-up gifts as the Holy Spirit impresses this upon you: a free Bible or QR code for a free Bible, the business card of one or more Bible teaching, Spirit filled churches, a Christian music CD (especially one that features singing in tongues!), and anything else that would be helpful to continue the journey toward Jesus.

WHETHER TO IDENTIFY THE SOURCE OF THE GIFTS

Should you identify Jesus, the Heavenly Father or more vaguely "the Christian God" as the source of tongues and interpretation? That depends. In general, those who were raised in a Christian household, no matter how nominal the faith and no matter what the denomination, whether Catholic, Baptist, Methodist, Presbyterian or some other Protestant group, as well as those who gravitate toward non-denominational, seeker sensitive Christianity (Joel Osteen fans, for example), tend to have a favorable impression of Christ, Christians, and Christianity. In such case, identifying the source of the vocal gifts is helpful, even advantageous to those who minister and beneficial for those who receive. You can educate these recipients about the faith of their childhood and youth or their current interest in Christ by pointing to Bible passages that instruct in these gifts (Acts 2, 1 Corinthians 12 and 14). Exposure to tongues and interpretation is a great opportunity for proto-Christians and nominal Christians to explore deeper and richer aspects of the faith and for non-Bible trained, drifted or backslidden Christians to rededicate their lives. (Unfortunately, many Christians attend New Age events because they do not know any better: they have not read their Bibles, or they do not take seriously the admonitions in the Bible against occult practices; or they do not understand how these admonitions apply. Participation in any and all forms of spirituality indicates a profound level of ignorance, deception, confusion, and mixture in the body of Christ.)

There is one prominent exception to the general rule of favor with Christians: when a person has suffered spiritual abuse through a distorted or perverted version of Christianity. In this case a person can be triggered in trauma memory. At a recent New Age outreach, for example, my partner and I ministered to an older woman from a Catholic background who was currently attending a Unity Church. The Unity Church denies the divinity of Christ; Unity considers Jesus a mere human teacher and not Immanuel, God with us, God in the flesh (Isa 7:14; Matt 1:23). My partner, supposing her to be amenable to a hard sale of the gospel on account of her Catholic background, urged her to commit to Christ, and the woman, though polite, reacted negatively and entered into "lockdown". She admitted to us that the encounter reminded her of past experiences when she felt cornered and pressured to confess Christ. Her right eye twitched spastically, and my partner, who has the gift of discerning spirits, smelled a rotten odor. Clearly, a turf war was going on inside of her due to demonic opposition. When my partner and I debriefed, I recommended a more soft pedaled approach for people like her. This woman had suffered some spiritual abuse and needed a love encounter even more than a truth encounter.

New Agers tend to be open to the identification of the source of tongues because they believe in religious tolerance, practice religious fusion, and entertain the metaphysical idea of Oneness. Similarly, Buddhists and Hindus often allow Christians to minister to them because they are polite, they want a benefit, and they do not regard submission to the ministry of another religion as a threat to their belief system or spiritual security. Identifying the source of tongues and interpretation to recipients who practice some form of eastern mysticism is generally safe, or at least not controversial or divisive. Realize, however, that their understanding of Jesus is likely to be distorted. New Agers tend to regard Jesus as just one of many enlightened masters who modeled the realization of God within oneself. Hindus tend to regard Jesus in a similar way (as a guru), or they identify Jesus as one of many human avatars or incarnations of the Divine, all of which are mere names and forms of the nameless and formless supreme reality of Hinduism, Universal Being or Consciousness (Brahman). Buddhists tend to respect Jesus for traits they associate with the Buddha—compassion, wisdom, and sacrifice—but deny his divinity, atoning death, and resurrection.

Pagans and occult practitioners are generally not open; in fact, many are contemptuous of Christianity and hostile toward Christianity. Identifying the source of your inspiration probably would result in an antagonistic confrontation or a disgusted withdrawal and aborted ministry. For these people, it is best to withhold information about the source and simply let them experience the goodness of God unaware. Let God court them with supernatural gifts that bypass their prejudices. Despite the need for discretion, be careful not to misrepresent tongues and interpretation as just another form of divination or fortunetelling. You do not want to mislead them to draw the wrong conclusion about the gifts. Refer to tongues as a heavenly language or a mystery language from God and interpretation as the decoding of an encoded message. This explanation should be sufficient to distinguish the vocal gifts from other occult services. Leave them with a good impression, and let God explain in His own way and His own time.

CASE STUDIES: GOD'S COUNSEL AND COMFORT THROUGH INTERPRETATION

The combined gifts of tongues and interpretation can minister in a great way to God's people. The Holy Spirit excels at giving comfort and counsel through this beautiful gift combination, which equals prophecy. When you are by yourself or when your burden cannot be shared with others or understood by others, you can speak in tongues over yourself and interpret and get the mind of the Lord on the matter. When you are with a friend who operates in these gifts, the two of you can present a matter of concern to the Lord and take turns speaking in tongues as both of you interpret. Several rounds of this can yield great counsel and comfort straight from the Holy Spirit. Let's look at some examples. First we will study one open-ended session in which the partners had no specific agenda but simply let the Holy Spirit speak. Then we will study five closed sessions in which the partners brought one partner's specific personal concerns before the Lord.

OPEN-ENDED SESSION

Dana and Dasha

Let's call the two interpreters Dana and Dasha. Their goal was to let God speak to them about whatever was important to Him. They took turns speaking in tongues. One would speak in tongues and both would interpret, so each message in a tongue got two interpretations, one from Dana and one from Dasha. They did three rounds of this. At the end of each round, they compared notes.

Interpretation 1, Dana got a strong impression that the tongues and interpretation session would focus on developments in the upcoming new year, 2020, and onward into the new decade. She felt prompted to research the Hebraic meaning of the year 2020. The year 2020 in the Gregorian calendar corresponds to the year 5780 in the Hebrew calendar. The Biblical significance of this year can be determined by studying the alphabetical correlates to the numbers. The letters of the Hebrew alphabet are pictographic: they are word-pictures that convey meaning. Every letter is also assigned a number. So the numbers in a year correspond to letters that carry a message.

After quickly scanning an online article, Dana discovered that the last decade of 2010-2019 (which was the Hebrew decade 5770-5779) had a theme associated with the Hebrew letter "Ayin," which is a symbol for the "eye" or "seeing". The next decade of 2020-2029 (which is the Hebrew decade 5780-5789) has a theme associated with the Hebrew letter "Pey," which is a symbol for the mouth or "speaking". To summarize, the last decade was about gaining divine insight, hindsight, and foresight (for those who sought God's perspective), while the next decade will be about divine communication or sharing the insight previously gained (for those who seek to represent God as spokespersons).[1] Dana felt certain that God was going to speak to them about ministry emphasis in the next decade.

Interpretation 1, Dasha got:

> Rejoice in the Lord
> Sing songs
> Bring sacrifices
> The feast is prepared
> The guests are invited, open up the gates
> Come and dance before the Lord
> Come and praise His Name
> The Name from above
> The Morning Star shines
> Let the people rejoice

After Dasha shared this interpretation, Dana commented. Dana noted that a prominent theme was minstrelsy or worship arts ministry and that the nature of this minstrelsy was evangelistic, resulting in a greater number of guests in God's household. She drew this conclusion on the basis of imagery of the wedding feast: "the feast is prepared" and "the guests are invited," which alludes to the marriage supper of the Lamb, whose guests are those who have entrusted their lives to God (Matt 22:1-14; Rev 19:7-9).

Dana recognized the phrase "Morning Star" and shared these two verses: "And so we have the prophetic word confirmed, which you do well to heed as a light that shines in a dark place, until the day dawns and the morning star rises in your hearts" (2 Pet 1:19). And, "I, Jesus, have sent My angel to testify to you these things in the churches. I am the Root and Offspring of David, the Bright and *Morning Star*" (Rev 2:28; Rev 22:16). The supporting scriptures indicate that in the immediate and not-so-distant future (2020 and beyond), it would be important to "heed prophecy," which would provide "a light that shines in a dark place". The scriptures also indicate that Jesus "the Bright and Morning Star" would radiate through the hearts of His people who heed the prophetic word: "until the morning star rises in your hearts".

Interpretation 2, Dana got:

> I am the God of advancement. Look to Me.
> I direct the strikes (strike the enemy; strike camp). Look to Me.
> Return day by day for marching orders.

Dana remembered that in the Old Testament the Israelites who sojourned in the wilderness had to strike camp whenever the Lord prompted them, and they had to strike camp in a certain order, starting with Judah, whose name means "praise"; followed by Reuben, whose name means "see, a beloved son"; followed by Ephraim, whose name means "fruitfulness"; followed by Dan, whose name means "judge" (see Num 2; Gen 29:35; Gen 29:32; Gen 41:52; Gen 30:6). Dana sensed that they would be directed to "strike camp," to leave certain places and relocate and settle elsewhere. Indeed, both Dana and Dasha recently had been compelled to resign from substantial, long-term commitments to certain ministries and to join others. What Dana did not know was that in the coming year 2020 God would direct her to quit a secular job that she had worked for 15 years and to let two trade certifications expire, one in allied health care that she had maintained for 25 years, and the other in exercise science that she had maintained for 18 years. Ministry was to replace these trades, but the process would require extreme faith to relinquish worldly security and self-reliance for the invisible arms of the heavenly Father.

Dana sensed that praise, sonship (appreciating God as Father and oneself as beloved), fruitfulness or productivity, and judgment of the adversary would manifest in coming years. She noted that the tribe of Dan, which represents judgment, moves out last, only after the tribes of Judah, Reuben, and Ephraim are already on the move; these other tribes represent praise, sonship, and fruitfulness. Dana realized that she had had the order of ministry backwards. For years, she had emphasized judgment (spiritual warfare and deliverance), but now she saw that praise, sonship, and fruitfulness must precede that. She began to understand at least one reason for the delay in her call: she needed to put love before war.

Interpretation 2, Dasha got:

> Speak the Word
> The story of God is told on highways and byways
> Speak the Word
> Be bold
> Say what you hear
> Do not be ashamed
> Do not let the enemy dismay you
> Repeat it for deaf ears
> Speak and laugh in the face of the enemy
> The Word will conquer
> The Word will overcome
> The Word will break down the strongholds
> Speak the Word

Dana noticed that Dasha's interpretation of "Speak the Word; The Word will conquer; The Word will overcome; The Word will break down strongholds" reinforced Dana's earlier interpretation about the Hebrew year and decade as the year and decade of the mouth.

Dana recognized another allusion to the parable of the wedding feast in "the story of God is told on highways and byways": "Therefore go into the highways, and as many as you find, invite to the wedding" (Matt 22:9). Dana wondered whether the audience of the spoken Word would be people they meet in their travels or via the virtual highways and byways of the Internet. As the year unfolded, Dana's ministry website and YouTube videos got more and more viewing traction despite (or perhaps because of?) travel restrictions due to the COVID-19 pandemic.

Interpretation 3, Dana got:

> I am releasing My whirlwind,
> My windstorm, My twister;
> You will celebrate,
> Many will decry and declaim.
> You will exult in My triumph,
> Many will moan and groan and lament.
> How awesome are the victories of God!
> Long awaited; hard fought; blood wrought.
> Time to take the spoil:
> They shall plunder those who plundered them.

Concerning the statement, "They shall plunder those who plundered them," Dana got the following scripture as confirmation:

> They will not take wood from the field nor cut down any from the forests, because they will make fires with weapons; and they will plunder those who plundered them, and pillage those who pillaged them.—Ezekiel 39:10

Dana sensed that God's redemption and restitution and vindication would finally manifest in the next decade. She also sensed that there would be a division, not only between the people of God and the people of the world, but also between the consecrated people of God who follow holiness and the compromised people of God who follow the world. She sensed that the enemy's past weapons would serve as fuel for a holy fire in God's people, and she rejoiced in God's promise that His people would raid, ransack, and ravage their spiritual enemies.

Interpretation 3, Dasha got:

> The anger of the Lord is awesome
> Fear not the enemy
> Fear Him who can destroy both body and soul
> The fear of the Lord is the beginning of wisdom
> Stand in awe and see His glory
> See His ax coming down on the wicked
> His hammer on the hairy head of the enemy
> The Mighty One will laugh
> Those who boast in their might
> Will break their teeth on this stone

Dasha got the following supporting scriptures for "The Mighty One will laugh":

> He who sits in the heavens shall laugh;
> the Lord shall hold them in derision.—Psalm 2:4

> The Lord laughs at him,
> for He sees that his day is coming.—Psalm 37:13

> But You, O LORD, shall laugh at them;
> You shall have all the nations in derision.—Psalm 59:8

Dana recognized and identified several scriptures embedded in the interpretation, namely:

> "And do not fear those who kill the body but cannot kill the soul. But rather fear Him who is able to destroy both soul and body in hell."
> —Matthew 10:28

> The fear of the Lord is the beginning of wisdom.
> —Psalm 111:10; Proverbs 9:10

"Even now the ax is laid to the root of the trees."—Matthew 3:10

But God will wound the head of His enemies,
the hairy scalp of the one who still goes on in his trespasses.—Psalm 68:21

Interpretation 4, Dana was on a roll and did a fourth tongue and interpretation even though they had agreed to do only three. She got:

Bubbling up, bubbling up,
a continual flow of inspiration.
Ah, living in the flow of inspiration!
"The words that I speak [and the songs that I sing],
they are spirit and they are life."—John 6:63

In her mind's eye, Dana saw an image of Daybreak (1922), by the artist Maxfield Parrish (1870-1966), which she found online and shared with Dasha. (Daybreak is the most popular American art print of the twentieth century.)[2] The image conveys the grandeur of nature, classic beauty, and serenity. This could refer to the refreshing influence of the Presence of the Holy Spirit.

We see several themes emerging from this open-ended session of tongues and interpretation: evangelistic worship arts or singing and dancing for God as a way to attract others to Him; preaching and teaching with boldness messages that challenge or disturb listeners; poetic justice for the aggrieved, and divine judgment on the adversary. These interpretations confirmed the burgeoning ministries of these women: Dana was getting more speaking engagements at churches to present on the subject of deliverance and the gifts of the Spirit. Dasha was getting more singing and keyboard engagements.

Now let's transition to closed interpretations of tongues, those that present a particular question or concern before the Lord.

CLOSED SESSIONS

Leonora

Let's call her Leonora. Leonora suffers from a host of maladies that often drive her to bedrest. She has a life-long history of hormonal imbalances, mood disorders, and physical trauma, including head concussions and back injuries from auto collisions and accidents on the job. Leonora is on disability for some of these conditions. When Leonora was growing up, her mother often had been incapacitated (relegated to bed) by hormonal imbalances, mood disorders, and her husband's emotional abuse. Her mother's resignation and passivity had imprinted powerfully on Leonora in a negative way and had created a similar dysfunctional pattern in Leonora's life. Leonora forgave her mother and her father for their behavior, but she was still suffering.

After speaking in tongues for an extended period of time over Leonora and proclaiming deliverance scriptures and ordering the demonic to vacate and go to its judgment in Christ, her friend saw a big fishing net being cast into the black velvet night of the universe. The net was hauling in a great cluster of stars, each one coruscating like a diamond. Her friend understood this as Leonora's ministry as a mass evangelist; the stars were the seed of Abraham that Leonora was gathering for God; they were spiritual offspring. This vision was of Leonora's sacred purpose in life. This was God's promise for Leonora.

Then her friend saw a deliverance vision. She saw a balloon shaped like a dragon pierced by an arrow. The dragon balloon whistled as it released hot air and shriveled into a rumpled pile of plastic. After that, her friend saw an effigy of Leonora lying recumbent on a sickbed. The effigy was also a balloon, a blow-up doll resembling Leonora. Leonora entered the room with a big sword and drove it into the belly of the dummy of herself, puncturing and deflating the hollow image, which collapsed. Then her friend heard the scripture verse, "Your arrows are sharp in the heart of the King's enemies. The peoples fall under you" (Ps 45:5). The deliverance vision spoke of Leonora's active role in destroying a false image of herself that had relegated her to a sickbed. The evil one was behind this, but his power was no more than hot air or false speech that could be dispatched by an arrow of truth.

After this, Leonora had a breakthrough and felt much better. Most likely, Leonora will have to continue destroying the false image of herself every time she is tempted to identify with it and resign herself to a sickbed.

Daisy

Let's call her Daisy. Lately, Daisy had been feeling depressed and had been isolating herself. Her church attendance was patchy; there seemed to be some kind of psychological block to her attending. On Sunday, duties loomed like an endless series of hurdles; dressing was a fiasco, a fussy and fretful affair; the prospect of going to church seemed HUGE. During the workweek, Daisy's daily routine was burdensome and boring. After work, she could only muster the energy to drive home, clean house, prepare dinner for her brain injured son, and sack out on the couch and watch movies. This had been going on for some time. She admitted that "I need to return to my first love (the Lord)".

Daisy and her friend wrote "return to my first love" at the top of a sheet. Her friend spoke in tongues, and they both interpreted, jotting down impressions and scriptures. Then Daisy spoke in tongues, and they both interpreted. They completed three rounds of this to get the mind of the Lord for Daisy. Here's what they got (not exactly in this order, but paired thematically as much as possible):

Interpretation 1, Daisy heard:

> Don't touch anything dead. (Num 19:11, 18; Hag 2:13)
> Black and blue black and white.
> Don't touch anything dead.
> Have I not told you what to fight?
> Have I not told you:
> Two can put ten thousand to flight! (Deut 32:30)

Interpretation 1, Daisy's friend heard:

> Awake, you sleeper!
> Walk in the light!
> Awake, you who sleep,
> Arise from the dead,
> and Christ will give you light!—Ephesians 5:14

Interpretation 2, Daisy's friend heard:

> Oh, how often I have wanted to cuddle you,
> huddle with you,
> like a hen gathering her chicks,
> but you would not be consoled! (Matt 23:37)
>
> Come to the mother heart of God!
> You are a mother to others.
> Let Me be this to you.
> Be then like a weaned child,
> stilled and quieted,
> dandled on her mother's knee. (Isa 66:12-13; Ps 131:2)

Daisy's friend knew the scripture references to a hen gathering her chicks and a weaned child quieted by its mother. She was less sure about the location of the phrase "dandled on her mother's knees". A word search on "dandled" yielded this result, which is replete with references to the mother heart of God operating through His people:

> That you may feed and be satisfied
> With the consolation of her bosom,
> That you may drink deeply and be delighted
> With the abundance of her glory.

> Behold, I will extend peace to her like a river,
> And the glory of the Gentiles like a flowing stream.
> Then you shall feed;
> On her sides shall you be carried,
> And be dandled on her knees.
>
> As one whom his mother comforts,
> So I will comfort you.—Isaiah 66:11-13

Interpretation 2, Daisy heard the opening line of Elizabeth Barrett Browning's Sonnet 43, which she identified as her love letter to the Lord and His love letter to her; this bridged into the Lord's appreciation of the many roles she fulfills as a woman:

> How do I love thee? Let me count the ways:
> Mama, daughter, sister, aunt, friend.
> I have called you to the meadow,
> To the secret place of meeting
> Where the fern and the lily grow.

Daisy had never read Browning's entire sonnet. When she found it, she recognized it as "a divine kinship of LOVE" and found it deeply comforting:

"How Do I Love Thee?" (Sonnet 43)

> How do I love thee? Let me count the ways.
> I love thee to the depth and breadth and height
> My soul can reach, when feeling out of sight
> For the ends of being and ideal grace.
> I love thee to the level of every day's
> Most quiet need, by sun and candle-light.
> I love thee freely, as men strive for right.
> I love thee purely, as they turn from praise.
> I love thee with the passion put to use

In my old griefs, and with my childhood's faith.
I love thee with a love I seemed to lose
With my lost saints. I love thee with the breath,
Smiles, tears, of all my life; and, if God choose,
I shall but love thee better after death.
—Elizabeth Barrett Browning (1806-1861)[3]

Interpretation 3, Daisy's friend heard snatches of verses from the Song of Solomon:

My love! My love!
My sister, my spouse.
A spring shut up.
A fountain sealed.
A garden enclosed. (Song 4:9, 12)

Come, O north wind.
Blow, O south!
Blow upon my fountain of gardens,
That its fragrance may flow out. (Song 4:16)

Interpretation 3, Daisy heard:

Sweep with My love.
Walk in My works.

Give praise to the Lord on high,
the Lord most High,
Give praise to the God of Abraham!

Daisy was so moved by the message that she confided in her friend that years ago during the Shepherding or Discipleship Movement, she had asked her pastor for guidance on whether or not to date a man in the church, a NASA engineer who was undergoing a divorce from his wife. The wife was mentally unstable and had had multiple affairs. Daisy's pastor encouraged her to date the man. Not long afterward, the man's soon-to-be ex-wife committed suicide, and Daisy was blamed for the suicide and called into the office for what felt to her like a Star Chamber Court proceeding with the pastor presiding. As she was being interrogated and reproved, she felt herself disintegrating at a molecular level. The pastor's wife put her hand on Daisy's back for support, which was the only adhesive that held her together. Daisy never mentioned to her panel of accusers that she had submitted the decision to date the man to the pastor and that he himself had endorsed the dating relationship. While the pastor exposed her, she covered him.

Obviously, the memory of this deeply traumatic event was a block to her enjoying church and God. So the Lord's counsel to her was threefold. The first order of business was for her to leave her graveyard memories and soul bruises behind: "Don't touch anything dead. Black and blue black," and "Arise from the dead!". The second order of business was for Daisy not to be disconsolate, not to wallow in anguish, but to allow God to comfort her with a mother's heart: "How often I wanted to gather you as a hen gathers her chicks under her wings, but you were not willing!" and "I have calmed and quieted my soul, like a weaned child with its mother is my soul within me". The third order of business was for Daisy not to live any longer as a spring shut up and a fountain sealed, but to let the spices of her garden flow out and share with others what the Lord has planted and cultivated in her over the years. She is to revel in lavishing her nurturing gift on others.

Daisy was greatly encouraged and made a decision to use her gift of communication to write a book of comfort and counsel on how to navigate grief for a young woman whose mother had recently died. Another good outcome of the session was that Daisy realized that the Holy Spirit speaks through her in many ways, including tongues and interpretation, even when Daisy feels far from spiritual. Daisy realized more than ever that all of her spirituality comes from the Holy Spirit who is always ready, willing, and able, even when she is not. As the year unfolded, she found a compatible church, forged friendships, and actively participated in ministry.

Clara

Let's call her Clara. In the last year, Clara had received a very hopeful prophecy from a trustworthy, proven prophet that Clara would "fix foundations of truth, foundations of scripture that others had cracked". This call or commission would be supported by several things: a laser sharp gift of discernment to divide the authentic from the counterfeit, "an increase in His might upon her life" for deliverance, and "destiny relationships and companionship". Clara rejoiced in this, that "the desires of her heart would be brought into the front lines" for fulfillment. The prophecy had a catalytic effect and started to activate a gift set in Clara. Clara found herself operating in the gift set more and more, both inside and outside the church, and she became zealous about the gift set.

The Lord began to give Clara more and more revelation as she studied scripture and practiced the gifts. Clara completed one project showcasing the gifts and started another. She wanted to launch a focus group at her church for training and equipping in the gifts. She mailed the first project to several key people in leadership, but neither her pastor, nor the administrative pastor, nor the event coordinator for outreaches, nor a lay leader even acknowledged receiving her project, much less reviewing it. Several times she requested an appointment to meet and was given a hopeful response, but no firm date. She thought to herself, "What is going on? Why is the church leadership ignoring my requests to meet and discuss possibilities?" Clara realized there was an unusual pattern here; she wasn't sure whether it was due to busyness and distraction, indifference and disinterest, or guardedness and wariness toward her. She felt tempted to become resentful about being overlooked or disregarded, and she contended against the growth of a grudge in her heart. Knowing the call was from God, Clara forged ahead to recruit other members for an unofficial focus group (unapproved by church leadership). After a while it became apparent that these people lacked the necessary vision, commitment or discipline for the undertaking. Clara thought to herself, "Where are my compatriots in the spiritual gifts? Where are the visionaries? Where are the committed believers? Where are the people who were promised to me by prophecy? Where are they?"

In this predicament, Clara and a friend sought the mind of the Lord. They wrote "How should Clara form a core group of like minded, like hearted, like spirited believers?" What she got was a confirmation of the call and also a strategy to wait for God to motivate and inspire people, rather than to actively head hunt and scout for talent:

Interpretation 1, Clara heard:

> Go into all the world and preach the gospel of peace. And these signs will follow those who believe: In My name they will cast out demons; they will speak with new tongues; they will take up serpents; and if they drink anything deadly, it will by no means hurt them; they will lay hands on the sick, and they will recover.—Mark 16:15-18 (abridged, adapted)

Interpretation 1, Clara's friend heard:

> A gathering of the remnant.
> I, the Lord, will gather:
>
> "But I will gather the remnant of My flock out of all the countries where I have driven them, and bring them back to their folds; and they shall be fruitful and increase."—Jeremiah 23:3 (see context verses 4-8)

Interpretation 2, Clara heard:

> Continue.
> Continue to strengthen yourself in Me.
> Continue to strengthen your ministry friendships.
> Break bread together in house:
>
> "And they continued steadfastly in the apostles' doctrine and fellowship, in the breaking of bread, and in prayers."—Acts 2:42

Interpretation 2, Clara's friend heard:

> The Spirit will blow people to the door.
> "The wind blows wherever it pleases,
> but you cannot tell where it comes from and where it goes.
> So is everyone born of the Spirit."—John 3:8

Interpretation 3, Clara heard:

> Rest, rest, rest in knowing that this is indeed My will,
> and being My will, it must come to pass,
> without machinery and without machinations,
> for "My yoke is easy and My burden is light."—Matthew 11:30

Interpretation 3, Clara's friend heard:

> "Not by might, nor by power, but by My Spirit," says the LORD of hosts.
> —Zechariah 4:6

> Yet I will have mercy on the house of Judah,
> Will save them by the LORD their God,
> And will not save them by bow,
> Nor by sword or battle,
> By horses or horsemen.—Hosea 1:7

After this, Clara shared her perplexity about the lack of response of point people in her church to another friend who operates in the gifts. Clara and her friend wrote "squelched prophetic voice" at the top of the sheet. Here is what they got:

Interpretation 1, Clara heard an echo of the word her other ministry partner had given:

> Not by power, nor by might, but by My Spirit, says the LORD.
> —Zechariah 4:6

> So then, it is not of him who wills, nor of him who runs, but of God who shows mercy.—Romans 9:16

Interpretation 1, Clara's friend heard:

> I am raising up a sure foundation, a tried stone, a precious cornerstone.
> —Isaiah 28:16

Clara looked up the verse and saw that it included the following line, which was a bit ouchy or soul-crushing to her:

> Whoever believes will not act hastily.

Interpretation 2, Clara heard:

> This is the rest, and this is the refreshing.—Isaiah 28:12
> Just enjoy Me, and others will come around.
> Don't worry about traction and progress.
> I can build in a day.
> One can become a nation:
>
> A little one shall become a thousand,
> And a small one a strong nation.
> I, the Lord, will hasten it in its time.—Isaiah 60:22

Interpretation 2, Clara's friend saw in her mind's eye an old woman standing alone in a southwestern wilderness of sun, mountains, sand, and sky. The scene conveyed a sovereign stillness. The woman was declaring the Lord's love song for Clara in and through creation. Creation was expressing the Lord's majestic heart to Clara. Then the Lord put Clara inside the southwestern landscape. Her friend heard:

> From the rising of the sun to its going down
> The Lord's name is to be praised.—Psalm 113:3
> Sun, moon, and galaxies inhale and exhale My love for you.
> The Lord's creation is breathing His love for you.

Clara's friend found two more scriptures about sunrise and sunset:

> From the rising of the sun to its going down,
> Out of Zion, the perfection of beauty,
> God shines forth and reveals Himself in glory.
> —Psalm 50:1-2

> For from the rising of the sun, even to its going down,
> My name shall be great among the Gentiles;
> In every place incense shall be offered to My name, and a pure offering;
> For My name shall be great among the nations," says the Lord of hosts.
> —Malachi 1:11

After these sessions, Clara felt pierced. She realized that the obstructions were exposing a deep sense of helplessness, vulnerability, and dependence, a sense of being as weak and defenseless as a nursing infant. Clara hated this. She wanted to make things happen, to force change. She realized acutely in the core of her being, "I'm not in charge. I'm not in control. I have zero power. I am incapable of producing anything I want." Then she remembered what Jesus said, "I can of Myself do nothing," and "Most assuredly, I say to you, the Son can do nothing of Himself, but what He sees the Father do" (John 5:19, 30). She also remembered that Jesus said to a Roman ruler who boasted of his authority to execute or exonerate Jesus: "You could have no power at all against Me unless it had been given to you from above" (John 19:11). Clara realized that she needed a radical shift in orientation from her efforts, which were making her feel inadequate and incompetent in the face of negligible results, to an admission of utter helplessness and complete dependence on God who alone can orchestrate a desired outcome. Clara felt she was learning a painful truth about God's sovereignty. She began to ask, "Who are you, Lord?" and "Who are you to me?"

Clara was most impressed with the strange paradox of her own forceful belting in an Asian tongue (a warring tongue) and the series of interpretations that followed. To her, the Asian tongue felt like an assertion of her rights in God and an aggressive conquest of the kingdom, as in maxim, "The kingdom of heaven suffers violence, and the violent take it by force" (Matt 11:12), but the series of interpretations that followed indicated that outcomes had nothing to do with her fierceness or zeal or bravado: "I, the Lord will gather. I will blow on them. I will hasten it in its time. I will build the temple. I am sovereign". After the session, Clara felt acutely empty and realized that all her hope of fullness is in God: "You make fruitful". She wanted to take a child's relaxed posture of reliance on her papa. Not long afterward, Clara had an inspirational dream about her desire and got an invitation from another church to facilitate the focus group on the gifts.

Sofia

Let's call her Sofia. Sofia's family has a generational history of sensitivity to the spirit realm and schizophrenia. Sofia was extremely burdened for one of her sons, Sebastian (not his real name). After Sebastian's divorce and a rebound relationship that proved to be an Internet scam, Sebastian supposedly met a woman who worked as an undercover agent for the government and used her psychic and paranormal powers in sting operations to entrap and prosecute witches who murder people without a trace. This woman taught Sebastian an astral projection technique called "synergy," in which his spirit could take flight and visit others. Through this technique, Sebastian had sexual relations with the woman as well as with his brother's wife, which he later regretted and considered a mistake. Sebastian is now exceedingly tormented. He thinks seven people want to murder him, including his own brother. He has pain all over his body. He is addicted to marijuana. He uses profanity compulsively. He suffers from rage and homicidal ideation. Sebastian believes in Jesus but has a distorted understanding of the Savior and the faith. He judges most Christians as powerless and passionless and their help as worthless and so refuses to seek help.

Sofia visited her son for three months to help him purge his life. During this time, she prayed constantly for him and observed strange behaviors that seemed demonic: eyes rolling back in his head and weird body movements. At one point, he had a short interim of lucidity after listening to a teaching video of a Spirit-filled preacher. One day while Sofia was praying in tongues, she had an extraordinary experience in which she lost consciousness of herself and felt the Spirit of God lifting her up into a heavenly realm. She heard exquisite heavenly melodies. After that, her son had another brief interval of mental clarity and emotional stability and made peace with his brother, but then relapsed again. Sofia is convinced that Sebastian is suffering from schizophrenia and that he needs deliverance from a spirit of witchcraft. She believes that the sexual encounters Sebastian had in the spirit realm with the purported undercover agent, his brother's wife, and other women were succubus encounters—interactions with a sex demon that impersonates female sex partners.

Sofia and her friend wrote "Sebastian" at the top of a page. Because of the gravity of the situation, they spent a couple hours seeking the counsel and comfort of the Holy Spirit. Here is what they got:

Interpretation 1, Sofia's friend saw a body of water, the surface of which was covered with gentle ripples or small waves. She heard the word "newborn," and the phrase "born of the Spirit and of water". She got the following scripture:

> Jesus answered, "Most assuredly, I say to you, unless one is born of water and the Spirit, he cannot enter the kingdom of God. That which is born of flesh is flesh, and that which is born of the Spirit is spirit. Do not marvel that I said to you, 'You must be born again.' The wind blows where it wishes, and you hear the sound of it, but cannot tell where it comes from and where it goes. So is everyone who is born of the Spirit."—John 3:5-8

Interpretation 1, Sofia heard: "Broken gates will be repaired". She also heard, "Seek that which was lost and bring back that which was driven away. Bind up that which was broken and strengthen that which was sick," from Ezekiel 34:16. She had an impression of a multi-generational assignment of restoration, in which she would help restore her son and then her son would help restore others, as prophesied in the following verses in Isaiah:

> Those from among you
> Shall build the old waste places;
> You shall raise up the foundations of many generations;
> And you shall be called the Repairer of the Breach,
> The Restorer of Streets to Dwell in.—Isaiah 58:12
>
> And they shall rebuild the ancient ruins;
> They shall raise up the former desolations,

> And renew the ruined cities,
> The devastations of many generations.—Isaiah 61:4 AMPC

Interpretation 2, Sofia's friend had an impression of the Lord as a Man of War. She heard, "I will deal with your oppressors who afflict you," from Zephaniah 3:19. Then she got another impression of David confronting the Philistine giant with a bold attitude, "For who is this uncircumcised Philistine that he should defy the armies of the living God?" and of David prophesying doom to the giant and nullifying his curses (1 Sam 17:26):

> Then David said to the Philistine, "You come to me with a sword, with a spear, and with a javelin. But I come to you in the name of the LORD of hosts, the God of the armies of Israel, whom you have defied. This day the LORD will deliver you into my hand, and I will strike you and take your head from you. And this day I will give the carcasses of the camp of the Philistines to the birds of the air and the wild beasts of the earth, that all the earth may know that there is a God in Israel. Then all this assembly shall know that the LORD does not save with sword and spear; for the battle is the LORD's, and He will give you into our hands."—1 Samuel 17:45-47

Interpretation 2, Sofia remembered a vision she had of her son while she was still pregnant with him in her womb: she saw him suffused in a shaft of light and the power of the Holy Spirit upon him; her son was pure and full of light. She heard the lyrics of the song, "Love Lifted Me," an American hymn published in 1912:

> Love lifted me! Love lifted me!
> When nothing else could help, love lifted me!

The rest of the lyrics, which were personally meaningful to her are:

> **"Love Lifted Me"**
>
> I was sinking deep in sin
> Far from the peaceful shore,

Very deeply stained within,
Sinking to rise no more.
But the Master of the sea
Heard my despairing cry,
From the waters lifted me,
Now safe am I.

Love lifted me! Love lifted me!
When nothing else could help, love lifted me! (2x)

All my heart to Him I give,
Ever to Him I'll cling,
In His blesséd presence live,
Ever His praises sing.
Love so mighty and so true,
Merits my soul's best songs,
Faithful, loving service too,
To Him belongs.

Refrain

Souls in danger, look above,
Jesus completely saves;
He will lift you by His love,
Out of the angry waves.
He's the Master of the sea,
Billows His will obey;
He your Savior wants to be,
Be saved today.

Refrain.

—lyrics by James Rowe; melody by Howard E. Smith[4]

Interpretation 3, Sofia's friend saw an eagle. She remembered a verse from Exodus in which the eagle is a metaphor for the Lord's deliverance:

> "You have seen what I did to the Egyptians, and how I bore you on eagles' wings and brought you to Myself."—Exodus 19:4

A word search on "eagle" in a Bible application yielded another verse in Revelation that connects the eagle with deliverance:

> But the woman was given two wings of a great eagle, that she might fly into the wilderness to her place, where she is nourished for a time and times and half a time, from the presence of the serpent.—Revelation 12:14

Sofia told her friend that she associates the eagle with "complete freedom". Sofia had previously wanted to paint a painting of an eagle, which she now considered doing as a prophetic act of freedom for her son.

Interpretation 3, Sofia felt travail, a physical agony and a mental anguish in laboring for the manifestation of her son as a son of God. Just as Sofia had physically brought her son into the earth, she now felt herself spiritually bringing him to God, and there was a continual wrenching or convulsion in the delivery. She got the following passage:

> For I consider that the sufferings of this present time are not worthy to be compared with the glory which shall be revealed in us. For the earnest expectation of the creation eagerly waits for the revealing of the sons of God. For the creation was subjected to futility, not willingly, but because of Him who subjected it in hope; because the creation itself also will be delivered from the bondage of corruption into the glorious liberty of the children of God. For we know that the whole creation groans and labors with birth pangs together until now. Not only that, but we also who have the firstfruits of the Spirit, even we ourselves groan within ourselves, eagerly waiting for the adoption, the redemption of our body.—Romans 8:18-23

Interpretation 4, Sofia's friend heard, "Hades must deliver Him up. Hell must disgorge him. Hell must spew him out." She remembered the story of Jonah who had deliberately disobeyed God. The Lord prepared a great fish to swallow him until he had a change of mind and heart, after which the fish regurgitated him onto the shore. Jesus said that just as Jonah was in the bowels of a fish for three days, Jesus would be in the bowels of the earth or Hades for three days for our sake, to deliver us from the wrong decisions we make that land us in the netherworld (Matt 12:40):

> Out of the belly of Sheol I cried,
> And You heard my voice.
> For You cast me into the deep,
> Into the heart of the seas,
> And the floods surrounded me;
> All Your billows and Your waves passed over me.
> Then I said, "I have been cast out of Your sight;
> Yet I will look again toward Your holy temple."
> The waters surrounded me, even to my soul;
> The deep closed around me;
> Weeds were wrapped around my head.
> I went down to the moorings of the mountains;
> The earth with its bars closed behind me forever;
> Yet You have brought up my life from the pit,
> O LORD, my God.
>
> So the LORD spoke to the fish, and it vomited Jonah unto dry land.
> —Jonah 2:1-6, 10 (abridged)

Interpretation 4, Sofia saw her son Sebastian standing in his destiny, worshipping God in spirit and in truth: "But the hour is coming, and now is, when the true worshipers will worship the Father in spirit and truth; for the Father is seeking such to worship Him" (Jn 4:23). She saw him singing and bringing other people into their destiny.

The messages sketch the spiritual journey that is ahead for Sofia's son Sebastian. Even though her son confesses faith in Jesus, the message about being "born of the Spirit and of water," suggests that he needs to undergo water baptism, which represents conversion, as well as Spirit baptism. There may have been something faulty about his conversion or he may have believed in a false Jesus. Paul indicates that there are faulty or perverted versions of the gospel that present "another Jesus" than the real Jesus and impart "a different spirit" than the Holy Spirit (see Gal 1:6-9; 2 Cor 11:4). If this is the case, then Sebastian might need deliverance from a false spirit of Christ, that is, a demon that impersonates Christ.

Certainly, the messages about deliverance confirm that Sebastian is not just mentally ill but demonically tormented and oppressed: the defiant giant Goliath must be slain; Sebastian must be airlifted out of bondage on the eagles' wings of God; "hell must disgorge him" the way the whale regurgitated Jonah on shore.

Sofia's memory of the vision she had of her son radiant with light while she was still pregnant, her current vision of him leading worship "in Spirit and in truth," and the scripture about generational ruins being rebuilt all point to future restoration. Sofia is clearly the most important intercessor for her son, as indicated by the scripture about her birthing him through the Spirit just as she had birthed him through her body.

The strategy is outlined: she must prosecute war in the Spirit against the enemies of his soul the way David prosecuted war against Goliath; she must pray for him to respond the way Jonah responded to his plight: he himself must cry out to God for deliverance from the belly of Sheol.

Wendi Nixon

Now here's Wendi (Wendi gave me permission to use her real name!). Wendi is a very productive person who often burns the candle at both ends without running out of fire or wax. She is a counselor who specializes in trauma cases, especially trauma in children but also trauma in adults that stems from childhood. Wendi operates a small horse farm and teaches riding lessons. She is pursuing her doctorate in counseling as well as grant funding for equestrian therapy. Wendi is married to an agronomer who advises farmers on how to obtain a better crop yield. Being a farmer's wife, Wendi is a good cook and baker to boot!

Several years ago, she pursued a dream of running a tea shop as a quasi-ministry to the general public. She went out of business within a year, and she and her husband lost a lot of money in the venture. Recently her thoughts returned to the tea shop. She thought she had heard from the Lord to start the business, but in the face of failure, she wondered what it was all about. She wanted better understanding and psychological resolution and closure. She was dogged by the memory of a meeting that she had had with a pastor many years prior who had seen in the Spirit a pair of sneakers running by themselves. She wondered whether she had run ahead of the Lord on the timing of the tea shop.

I recommended that we submit her concern to the Lord. We did four rounds of tongues and interpretation to get the mind of the Lord on the matter. In the process, Wendi got an unexpected surprise.

Interpretation 1, For the interpretation of the first tongue, I got a homey poem for Wendi:

> Mama's kitchen
> was never a business
> but the greatest business of life was run there—
> it was the business of growing up.
> There was no recipe for growing up
> and growing up was not a service
> and growing up charged no fee.
>
> Growing up was free,
> but it took all we had!
>
> Oh, mama's kitchen!
> What a great place to be.
> That's where we got to listen to the adults
> and play with the adults
> and try our hand at adulthood.

Interpretation 1, Wendi saw a sun rising over the horizon. She heard the words: "A start". Something was initiated and set in motion by the tea shop business that cannot stop or be reversed. She saw a metal ball rolling down a track. The tea shop was a beginning point, but there were two more points ahead of her. She heard the Lord say, "I've got my eye on you."

Interpretation 2, For the second tongue, I got a number statements centering on the theme of provision: serving meals to many; the kitchen and the field (or the cook and the farmer) and the close connection between the two; husbandry or crop cultivation as a necessity of life that elevates the farmer above a king; foreboding of hard times; and a promise of supernatural provision (during a time of dearth?). As much as I do not want to entertain the foreboding, my impression was that the interpretation pointed to a ministry of provision during a future time of famine due to some crisis: a war, disruption of trade or commerce, or exclusion from commerce.

> Cast your bread upon the waters,
> for after many days it will return to you.
> Give a serving to seven and also to eight,
> for you do not know what disaster may befall the land,
> what evil will be on earth. (Ecc 11:1-2)
>
> Even the king is fed from the field.
> "Moreover the profit of the land is for all;
> even the king is served from the field."—Ecclesiastes 5:9
> In time of war, farmers are kings.
>
> Husbandry was the first occupation.
> "The Lord planted a garden eastward of Eden and there He put the man whom He had formed. Then the Lord God took the man and put him in the garden of Eden to tend and keep it."—Genesis 2:8 and 2:15
>
> The kitchen isn't far from the field.
> (Or) The kitchen is next to the field.

Supernatural provision.
Production in latter years.

Interpretation 2, Wendi got a poem in the style of Dr. Seuss, which delighted both of us:

Do you not see it
Do you not know
My winds are blowing
To and fro

Winds of change
Coming near
From afar
For all to hear

Growing fast
Growing strong
Soon you will find out
Where you belong

Don't be afraid
And never doubt
The tide is changing
And coming about

Debts are cancelled
Stains washed away
Things will be white (and pure)
Which once were gray

(Dear one)
Do you not see it
Do you not know

> My winds are blowing
> To and fro

Interpretation 3, For the third tongue, I got a theme of communion. Serving food and enjoying food together is an expression of friendship or close relationship. In the Bible it is taken for granted that meals are shared with family or friends (not strangers or enemies). (So meals were never meant as business only!) The full understanding of the significance of a meal is found in communion when Jesus said, "My flesh is food indeed. My blood is drink indeed" (Jn 6:55). When you share a meal with someone, you share your life with that person during the process: the meal is a celebration of life. The meal also sustains life; it requires the sacrifice of a life to preserve life.

Interpretation 3, Wendi got a picture in her mind's eye of Jesus creeping over the horizon, pulling back folds of fabric in search of her. Here is what she wrote:

> Jesus is creeping over the horizon,
> pulling back fabric (curtains maybe?).
> He's looking for me in the fabric;
> He's calling me—"Where are you?"
> It feels a little like a game of hide and seek.
>
> "You are hiding because you felt ashamed—
> felt like you had mismanaged resources,
> felt like you had missed the mark.
>
> I'm calling you out of hiding, my dear one.
> Come back to Me and give Me your shame.
> That was not from Me.
>
> Let me touch Your heart and heal
> the pain—give it to Me.
> Let's run on to the future of
> new things,

glorious things,
Me and you things.

I have finished the work and
you do not have to carry this burden."

Wendi got all choked up when she read this interpretation to me. I was surprised by her emotional response, for she is a steady, stalwart type—unflappable in the main—the kind of person others lean on for stability. She, too, was surprised by her distress, a mingling of sorrow and embarrassment. She had no idea that she still felt demoralized over the loss of the business and their investment and that downheartedness had been lingering in the shadows of her mind all the while. The recognition of this was a revelation to her and so too was the Lord's dismissal of it and His invitation to a bright future.

Interpretation 4, The last interpretation was of an unusual tongue: a languid yet rollicking song with a lilting melody in a French-sounding language. I got a marriage supper of the Lamb wedding theme and the following scriptures, beginning with a statement Jesus made at the last supper:

"I will not drink of the fruit of the vine again until I drink it in My Father's kingdom."—Matthew 26:29; Luke 22:18

I have drunk my wine with my milk. Eat, O friends!
Drink, yes, drink deeply,
O beloved ones!—Song of Solomon 5:1

On this mountain the LORD Almighty will prepare
a feast of rich food for all peoples,
a banquet of aged wine—
the best of meats and the finest of wines.
On this mountain he will destroy
the shroud that enfolds all peoples,

> the sheet that covers all nations.
> —Isaiah 25:6-7 NIV

On closer examination of the last passage from Isaiah, I was surprised to see the correlation between that passage and Wendi's earlier vision of the Lord searching for her in folds of fabric like curtains. The feast that God prepares removes a "shroud that enfolds the peoples," a "sheet that covers the nations". This indicates the purpose of every meal, not just the great one that culminates the end of the age. The purpose of every meal shared with good company is to know and be known: meals are (or should be) about revealing yourself to others and others revealing themselves to you. Meals are relational. Meals are heart to heart.

Interpretation 4, Wendi wrote:

> Song of camaraderie
> Sung with best friends
> [at a] French café
> [reminds me of my distant heritage]
> Celebration of the victory
>
> The whole café is singing with you and for you
> This is a community event
> The song will cover the community
> and release healing, unity, and peace.
>
> Angels are bringing bowls
> —of peace
> —of provision / gold
> These are answers to prayer,
> for the incense of the prayers
> have reached My throne,
> and they are sweet.

After the session I shared with Wendi that in my experience tongues and interpretation usually do not yield strong, specific directives on what to do and how to do it. Rather, tongues and interpretation seem to deal with matters of the heart. Wendi commented that the session was very deep. She was surprised by her emotional response to the Lord's comfort. She had not even realized that she felt a sense of shame over the failed business, but God put His finger on the wound, and His finger was a balm. Wendi felt that there was tremendous value in the psychological awareness and support that the Holy Spirit brought through the session. As a professional counselor, Wendi's opinion meant a lot to me. I think it's safe to say that tongues plus interpretation are a great way to minister to a person's heart. I recommend this gift combination for emotional healing!

Tongues and interpretation are also prophecy. There were many sneak previews of Wendi's future in the session, but the one that struck me the hardest was the statement: "In time of war, farmers are kings," backed by the scripture from Ecclesiastes that serving meals to many in a time of abundance is a spiritual security against lack when evil overruns the earth. Wendi told me that she and her agronomist husband had recently sampled a peanut bread recipe. They did so out of sheer curiosity and because her husband advises peanut farmers on improved crop yield, so information about what you can do with peanuts is always welcome. But the history of the recipe is sobering: it was invented during the food shortage of the Great Depression (1929-late 1930s). The recipe called for a minimal number of cheaper, more accessible, and more filling ingredients that women were likely to have on hand in a time of dearth. This seemed to be a confirmation of the prophetic nature of the message I got.

Friends, let's stay close to God. We do not know what is ahead, but the Almighty provides and protects. Let's develop our ability to hear Him better. Let's use our gifts of tongues and interpretation.

APPENDIX: THE ENNEAGRAM, AN OCCULT BLOCK TO THE HOLY SPIRIT

The Enneagram is a New Age and occult personality inventory and guide to spiritual growth that has become popular within the Evangelical community in recent years. Books on the Enneagram have been written by Christian authors and published by well-respected, trusted Christian publishers such as Zondervan and InterVarsity Press (IVP). The Enneagram has been promoted by pastors and elders, and churches have hosted and sponsored workshops. This widespread endorsement indicates a lack of inquiry or discernment among Christians and a breakdown in the gatekeeping function of church leadership and publishing houses, which have a sacred trust to screen for orthodoxy. The popularity of the Enneagram among Christians also suggests that deception and error within Christianity is systemic and cultural.[1]

This index provides a synopsis of what is wrong with the Enneagram. Much of the research has been done by Don and Joy Veinot and Marcia Montenegro who co-authored an exposé and apologetic on this subject entitled *Richard Rohr and the Enneagram Secret* (2020). I recommend their book for further study and freedom. Please share this information with those who need to hear it. We are our brother's keeper (Gen 4:8-10).

EFFICACY

There are two ways to evaluate the Enneagram: scientifically and theologically. The science of personality measures the effectiveness of an instrument: whether or not it is a reliable indicator of human personality. On the other hand, the Bible measures whether the instrument is true or false, right or wrong, good or evil by the law of God. These are fundamentally different and dissimilar standards of evaluation. Let's start with science, with the efficacy of the Enneagram as an instrument for measuring personality and for making recommendations for personal development. For now, we will leave theological concerns aside.

Is the Enneagram an effective psychological instrument? Is it accurate in assessment and guidance? To date, the Enneagram has not been adequately tested for validity as a personality inventory, nor has it been approved for use by any authority in the field of psychology or counseling. As long ago as 1992, Mitch Pacwa, a Roman Catholic Jesuit priest who renounced the Enneagram, expressed concerns about the lack of objective testing and quality assurance and the fact that recommendations were based on anecdotal reports from Occultists who had a vested interest in promoting the practice. Pacwa also pointed out that there is no standard for determining who is a qualified, competent trainer and who has the necessary expertise to profile your identity and recommend how you can improve yourself:

> No test, no standards, no board of examination exists, so most enneagram "experts" have that title through self-declaration and workshop advertising. People do not go to doctors and psychologists unless that practitioner is tested and licensed. Should not some similar requirement be made of enneagram teachers, who not only explain what your personality is like but make recommendation about what you should be like?[2]

The only scientific evaluation that has been performed is a psychometric analysis by Jay Medenwaldt, an apologist who was pursuing his Ph.D. in Social Psychology at the time. (Medenwaldt already had an MA and BS in psychology and had served as a behavioral scientist in the Air Force for nine years and taught psychology as an adjunct.)

Medenwaldt published his findings in January of 2019 in "The Enneagram, Science, and Christianity—Part 1". In his introduction he noted that "the enneagram is not a scientifically validated tool nor is it used by therapists (although there are some rare exceptions)". He also noted that it was not mentioned in "any textbooks on personality, counseling, or the psychology of religion". Only a few scientific studies had examined it; "none of them were in top-tier journals," and "their methodology was questionable". He checked the credentials of "20 or so different enneagram experts," many of whom had theology degrees, but only one had "training in psychometrics, test construction, and personality," which are necessary to verify the accuracy of such an instrument.[3]

Medenwaldt identified the following flaws in the Enneagram or in tests that have been conducted to determine its accuracy:

- One measure is "test-retest reliability". Test-retest reliability measures whether a test produces consistent results when subjects take the test over again. The only study that investigated this factor was biased: the research subjects were trained in the Enneagram and self-selected their own personality types. The results of that study, which were good, must be discounted on the basis of research subject bias. A related problem is that Enneagram practitioners claim that the human personality remains the same from childhood onward whereas research shows that the human personality gradually changes over time.

- Another measure is "inter-rater reliability". Inter-rater reliability measures the degree of consensus among personality type assessors: to what extent two people agree that a person is a particular type. This measure was low even among experienced Enneagram practitioners; and the less experience a person had, the lower the inter-rater agreement was.

- Another measure is "internal consistency". Internal consistency measures the congruence in questions for each personality type—whether the questions test the same thing. The Enneagram was below the acceptable threshold for internal consistency on three personality types. Medenwaldt explained that this was due to the "ipsative" structure of the questions, which force a person to choose between two alternatives rather than a range of alternatives on a spectrum of agreement/disagreement. The result of this design flaw is that most people exhibit characteristics of several Enneagram personality types rather than one.

- Another measure is "predictive validity". Predictive validity determines how accurately the test predicts behavior. The only study that investigated this factor was flawed (the reasons are too complex to review here).

- A final concern is the organization of types in the Enneagram. When research subjects were asked to organize the types by similarities, the results were radically different, suggesting that the current organization of types is "arbitrary".[4]

After performing this psychometric analysis, Medenwaldt's conclusion was that the Enneagram is not reliable enough to be helpful, and there is risk of harm:

> Overall, the psychometric properties of the enneagram are mixed. Some properties are below standard thresholds, a few a very good, and a lot of them are right around minimally acceptable standards. It's not a terrible test, but it's not good either.
>
> For those who have studied psychometrics, it's a no-brainer that the enneagram simply cannot do all its proponents claim it can. Any scientist who studies personality would simply look at the reliability scores and conclude the test is not accurate enough to be helpful, and therefore, they wouldn't use it because the potential for harm would be too high.[5]

Christians who are interested in a personality test would be better off taking the NEO (commonly called "the big five" traits of openness, conscientiousness, extraversion, agreeableness, and neuroticism) or alternatively, the Minnesota Multiphasic Personality Inventory (MMPI), which is more expensive to administer. These two personality tests are considered the "gold standard". The reader may be interested to know that scientists do not endorse the popular Meyers-Briggs Type Indicator (MBTI) because of its questionable validity.[6] Ultimately, Christians have a duty to go beyond the humanistic standard of what is acceptable in the field of science. They have a duty to honor the higher standard of God's law and what is true, right, and good by that standard. The rest of this index addresses these theological concerns.

BOGUS PROVENANCE

The origin of the Enneagram has been the subject of much speculation and debate. Ian Cron (1960-), co-author of one of the Enneagram books used by Christians, says of its provenance:

> If its sketchy origins weren't enough to spook the mules, there is no scientific evidence that proves the Enneagram is a reliable measure of personality. Who cares that millions of people thought it was accurate? Grizzly man thought he could make friends with bears and we know how that turned out.[7]

Cron's cavalier attitude and grim gallows humor are startling. He implies that there is something eerie or uncanny about the origin of the Enneagram: "sketchy enough to spook the mules". He jokes that playing with the Enneagram might not turn out well for us, just as befriending bears did not turn out well for grizzly man. Is this off-the-cuff scoffing warning laughable or not?

Several bogus theories of antiquity have been advanced to bolster the credibility of the Enneagram. One secular theory is that the Greek philosopher Pythagoras (570-c. 490 BCE)

> used a drawing resembling the Enneagram symbol as his spiritual signature after learning of it in Heliopolis, which was the center of worship of the Ennead or nine deities of ancient Egyptian mythology.[8]

There are two major problems with this claim from a Christian standpoint. First, as the *Stanford Encyclopedia of Philosophy* points out, "Pythagoras wrote nothing, nor were there any detailed accounts of his thoughts written by contemporaries," though many forged posthumous works in his name gave rise to a distorted tradition in which Pythagoras became the source of all that is great about Greek philosophy. Zero evidence exists to support the claim that Pythagorus was the putative author or even partial author of the Enneagram. This claim is a fabrication. Second, Pythagorus was renowned as an expert in Greek religion (mythology), not a mathematician or scientist.[9] The nature of his ideas (Greek mythology) would preclude their acceptance by any serious Christian.

Jim Aldrich, a proponent of the New Age version of the Enneagram, points out that an independent scholar, James Webb, diligently researched the origin of the Enneagram and found no evidence to support any of the theories of antiquity being offered, including (but not limited to) the cognate materia in the Kabbalah and in the *Ars Magna* of Ramón Lull (c. 1232-1315), and the *Arithmologia* of the Jesuit Athanasius Kircher (1601-1680). His conclusion:

> The enneagram is sui generis [unique; peculiar; singular; the only example of its kind] and G.I. Gurdjieff, if not its author, is at least its first modern proponent.[10] (interpolation mine)

We will discuss Gurdjieff in a moment, but first let's dispatch a few more myths of origin.

Christians try to make a case for the Enneagram's Christian origins to validate their use of it, but the evidence is contrary. Richard Rohr, the chief promoter of the Enneagram to Christians, and his co-author Andreas Ebert made the following statements in an earlier edition of their book, *Discovering the Enneagram: An Ancient Tool for a New Spiritual Journey* (1992):

> The Enneagram is a mysterious model of the psyche that is *not originally Christian*.

> I believe that the Enneagram can help us to find a deeper and more authentic relationship with God—even though it was *not discovered by Christians*.[11] (italics mine)

Later, when the authors wanted to curry the favor of a Christian audience, they reneged their "not Christian" position in a later edition of the book and retitled the book to align with Christianity: *The Enneagram: A Christian Perspective* (2001). In this later edition, Rohr and Ebert claim that a Christian monk, ascetic, theologian, and desert father of the fourth century, Evagrius of Ponticus (345-399 CE) had the Enneagram in mind—a highly specific geometric diagram—when he wrote about the "shape" of numbers. The "shape" of numbers was a common concept at the time. (For example, if the number one were a shape, it might look like a circle. If the number three were a shape, it might look like an equilateral or an isosceles or a scalene triangle. If the number four were a shape, it might look like a square or parallelogram. If the number six were a shape, it might look like a hexagon.) But the Enneagram is not a simple geometric shape. It is a complex design. Rohr and Ebert projected the Enneagram figure into Evagrius' text to substantiate their claim of antiquity. This is more than a misinterpretation; it is a fabrication.[12]

Doctor of Theology Ronald V. Huggins describes Rohr and Ebert's efforts to peg Evagrius as the putative author of the Enneagram as "promiscuously fishing about in the Patristic texts for some support, any support that they might find for their Enneagram symbol along with its attendant personality test". He says:

> The Enneagram symbol cannot be shown to predate 1916, and the link between the symbol and the text can be fairly confidently dated as occurring for the first time in c. 1969.[13]

Rohr and Ebert also fabricate a connection to the thirteenth century "mathematician, polymath [a person of great and varied learning], philosopher, logician, Franciscan tertiary and writer" Ramón Lull (1232/33-1315/16; interpolation mine). Rohr makes the outrageous claim that:

> "...my fellow Franciscan, Blessed Raymond Lull [sic], who successfully used the ancient Enneagram as a lingua franca to mutually evangelize warring Christians and Moslems. This is a very proven, traditional, and tested tool for both the 'conversion of morals' and the 'discernment of spirits'"...[14]

There is no evidence that Raymón Lull drew a nine-pointed Enneagram, much less that this was a tool of reconciliation between Christians and Muslims (!). Lull did draw many diagrams of overlapping geometric shapes, including those that featured two, three, five, nine, fourteen, and sixteen triangles, but none of these and none of his other symbols was the nine-pointed Enneagram symbol.[15]

REAL PROVENANCE

What is the real origin of the Enneagram? In actuality, it is the product of contributions from several occult sources. We trace the origin here and ask the reader to consider the spiritual implications in terms of fitness for Christian use, especially in light of the injunction in the book of Acts to:

> abstain from and avoid anything that has been polluted by being offered to idols.—Acts 15:20, 29 AMPC

Paul explains that idols represent evil spirits or demons:

> [...] what the pagans sacrifice they offer [in effect] to demons (to evil spiritual powers) and not to God [at all]. I do not want you to fellowship and be partners with diabolical spirits [...].—1 Corinthians 10:20 AMPC (abridged)

The origin of the Enneagram, the way it is used, and claims about it indicate that it is an idol backed by demonic power. It was made and developed through the use of divination and witchcraft. As a product of divination and witchcraft, it continues to host spirit power. Divination and witchcraft are explicitly forbidden by God and prohibited in the Bible:

> You are not to practice divination or witchcraft.—Leviticus 19:26 CSB (abridged)

> There shall not be found among you anyone who uses divination and fortune-telling, one who practices witchcraft, or one who interprets omens, or a sorcerer, or one who casts a charm or spell, or a medium, or a spiritist, or a necromancer [who seeks the dead].—Deuteronomy 18:10-11 AMP (abridged)

George Ivanovich (G.I.) Gurdjieff (c. 1866/1872/1877-1949), a mystic teacher who abandoned the Eastern Orthodox faith, created the geometric diagram known as the Enneagram—a nine-pointed figure somewhat reminiscent of a jagged crown inside a circle. At first the Enneagram had nothing to do with a personality or character inventory. Rather, it was a symbol for—and an esoteric container of—the totality of all knowledge in the universe. Knowledge could be retrieved from the Enneagram by consorting with the Enneagram. But the inquirer could only retrieve as much knowledge as the inquirer possessed or could understand. Gurdjieff created a "sacred dance" resembling whirling dervish movements to be performed in front of the Enneagram. The movements were the interpretation of the knowledge received from the Enneagram.[16]

Gurdjieff regarded the Enneagram as all knowing or omniscient (basically a substitute for God). He seems to have used it as a divinatory tool and paid homage to it. As a focal point for the "sacred dance," the Enneagram seems to have functioned both as an altar and a contact object or object of meditation for the transmission of information from the spirit realm. The "sacred dance" seems to have been both a ritual offering to the spirit power that informs the Enneagram as well as a lyrical method of channeling the message from the spirit realm through body language or movement. If so, his worship and consultation of the Enneagram combined sorcery and divination.

Gurdjieff created his own path to spiritual awakening and transformation, which involved monitoring the body as an object of meditation to the point of alienating the observer from any identification with his body and any identification with himself as a doer or actor. The awareness that remained that was not centered in the body or in the self as a doer or actor was supposedly the true self.[17] This practice is akin to eastern mysticism in its deconstruction of the human personality and its deconstruction of the sense of oneself as a unique embodied being.

Rodney Collin (1909-1956), who studied Gurdjieff's teachings and who wrote *The Christian Mystery* (1952), was the first to apply or adapt the Enneagram to the human personality. Collin was a proponent of astrology and medieval alchemy, especially the four humours, a pseudo-medical and psychological typing system that categorized human temperaments by the supposed predominance of certain bodily fluids (blood, phlegm, yellow bile, and black bile). Inspired by this, Collin created profiles of six different temperament types plus subsets based on the predominance of glandular/endocrine activity in a person and the supposed planetary influence upon the glands. Here are his temperament types:

- the martial temperament governed by Mars;
- the jovial temperament governed by Jupiter;
- the saturnine temperament governed by Saturn;
- the lunar temperament governed by the Moon;
- the mercurial temperament governed by Mercury;
- the venusian temperament governed by Venus.

Collin claimed that you could improve your own planetary-glandular personality type by incorporating attributes of the two planetary-glandular types in the Enneagram sequence downstream of you according to a particular formula.[18] Collin's contribution to the development of the Enneagram is a product of divination (astrology) and sorcery (alchemy). At this point, the Enneagram was an astrological and alchemical typing of personality.

Oscar Ichazo (1931-2020), an occult teacher who founded the Arica Institute in Arica Chile in 1968, added to the Enneagram typing system three self-preservation drives of "conservation" (digestion), "relation" (circulation), and "adaptation" (the nervous system) and two self-perpetuation drives, "sexual" and "spiritual". Ichazo taught his students to dis-identify from the "false self" or "ego" with its "fixations" developed in childhood and return to the "true self" that is perfect and divine. This is a New Age concept that combines popular psychology with Hinduism. Ichazo's inspiration for his work on the self seems to have derived from supernatural sources. He incorporated psychedelics and shamanism into his work; he carried out orders from "a higher entity called Metatron," and his Institute was "guided by an interior master," presumably a spirit that controlled Ichazo.[19] Ichazo's contribution to the development of the Enneagram typing system is a product of witchcraft (channeling spirit guides) and sorcery (psychedelics, shamanism).

Ichazo taught **Claudio Naranjo** (1932-2019), a psychiatrist and New Ager, who is largely credited with formulating the temperament types. Naranjo introduced the Enneagram to the Esalen Institute in Big Sur, California, in 1971. The Esalen Institute is a boundary bending and boundary breaking New Age exploratorium aptly described by Doctor of Theology Ronald V. Huggins as "a place where people were likely to get naked, take LSD, and beat on native drums". Naranjo attributed the source of his inspiration to "automatic writing". Automatic writing is the occult art of channeling messages from the spirit realm by yielding motor control to a spirit that dictates the content of a message and directs the movements of the hand in writing or typing.[20] Naranjo's contribution to the development of the Enneagram typing system is a product of witchcraft (channeling messages from a spirit through automatic handwriting).

Naranjo taught psychic Helen Palmer, who later collaborated with David Daniels, a professor of psychiatry at Stanford University and a New Ager, to create a "Narrative Tradition" of the Enneagram in 1988. Naranjo also taught Bob Ochs (1930-2018), a Jesuit, who presented the Enneagram at a Roman Catholic seminary in Chicago in the 1970s. From there, it began to infiltrate Christianity. At the seminary, Richard Rohr (1943-), a Roman Catholic Franciscan priest, and Mitch Pacwa (1949-), a Roman Catholic Jesuit priest, studied it. Richard Rohr became the chief proponent of the Enneagram and wrote several books on it: first a book in German, *Discovering the Enneagram: An Ancient Tool for a New Spiritual Journey* (1989); then an English translation (1990); then he a co-authored book with Andreas Ebert, *Discovering the Enneagram* (1992), which was revised and expanded into *The Enneagram: A Christian Perspective* (2001). Rohr is largely responsible for the Enneagram's current popularity among Evangelicals.[21]

By contrast, **Mitch Pacwa** became an early opponent, warning Catholics against the Enneagram in his book *Catholics and the New Age: How Good People Are Being Drawn into Jungian Psychology, the Enneagram, and the Age of Aquarius* (1992) and later warning Protestants in his article, "Tell Me Who I Am, O Enneagram," published in the *Christian Research Journal* (June, 2009). Pacwa became disenchanted with the Enneagram when he noticed that he tried to force fit his own life and the lives of others into the typing system and he caught himself dismissing information that did not conform with the system. He also became increasingly suspicious about the provenance of the work after discovering that the typing system did not actually originate with Gurdjieff or his immediate followers. After being alerted about the occult origin in a booklet targeting Catholics (*A Closer Look at the Enneagram* by Dorothy Ranaghan), he became deeply disturbed about the occult inspiration and occult content embedded in the design and mechanics of the typing system.[22]

Meanwhile, **Richard Rohr** popularized the Enneagram among Evangelicals. All who have been taught by Rohr, including authors of Christian versions of the Enneagram that are now studied by Evangelicals, have been influenced by Rohr and share his world view (and spirit power) to some extent. A brief overview of Rohr's beliefs as articulated on his website and in his book *The Universal Christ* (2019) reveals that Rohr subscribes to many heresies that violate Christian orthodoxy. Such heresies can be classified as "doctrines of demons" that offer alternative sources of knowledge to the Bible and alternate sources of power to the Holy Spirit (1 Tim 4:1).[23] Here is a summary of Rohr's views:

Panentheism: Rohr is a Panentheist who believes that God is in creation and creation is in God. In panentheism, God is co-extensive with the universe. God inhabits every being and every aspect and dimension of the universe: the whole universe is a manifestation of God, yet God is also greater than the universe and contains the universe within Himself. Panentheism negates the Biblical distinction between the Creator and His creation. In the Bible, creation is a work of God and not the very being of God. The Creator is superior in every way to His creation: superior in knowledge (omniscient), superior in power (omnipotent), superior in presence (omnipresent), superior in moral being (holy), and superior in beauty (glory). Despite Rohr's Catholic identification, he applies panentheistic ideas to Jesus, splitting Jesus into the "time-bound" and "culturally-bound" historic person and a "Universal Christ" or ubiquitous manifestation of Christ in the cosmos, of which we and everything else are a part. Rohr views the historic Jesus as one who modeled the right understanding of the "Universal Christ" or cosmic incarnation of God's being; the co-mingling of matter with the Spirit of God. In Rohr's mind, Christ inhabits everything, and all things are already in Christ: the body of Christ is "all creation," the totality of the universe, rather than redeemed people who have accepted His blood sacrifice for the remission of sins and who obey His teachings and His commands.[24]

Non-Dualism: Rohr is a Non-Dualist who believes that "there is only One Reality" and "Non-duality is the highest level of consciousness". This is yoga philosophy, the aim of which is the supreme reality of Hinduism: universal being-consciousness-bliss. Non-dualism goes beyond panentheism. Non-dualism denies the reality or existence of anything but God. God alone exists. God is all, and all is God. The ongoing drama of creation teeming with billions of individual beings is an illusion or transient enough to be of no consequence, and behind this illusion or transience is ubiquitous being-ness and ubiquitous awareness that is God. Rohr advocates a non-dual mystical practice called Contemplative

Prayer. Contemplative Prayer is an eastern meditation detachment technique that has been pawned off as a contemporary version of the monastic tradition of contemplating scripture to commune with God (Lectio Divina). In actuality, Contemplative Prayer is neither contemplation nor prayer; it is the practice of detaching from the mind and embodied existence to dissolve into cosmic being or cosmic consciousness (the Hindu supreme reality).[25]

Perennialism: Rohr is a Perennialist who believes that all religions advance the same truth, reality, or divinity and that every religion is just a different path to the same divine. He accepts all religions as right (except, of course, Biblical Christianity).[26]

Rohr denies the Bible as God-inspired, revelatory, and accurate despite Jesus's affirmation to the Father that "Your word is truth" and that "until heaven and earth disappear, not the smallest letter, not the least stroke of a pen, will by any means disappear from the Law until everything is accomplished" (Jn 17:17; Matt 5:18 NIV). Rohr regards the Bible as a journal of human experiences and commentaries on human efforts to connect with God:

> "It is an account of our very human experience of the divine intrusion into history. It was written by people trying to listen to God. We must know that humans always see 'through a glass darkly' and all knowledge is imperfect."[27]

Rohr also views the Bible as spiritually evolutionary, reflecting the different stages of spiritual development or consciousness of its many human authors.[28] In other words, he treats the Bible as humanistic, merely of human origin, whereas the Apostle Paul affirms, "All scripture is given by inspiration of God and is profitable for doctrine, for reproof, for correction, for instruction in righteousness" (2 Tim 3:16).

Because of his disregard for the Bible, Rohr denies or distorts all fundamental doctrines of Christianity. He denies original sin and the sin nature and redefines sin as the unfortunate, mistaken notion that we are separated from God, a notion that we must disabuse ourselves of through non-dual (yoga) meditation to realize that we are actually one with God.[29] Because Rohr denies the reality of sin, he also denies the redemptive purpose of Christ's crucifixion as the remission of sins. Rohr reinterprets the cross as "a statement from God that reality has a cruciform pattern".[30] Rohr believes in universal salvation, that everyone will be saved eventually: "salvation is not a question of if but when".[31] He counts "all who look at the world with respect even if they are not formally religious," as already "en Cristo, or in Christ".[32] Rohr denies the resurrection as a physical victory over death and the grave and a spiritual victory over sin and the Devil. He redefines resurrection as "Christ's consciousness" unbound and released "from a specific place and time". Similarly, Rohr denies the second coming or return of Christ in the flesh and redefines it as humanity's realization of the Incarnation in us, "the divine indwelling in all of us". To Rohr, "Incarnation is already redemption. Bethlehem was more important than Calvary".[33] By this he means that God affirmed our innate divinity by becoming human; and God affirmed the innate divinity of all creation by inhabiting creation. To Rohr, redemption is realizing that God is already in us and around us. Much of Rohr's thinking is Hindu yoga philosophy posing as Christianity, not well disguised.

From this overview, we see that Rohr preaches "another gospel" and "another Jesus" that hosts "a different spirit" than the Holy Spirit (2 Cor 11:4). This is what Paul warned about when he predicted an apostasy at the end of the age through doctrines of demons:

> Now the Spirit expressly says that in latter times some will depart from the faith, giving heed to deceiving spirits and doctrines of demons.
> —1 Timothy 4:1

Rohr passed on his views to countless New Agers, including the late Don Riso, former president of the Enneagram Institute, and Russ Hudson, current president of the Enneagram Institute. Riso and Hudson co-authored *The Wisdom of the Enneagram: The Complete Guide to Psychological and Spirit Growth for the Nine Personality Types* (1999).[34]

Rohr also passed on his views to authors of two Enneagram books that are favorites with Evangelicals: *The Road Back to You* (2016) by **Ian Cron and Suzanne Stabile**, and *The Sacred Enneagram* (2017) by **Christopher Heuertz**. Rohr's influence on these authors should not be underestimated. Rohr mentored Stabile for several years, and both Stabile and Cron teach at Rohr's Center for Action and Contemplation (CAC) in Albuquerque, New Mexico, indicating that they are aligned with his views. Rohr, Heuertz, and Heuertz's wife all serve in executive capacities in each other's organizations. Their relationships are not tenuous or casual, but serious and collaborative. These Christian authors are agreed in ideology and spirit with Rohr: "Can two walk together, unless they are agreed?" (Amos

3:3). All current Christian Enneagram authors and coaches, including **Beth McCord**, were trained by New Agers and Occultists and are implicated in that lineage of spiritual transmission and are promoting a work that is the product of spirits that are not the Holy Spirit.[35] Even if future Christians learn about the Enneagram solely from other Christians, the spirit realm knows what belongs to it and will piggyback on its own property, even scrubbed versions of it.

Pelagianism: Rohr's teaching on the Incarnation as the universal divine or Christ in all creation is presented in Christianized form in Heuertz's book. Heuertz emphasizes "the goodness in humanity" and our ability to improve ourselves through self-help measures. He, too, reinterprets the significance of Christ's Incarnation as proof that we are all fundamentally good, not proof that we are all fundamentally sinful and need the intervention of a divine Savior to rescue us from ourselves. The presentation of humanity in a positive light and capable of self-reform is highly complimentary and appealing and empowering, but these notions are totally unBiblical and unreal. They constitute a heresy known as Pelagianism that was denounced by two councils in the late fourth century. Pelagianism is the belief that mankind is inherently good and capable of self-reform. The heresy denies original sin, that we are born with a sin nature and a proclivity and desire to sin; it denies the need for a Savior or salvation; it denies the need for the Holy Spirit to awaken conscience and grant power over sin. The heresy assumes that humans have the desire and ability to know and do what is right apart from divine help. The heresy also assumes that humans can merit salvation through good conduct.[36] The influence of such heresies in the Enneagram may be subtle, but they are nonetheless powerful.

Rohr's teaching on the universal Incarnation of Christ is even more evident in Cron and Stabile's views. In an interview, Cron and Stabile were asked which type Jesus was. They said:

> "Jesus represents all numbers. It has been said in Christian Enneagram tradition that *the Enneagram is the face of God*".[37] (italics mine)

This claim is incredible. It asserts that the Enneagram provides direct revelation and experience of God in the same way that an actual encounter with God would. This puts a man-made work produced in partnership with demons in the place of God. Let's contrast Cron's and Stabile's statement with scripture. Scripture says that no one has ever seen God except Jesus, and Jesus is the only face of God that we can see (not the Enneagram):

> *No one has ever seen God, but the one and only Son,* who is himself God and is in closest relationship with the Father, has made him known.
> —John 1:18 NIV (italics mine)

> *No one has seen the Father except the one who is from God*; only he has seen the Father.—John 6:46 NIV (italics mine)

> For God who said, "Let light shine out of darkness," made his light shine in our hearts to give us the light of the knowledge of *God's glory displayed in the face of Christ.*—2 Corinthians 4:6 NIV (italics mine)

> He [Jesus Christ] is the divine portrait, the true likeness of the invisible God, and the first-born heir of all creation.—Colossians 1:15 TPT

> He [Jesus Christ] is *the sole expression of the glory of God* [the Light-being, the out-raying or radiance of the divine], and *He is the perfect imprint and very image of [God's] nature.*—Hebrews 1:3 AMPC (italics mine)

According to scripture, the only face of God that we can seen is the face of Jesus. To claim, as Cron and Stabile do, that the Enneagram is the face of God is to promote an imposter. Cron and Stabile superimpose the Enneagram over the face of God in place of God; they put a man-made, occult diagram and the syncretistic occult meaning that it represents and the spirit power vested in it as a mask over God. This is a breach of the first commandment not to entertain other gods before Him or beside Him and the second commandment not to fashion an image of anything in heaven, on earth, or beneath the earth and revere or serve it (Ex 20:1-4).

Some Christian Enneagram coaches are equally outrageous in their claims. **Bill Gaultiere**, a licensed psychologist who "pastors/mentors pastors" and who taught an Enneagram seminar at Saddleback Community Church in California, said: "At the center of the Enneagram is our Lord Jesus Christ". Most emphatically, Jesus is not at the center of an occult art, nor will He ever be. Gaultiere said, "He [Jesus] is the perfection of all nine types."[38] But Jesus cannot be typecast, not even as the perfect human personality. He is not the consummation of any human typing system. He is God: not just human, but divine:

> "For My thoughts are not your thoughts,
> Nor are your ways My ways," says the LORD.
> "For as the heavens are higher than the earth,
> So are My ways higher than your ways,
> And My thoughts than your thoughts."—Isaiah 55:8-9

Gaultiere said, "They [all nine types] integrate in Him." Human personalities are not dissociated parts of God that need to "integrate" back into Him, and the Enneagram is not a tool for integrating the human personality in any case. Gaultiere said, "When you see Jesus in the Enneagram, you see who you are meant to be".[39] If you see Jesus in the Enneagram, you are seeing another Jesus, not the real Jesus. To see the real Jesus, you need to look directly at Him, not indirectly through a medium that was invented by men who were inspired by demons. The Enneagram does not reveal Jesus. Jesus reveals Himself through His word and His Spirit. The Enneagram is a block to seeing Jesus and a block to hearing Him for ourselves.

CAN'T WE JUST REDEEM THE ENNEAGRAM?

"Can't we just redeem the Enneagram for service to God and God's people?"[40] The short answer is NO. No human being has the power to redeem anything. Only God redeems. God only redeems what He has made, not what humans have made in partnership with demons. God only redeems by the blood ransom of Christ, not by some other method. Jesus did not die to redeem the Enneagram. He died to redeem people. There is no acceptable version of anything occult. Occult arts cannot be expurgated (purged of offensive material) and sanctified and consecrated to God's use or human use. What God bans is slated for total destruction. There is nothing salvageable about something that is banned.

This includes divination and sorcery and witchcraft, which are elements in the creation, development, dedication, and workings of the Enneagram.

The Enneagram belongs to the spirit world. Why? Because the Enneagram was inspired by spirits. People partnered with the spirit world to create and develop the Enneagram. The Enneagram is not just a human invention but a collaborative work co-authored by people and the spirits they consulted. Since every author owns his own work, spirits own the work they helped produce. As co-authors, spirits retain rights of possession and control over the Enneagram. They participated in its creation; it was dedicated to them; and it operates by principles of the spirit world.

Christians who seek their God-given identity or perfect self through the Enneagram are relying on it as a divinatory tool, for they are seeking to understand themselves through a source other than the Bible and the Holy Spirit. Christians who seek personal transformation through the Enneagram are relying on it as an instrument of sorcery or magic, for they are seeking regeneration by a means other than the blood of Christ and the Spirit of Christ. Such activities God bans.

Consulting the Enneagram for spiritual guidance instead of—or in addition to—the Bible and the Holy Spirit is the error of Balaam. Balaam straddled spiritual kingdoms. He used the old world technique of omens or augury, which blends sorcery (witchcraft) with divination (fortune telling), yet he also received prophetic revelation from the Lord to bless Israel (see Num 23 and 24, esp. Num 24:1). Straddling kingdoms never ends well, and indeed Balaam's life was cut short (Num 31:8, Josh 13:22).

As a replacement for or supplement to the Bible and the Holy Spirit, the Enneagram and the spirits behind it can hinder the baptism in the Holy Spirit or block revelation that flows through the gifts of the Holy Spirit, especially the revelatory gifts of tongues, interpretation, word of knowledge, word of wisdom, and prophecy. Repentance and renunciation are necessary.

The Enneagram is only one of countless occult arts. My sincere hope is that this in-depth analysis will aid discernment and understanding about how the spirit world operates so that Christians will recognize and avoid other forms of compromise as well. For further study, the interested reader is referred to the well-researched treatise, *Richard Rohr and the Enneagram Secret* by Don and Joy Veinot and Marcia Montenegro, my primary source on the subject.

ENDNOTES

INTRODUCTION

1. Philip Botts, personal communication, May 27, 2020.
2. Philip Botts, personal communication, May 29, 2020.
3. Evan Hill, Ainara Tiefenthäler, Christiaan Triebert, Drew Jordan, Haley Willis, and Robin Stein, "8 Minutes and 46 Seconds: How George Floyd Was Killed in Police Custody," *The New York Times*, May 31, 2020, https://www.nytimes.com/2020/05/31/us/george-floyd-investigation.html/.
4. Caleb Parke, "From George Washington to Ulysses S. Grant: Statues, Monuments Vandalized Extend beyond Confederates amid Black Lives Matter Protests," *Fox News*, June 22, 2020, https://www.foxnews.com/us/statue-monument-vandalized-torn-down-protest; Rachel Scully and James Bikales, "A List of the Statues across the US Toppled, Vandalized or Officially Removed amid Protests," *The Hill*, June 12, 2020, https://thehill.com/homenews/state-watch/502492-list-statues-toppled-vandalized-removed-protests.
5. Philip Botts, personal communication, June 1, 2020.
6. "Door of Hope, Gray Scale" (April 6, 2020), Cassandra Donnelly, with kind permission. FaceBook: https://www.facebook.com/CreativePassages. Fine Art America: https://fineartamerica.com/profiles/cassandra-donnelly.
7. Randy Clark, "Session 18, Healing and Disbelief: Cessationism," *School of Healing and Impartation Essentials 2*, Global Awakening, 2008, audio teaching electronic download, 1:09:39.
8. Philip Botts, "Speaking in Tongues Workshop: The Benefits of Tongues for the Individual, Part 1," The River Room, August 15, 2019, YouTube video, 50:28, https://www.youtube.com/watch?v=xXCJk0d8A5c. Note: Philip's testimony is at the very end of the workshop.
9. Greg Horton and Yonat Shimron/Religion News Service, "Southern Baptists Change Policy on Speaking in Tongues," *Charisma News*, May 15, 2015, https://www.charismanews.com/us/49661-southern-baptists-change-policy-on-speaking-in-tongues.
10. Horton and Shimron/Religion News Service, "Southern Baptists Change Policy."
11. Ibid.
12. Ibid.
13. Botts, "Speaking in Tongues Workshop: The Benefits of Tongues for the Individual, Part 1."
14. Meghann Myers, "Horrific Cable Mishap caused by Maintenance Errors," *Navy Times*, July 14, 2016, https://www.navytimes.com/news/your-navy/2016/07/14/horrific-cable-mishap-caused-by-maintenance-errors-navy/.
15. Botts, "Speaking in Tongues Workshop: The Benefits of Tongues for the Individual, Part 1."

16. Ibid.
17. "Door of Hope, Colorful Burst of Sunlight" (April 6, 2020), Cassandra Donnelly, with kind permission. FaceBook: https://www.facebook.com/CreativePassages. Fine Art America: https://fineartamerica.com/profiles/cassandra-donnelly.
18. Botts, "Speaking in Tongues Workshop: The Benefits of Tongues for the Individual, Part 1.
19. Ibid.
20. Ibid.
21. North American Mission Board, "Baptists and Speaking in Tongues," March 30, 2016, https://www.namb.net/apologetics-blog/baptists-and-speaking-in-tongues/.
22. Ibid.
23. Botts, "Speaking in Tongues Workshop: The Benefits of Tongues for the Individual, Part1."
24. "Door of Hope, Collage Element" (April 6, 2020), Cassandra Donnelly, with kind permission. FaceBook: https://www.facebook.com/CreativePassages. Fine Art America: https://fineartamerica.com/profiles/cassandra-donnelly.

THE SHANTUNG REVIVAL: "LORD, DO IT AGAIN, AND BEGIN IN ME!"

1. Adam Augustyn, "Second Sino-Japanese War (1937-1945)," *Encyclopaedia Britannica*, accessed June 8, 2020, https://www.britannica.com/event/Second-Sino-Japanese-War.
2. C.L. Culpepper, "Prologue" in *The Shantung Revival*, The Gospel Truth dot net, March 25, 1968, https://www.gospeltruth.net/shantung.htm. Note: Culpepper credits Mary Crawford for compiling a treatise of reports of the revival in 1933; his book is an expanded revision with additions, reflections, and comments. The entire book is available in portable document format (PDF) online.
3. Culpepper, "Chapter One: The Shadow of a Mighty Rock" in *The Shantung Revival*, The Gospel Truth dot net, March 25, 1968, https://www.gospeltruth.net/shantung.htm.
4. Chet and Phyllis Swearingen, "The Shantung Revival (1927-1937)," *Beautiful Feet*, accessed June 5,2020, https://romans1015.com/shantung-revival/; Culpepper, "Chapter One: The Shadow of a Mighty Rock" in *The Shantung Revival*.
5. Swearingen, "The Shantung Revival (1927-1937)."
6. Culpepper, "Prologue"; "Chapter One: The Shadow of a Mighty Rock"; "Chapter Two: A Foundation—The New Birth" in *The Shantung Revival*.
7. *The Biographical Dictionary of Chinese Christianity*, "Marie Monsen: 1878-1962, Norwegian Missionary in China," https://bdcconline.net/en/stories/monsen-marie.
8. Culpepper, "Chapter One: The Shadow of a Mighty Rock" in *The Shantung Revival*.
9. Culpepper, "Chapter Two: A Foundation—The New Birth" in *The Shantung Revival*; Swearingen, "The Shantung Revival (1927-1937)."
10. Culpepper, "Chapter Two: A Foundation—The New Birth" in *The Shantung Revival*.
11. Ibid.
12. Ibid.
13. Culpepper, "Chapter Four: Permanent Results" in *The Shantung Revival*.
14. Culpepper, "Chapter Three: The Revival Spreads" in *The Shantung Revival*.

15. Ibid.
16. Culpepper, "Chapter Two: A Foundation—The New Birth" in *The Shantung Revival*.
17. Ibid.
18. Ibid.
19. Ibid.
20. Culpepper, "Chapter Three: The Revival Spreads" in *The Shantung Revival*.
21. Ibid.
22. Ibid.
23. Ibid.
24. Culpepper, "Chapter Four: Permanent Results" in *The Shantung Revival*.
25. Culpepper, "Chapter Three: The Revival Spreads" in *The Shantung Revival*.
26. Ibid.
27. Culpepper, "Chapter Four: Permanent Results" in *The Shantung Revival*.
28. Ibid.
29. Ibid.
30. Swearingen, "The Shantung Revival (1927-1937)."
31. Culpepper, "Epilogue" in *The Shantung Revival*.
32. Culpepper, "Chapter Four: Permanent Results," in *The Shantung Revival*; Swearingen, "The Shantung Revival (1927-1937)".
33. Swearingen, "The Shantung Revival (1927-1937)."
34. R. Cal Guy in "Introduction," *The Shantung Revival*, by C.L. Culpepper, The Gospel Truth dot net, March 25, 1968, https://www.gospeltruth.net/shantung.htm.
35. Baker James Cauthen in "Introduction," *The Shantung Revival*, by C.L. Culpepper, The Gospel Truth dot net, March 25, 1968, https://www.gospeltruth.net/shantung.htm.
36. Donald McGavran in "Introduction," *The Shantung Revival*, by C.L. Culpepper, The Gospel Truth dot net, March 25, 1968, https://www.gospeltruth.net/shantung.htm.
37. Culpepper, "Foreward," *The Shantung Revival*.
38. Ibid.
39. Culpepper, "Epilogue," *The Shantung Revival*.

"A MEGA PENTECOST"

1. Tim Sheets, "Pentecost and Divisions of Angels," Oasis Church, May 24, 2020, YouTube video, 41:19, https://www.youtube.com/watch?v=ZkHYPbERhQM&feature=youtu.be.
2. Sheets, "Pentecost and Divisions of Angels".
3. *Blue Letter Bible*, Strong's H6635: tsaba/host, https://www.blueletterbible.org/lang/lexicon/lexicon.cfm?Strongs=H6635&t=KJV.
4. Sheets, "Pentecost and Divisions of Angels".
5. Ibid.
6. The Editors of Encyclopaedia Britannica, s.v. "Legion: Military Unit," *Encyclopaedia Britannica*, July 20, 1998, https://www.britannica.com/topic/legion.
7. Sheets, "Pentecost and Divisions of Angels".
8. *Got Questions (Your Questions. Biblical Answers)*, "What is the definition of ekklesia?" last updated 2020, https://www.gotquestions.org/definition-ekklesia.html.

9. *Merriam-Webster dot com dictionary*, s.v. "Ecclesia," https://www.merriam-webster.com/dictionary/ecclesia.
10. *Got Questions*, "What is the definition of ekklesia?".
11. Sheets, "Pentecost and Divisions of Angels"; see also: Tim Sheets, "Shoulder to the Wheel," Oasis Church, August 17, 2020, YouTube video, 51:25, https://www.youtube.com/watch?v=yeX5KhewHz8.
12. Sheets, "Pentecost and Divisions of Angels."
13. Ibid.
14. "The Overflow" (June 6, 2020), Cassandra Donnelly, with kind permission. FaceBook: https://www.facebook.com/CreativePassages. Fine Art America: https://fineartamerica.com/profiles/cassandra-donnelly.
15. Cassandra Donnelly, "Speaking in Tongues Workshop: The Public Purposes of Tongues, Part 2," The River Room, June 19, 2020, YouTube video, 1:00:10, https://www.youtube.com/watch?v=hj6WaGQtyps. Note: Cassandra's talk is at the end of the video.
16. Donnelly, "Speaking in Tongues Workshop: The Public Purposes of Tongues, Part 2".
17. Cassandra Donnelly, personal communication June 14, June 29, and July 1, 2020.
18. Donnelly, "Speaking in Tongues Workshop: The Public Purposes of Tongues, Part 2".
19. Paula Price, *The Prophet's Dictionary: The Ultimate Guide to Supernatural Wisdom*, rev. ed. (Tulsa, OK: Whitaker House, [1999] 2006), 221-222.
20. Donnelly, "Speaking in Tongues Workshop: The Public Purposes of Tongues, Part 2".
21. Ibid.
22. Ibid.
23. *Wikipedia*, s.v. "Kintsugi," last updated May 30, 2020, https://en.wikipedia.org/wiki/Kintsugi.
24. Donnelly, "Speaking in Tongues Workshop: The Public Purposes of Tongues, Part 2".
25. Ibid.
26. [Computer screen shots of] Lindy's Post, "SUN, JUN 21 AT 2 PM—11 PM: Luciferian March for a One World Government Raleigh NC, North Carolina State Capitol," Public - hosted by the Disciples of Lucifer, Raleigh, North Carolina, and 3 others," FaceBook; SteveNoble Show, C2A Radio Network, "The Icing on the Cake: Satanic Spirit of the Age coming out of the Shadows and onto Main Street"; INTELLIHUB.
27. Donnelly, "Speaking in Tongues Workshop: The Public Purposes of Tongues, Part 2".
28. Ibid.
29. Ibid.

SPEAKING IN TONGUES TESTIMONY

1. *Blue Letter Bible*, Strong's G907: baptizo/baptize, https://www.blueletterbible.org/lang/lexicon/lexicon.cfm?Strongs=G907&t=KJV.
2. Sveta Spear at the keyboard (2019), with kind permission.

SPEAKING IN TONGUES IMPARTATION AND ACTIVATION

1. Corinna Craft, "Pentecost: the Gift of Tongues for Power Evangelism, Prayer, Prophecy and Spiritual Warfare," The River Room, May 23, 2021, YouTube video, 56:18, https://www.youtube.com/watch?v=e7kIwA4yYrQ&t=202s.
2. Marcus Rogers, "If You Love Smoking Weed or Drinking You Will Really Love Speaking in Tongues," November 9, 2019, YouTube video, 25:12, https://www.youtube.com/watch?v=7xXgPgyI16c.
3. Louis Prima (King Louie) and Phil Harris (Baloo the Bear), vocal performance of "I Wan'na Be Like You," by Robert Sherman and Richard Sherman (songwriters), with George Bruns (instrumentals) and Walter Sheets (orchestration), in Walt Disney's animated film, *The Jungle Book* (1967), posted November 7, 2013, YouTube video, 3:49, https://www.youtube.com/ watch?v=FOTZJ8EFgpk.
4. Ella Fitzgerald, "How High The Moon/Epic scat LIVE 1966 [RITY archives]," archived from Reelin' In The Years Productions, Posted July 18, 2018, YouTube video, 6:34, https://www.youtube.com/watch?v=1GUmxnYheK0.
5. Jennifer LeClaire, "Remove the Bottleneck from Your Life!" Jennifer LeClaire @ propheticbooks, January 17, 2020, Periscope TV.
6. Sid Roth, "God Talk: Doorway to the Supernatural!" *It's Supernatural!* FaceBook page, posted on FaceBook (Live), January 9, 2018, video 11:55, https://www.facebook.com/its.supernatural/videos/10155253197347263.
7. Kevin Zadai, interview by Sid Roth, *It's Supernatural!* ISN, January 5, 2020, television program, 28:30, https://sidroth.org/television/tv-archives/kevin-zadai-5/.
8. Ibid.
9. Ibid.
10. Ibid.
11. Sid Roth, "God Talk: The Key to Unlocking Your Destiny!" *It's Supernatural!* ISN, March 29, 2017, television program, 43:14, https://sidroth.org/god-talk/.
12. Corinna Craft, "Speaking in Tongues Workshop: For the Common Good or Profit of All," Ray Boetcher/The River Room, January 17, 2020, YouTube video, 48:13, https://www.youtube.com/watch?v=bk_fo-1ZUeY&list=PLGYFMQ8WuIJB29bXH1e_nPiG1aHWz4Y3G&index=4&t=2568s.

    Corinna Craft, "Speaking in Tongues Workshop: Praise, Worship, and Prophecy," The River Room, February 21, 2020, YouTube video, 48:42, https://www.youtube.com/watch?v=0CRktERo80c.

    Corinna Craft, "Speaking in Tongues Workshop: Unity in the Holy Spirit and the Royal Priesthood," The River Room, March 20, 2020, YouTube video, 1:11:29, https://www.youtube.com/watch?v=8lf0NmHLoKc&t=1740s.

    Corinna Craft, "Speaking in Tongues Workshop: The Royal Priesthood of All Believers, the Laity as Clergy," The River Room, April 17, 2020, YouTube video, 1:16:15, https://www.youtube.com/watch?v=N4dGBQM9-58.

13. Corinna Craft, "Speaking in Tongues Workshop: Praise, Worship, and Prophecy," The River Room, February 21, 2020, YouTube video, 48:42, https://www.youtube.com/watch?v=0CRktERo80c.
14. Corinna Craft, "Speaking in Tongues Workshop: Unity in the Holy Spirit and the Royal Priesthood," The River Room, March 20, 2020, YouTube video, 1:11:29, https://www.youtube.com/watch?v=8lf0NmHLoKc&t=1740s.

    Corinna Craft, "Speaking in Tongues Workshop: The Royal Priesthood of All Believers, the Laity as Clergy," The River Room, April 17, 2020, YouTube video, 1:16:15, https://www.youtube.com/watch?v=N4dGBQM9-58.
15. "Door of Hope" (April 6, 2020), Cassandra Donnelly, with kind permission. Fine Art America: https://fineartamerica.com/profiles/cassandra-donnelly. FaceBook: https://www.facebook.com/CreativePassages.

SINGING IN TONGUES TESTIMONY

1. Emily Blunt (Mary Poppins), vocal performance of "Can You Imagine That?" by Marc Shaiman (composer and lyricist) and Scott Wittman (co-lyricist), recorded 2018 with Pixie Davies, Joel Dawson and Nathanael Saleh, in *Mary Poppins Returns*, Burbank, CA: Walt Disney/Buena Vista Home Entertainment, 2018, DVD, 4:22. For a clip, see Emily Blunt, "Can You Imagine That?" Clip/*Mary Poppins Returns*, December 12, 2018, YouTube video, 1:03, https://www.youtube.com/watch?v=e_sV7hm179Q.
2. Jacob's Ladder, Nicolas Dipre (c. 1495-1532). Public Domain in country of origin and other countries and areas where the copyright term is the author's life plus 100 years or fewer. {{PD-US-expired}} Musée du Petit Palias, Avignon, France. Source/Photographer: Museum site: http://www.petit-palais.org/musee/fr/voir-la-collection-les-peintures-de-l-ecole-d-avignon/collection/les-peintures-de-l-ecole-d-avignon/tri-par/region/et/toutes/page/11. Wikimedia Commons: https://commons.wikimedia.org/wiki/File:Nicolas_Dipre._Le_songe_de_Jacob._c.1500_Avignon,_Petit_Palais..jpg.
3. Corinna Craft, Jutta Gay, and Sveta Spear. *Spirit Stairwell: A Cappella Voices Hosting the Presence*, CDBaby, 2019, compact disc. Available for free streaming (with commercial interruptions) on Spotify.
4. Ibid.

SINGING IN TONGUES PRACTICE

1. Corinna Craft, "Singing in Tongues Part 1: Spiritual Songs," The River Room, January 15, 2021, YouTube video, 53:15, https://www.youtube.com/watch?v=gdZeFBI0t2w.
2. Corinna Craft, "Singing in Tongues Part 2: Love, Transformation, Protection, Warfare," The River Room, February 16, 2021, YouTube video, 1:12:35, https://www.youtube.com/watch?v=6woH55dDhsE.
3. Corinna Craft, "Singing in Tongues Part 3: Power Evangelism," The River Room, March

12, 2021, YouTube video, 1:02:29, https://www.youtube.com/watch?v=o-fzcoQkorY.
4. Corinna Craft, "Singing in Tongues Part 4: A New Song," The River Room, April 9, 2021, YouTube video, 1:44:37, https://www.youtube.com/watch?v=hj7qrdb933s&t=4008s.
5. Corinna Craft, "Singing in Tongues Part 5: Tonal Quality and Mood of Different Themes," The River Room, May 14, 2021, YouTube video, 1:27:48, https://www.youtube.com/watch?v=THCQGOSuqWg&t=4256s.

INTERPRETING TONGUES TESTIMONY

1. Photograph used with kind permission from the photographer, Guillermo Torres (see Joetorres 98 on Instagram).

INTERPRETING TONGUES PRACTICE

1. Corinna Craft, "Interpreting Tongues (Part 1): Impressions of Meaning," The River Room, July 17, 2020, YouTube video, 1:46:23, https://www.youtube.com/watch?v=qzGcqb3KpBw.
2. Corinna Craft, "Interpreting Tongues (Part 2): Comparing Multiple Messages," The River Room, August 9, 2020, YouTube video, 58:58, https://www.youtube.com/watch?v=AnR6pBkmXHU.
3. Corinna Craft, "Interpreting Tongues (Part 3): Judging and Delivering an Interpretation," The River Room, September 20, 2020, YouTube video, 1:25:00, https://www.youtube.com/watch?v=H6HYywjzsRM.
4. *Answers*, "What is the distance in miles from Jerusalem to Babylon?" accessed May 13, 2020, https://www.answers.com/Q/Distance_between_Jerusalem_and_Babylon; *The Holy Bible: The New International Version Study Bible*, ed. Kenneth Barker (Grand Rapids, Michigan: Zondervan, 1985), 1238 (note on Ez 8:14).
5. Deeper Waters (2019), Eddy Cutrera, with kind permission. Website: https:// Christolution. weebly.com.
6. Lunar at Big House Church (2019), Eddy Cutrera, with kind permission. Website: https:// Christolution.weebly.com.
7. Open Heavens (2016), Acrylic on Wood, Alison Webster, with kind permission. Instagram:https://www.instagram.com/allyblingart. FaceBook: https://www.facebook.com/allyblingcouture.
8. Refiner's Fire (2017), Mixed Media on Wood, Alison Webster, with kind permission. Instagram: https://www.instagram.com/allyblingart. FaceBook: https://www.facebook.com/allyblingcouture.
9. Unquenched (2017), Acrylic on Wood, Alison Webster, with kind permission. Instagram: https://www.instagram.com/allyblingart. FaceBook: https://www.facebook.com/allyblingcouture.

10. Walk Ye (2017), Acrylic on Wood, Alison Webster, with kind permission. Instagram: https://www.instagram.com/allyblingart. FaceBook: https://www.facebook.com/allyblingcouture.
11. Grafted Olive (2017), Acrylic on Wood, Alison Webster, with kind permission. Instagram:https://www.instagram.com/allyblingart. FaceBook: https://www.facebook.com/allyblingcouture.
12. Forgive Them (2017), Acrylic on Wood, Alison Webster, with kind permission. Instagram: https://www.instagram.com/allyblingart. FaceBook: https://www.facebook.com/allyblingcouture.
13. Cleansing the Harvest (2017), Acrylic on Wood, Alison Webster, with kind permission. Instagram: https://www.instagram.com/allyblingart. FaceBook: https://www.facebook.com/allyblingcouture.
14. Job's Jar (2017), Acrylic on Canvas, Alison Webster, with kind permission. Instagram: https://www.instagram.com/allyblingart. FaceBook: https://www.facebook.com/allyblingcouture.
15. Seeds of Faith (4.17.2020), Cassandra Donnelly, with kind permission. FaceBook: https:// www.facebook.com/CreativePassages. Fine Art America: https://fineartamerica.com/profiles/ cassandra-donnelly.
16. Hope Arising (4.03.2020), Cassandra Donnelly, with kind permission. FaceBook: https://www.facebook.com/CreativePassages. Fine Art America: https://fineartamerica.com/profiles/ cassandra-donnelly.
17. Tree of Hope (4.17.2020), Cassandra Donnelly, with kind permission. FaceBook: https://www.facebook.com/CreativePassages. Fine Art America: https://fineartamerica.com/profiles/ cassandra-donnelly.
18. Nightly Blooms (2.21.2020), Cassandra Donnelly, with kind permission. FaceBook: https:// www.facebook.com/CreativePassages. Fine Art America: https://fineartamerica.com/profiles/ cassandra-donnelly.
19. Door of Hope, Colorful Burst of Sunlight (4.06.2020), Cassandra Donnelly, with kind per- mission. FaceBook: https://www.facebook.com/CreativePassages. Fine Art America: https://fineartamerica.com/profiles/cassandra-donnelly.
20. Out of the Clouds 'I' Come (2019), Jill Eulo, with kind permission. FaceBook: https://www.facebook.com/jill.eulo. Email: jilleulo@gmail.com.
21. Liberty's Vision (detail, 2016), Andre Dial, with kind permission. Website: https://www.oyacreativearts.com. Email: oyacreativearts@gmail.com.
22. *The Holy Bible: The New International Version Study Bible*, ed. Kenneth Barker (Grand Rapids, Michigan: Zondervan, 1985), 128-129 (notes on Ex 28:15 and Ex 28:30).
23. Robert Matthews, "Is Anything Truly Random?" *BBC Science Focus*, BBC, accessed October 16, 2020, https://www.sciencefocus.com/science/is-anything-truly-random/.
24. Ibid.
25. Ibid.
26. Andrew Zimmerman Jones, "Albert Einstein: What is Unified Field Theory?" ThoughtCo., last updated May 16, 2018, https://www.thoughtco.com/what-is-unified-field-theory-2699364.
27. Corinna Craft, "Casting Lots: Prophecies by Divine Design," The River Room, November 25, 2020, YouTube video, 59:38, https://www.youtube.com/watch?v=5ECisD3MQMI.
28. Corinna Craft, "Speaking in Tongues Workshop: Public Purposes of Tongues, Part 1,"

The River Room, May 22, 2020, YouTube video, 59:38, https://www.youtube.com/watch?v=Iby9VB6S9vQ.
29. Corinna Craft, "Speaking in Tongues Workshop: Public Purposes of Tongues, Part 2," The River Room, June 19, 2020, YouTube video, 1:00:10, https://www.youtube.com/watch?v=hj6WaGQtyps.

CASE STUDIES: GOD'S COUNSEL AND COMFORT THROUGH INTERPRETATION

1. Kim, "Hebrew Year 5780 (2020): A Year to Widen Your Mouth in Wisdom or Zip It Shut," *Sheerah Ministries - Waking Eve: Waking Sleeping Beauty* (blog), July 3, 2019, https://sheerahministries.com/?s=Hebrew+year+5780+2020.
2. *Wikipedia*, s.v. "Daybreak (painting)," last updated December 1, 2019, https://en.wikipedia.org/wiki/Daybreak_(painting).
3. Elizabeth Barrett Browning, "How Do I Love Thee?" (Sonnet 43), Academy of American Poets, https://poets.org/poem/how-do-i-love-thee-sonnet-43.
4. *Wikipedia*, s.v. "Love Lifted Me," last updated February 14, 2022, https://en.wikipedia.org/wiki/Love_Lifted_Me. This American hymn, based on Matthew 14:22, with melody by Howard E. Smith and lyrics by James Rowe, was first published in 1912. Many singers including Eddy Arnold and Kenny Rogers have performed this cover song with or without adaptations.

APPENDIX: THE ENNEAGRAM, AN OCCULT BLOCK TO THE HOLY SPIRIT

1. Don Veinot, Joy Veinot, and Marcia Montenegro, *Richard Rohr and the Enneagram Secret*, ed. Donna McGhee (Wonder Lake, Illinois: MCOI Publishing, 2020), 84-85, 91-93, 103.
2. Ibid., 128.
3. Ibid., 128; Jay Medenwaldt, "The Enneagram, Science, and Christianity—Part 1," *Jay Medenwaldt: Psychology, Apologetics, and Theology* (blog), January, 15, 2019, http://www.jaymedenwaldt.com/2019/01/the-enneagram-science-and-christianity.html.
4. Medenwaldt, "The Enneagram, Science, and Christianity—Part 1".
5. Ibid.
6. Ibid.
7. Veinot, Veinot, and Montenegro, "Chapter 3: Myth Taken," in *Richard Rohr and the Enneagram Secret*, ed. Donna McGhee (Wonder Lake, Illinois: MCOI Publishing, 2020), 55 (45-56 chapter page range); Ian Cron and Suzanne Stabile, *The Road Back to You: An Enneagram Journey to Self-Discovery* (Downers Grove, IL: InterVarsity Press, 2016), 11.
8. Veinot, Veinot, and Montenegro, *Richard Rohr and the Enneagram Secret*, 48-49; Christopher Heuertz, *The Sacred Enneagram* (Grand Rapids, Michigan: Zondervan, 2017), 43, Kindle Edition.
9. Carl Huffman, "Pythagorus," *Stanford Encyclopedia of Philosophy*, revised October 17,

2018, https://plato.stanford.edu/entries/pythagoras/.
10. Veinot, Veinot, and Montenegro, *Richard Rohr and the Enneagram Secret*, 56; James Moore, "The Enneagram: A Developmental Study," *The RunningFather* (blog), last updated March 25, 2004, https://runningfather.wordpress.com/2013/03/25/enneagram-a-developmental-study-james-moore/. First published in *Religion Today: A Journal of Contemporary Religions* (London) 3 (October 1986-January 1987): 1-5.
11. Veinot, Veinot, and Montenegro, *Richard Rohr and the Enneagram Secret*, 52; Richard Rohr and Andreas Ebert, *Discovering the Enneagram: An Ancient Tool for a New Spiritual Journey*, trans. Peter Heinegg (New York: Crossroad Publishing, 1992), xii-iii, xv.
12. Veinot, Veinot, and Montenegro, *Richard Rohr and the Enneagram Secret*, 50-52.
13. Ibid., 52.
14. Ibid., 53; "Richard Rohr says about Helen Palmer," last updated 2011, accessed June 29, 2020, Enneagram dot com, https://enneagram.com/helen_palmer.html.
15. Veinot, Veinot, and Montenegro, *Richard Rohr and the Enneagram Secret*, 53-54.
16. Veinot, Veinot, and Montenegro, "Chapter 4: Genesis of the Enneagram: From Gurdieff to Rohr," in *Richard Rohr and the Enneagram Secret*, ed. Donna McGhee (Wonder Lake, Illinois: MCOI Publishing, 2020), 60-61 (57-68 chapter page range).
17. Ibid., 61-62.
18. Ibid., 62-63; Rodney Collin, *The Christian Mystery* (1952), Holy Books dot com, https://www.holybooks.com/wp-content/uploads/The-Christian-Mystery.pdf. Note: Collin's entire book is in portable document format (PDF) online.
19. Veinot, Veinot, and Montenegro, *Richard Rohr and the Enneagram Secret*, 64-65.
20. Ibid., 63, 66-67; Claudio Naranjo, "The Origin of the Enneagram: Claudio Naranjo Speaks," June 18, 2010, YouTube video, 10:01, https://www.youtube.com/watch?v=wlO3KJWnNd8.
21. Veinot, Veinot, and Montenegro, *Richard Rohr and the Enneagram Secret*, 66-68, 70.
22. Ibid., 66-67.
23. Ibid., 68, 70.
24. Veinot, Veinot and Montenegro, "Chapter 5: Richard Rohr: Which God Does He Serve?" in *Richard Rohr and the Enneagram Secret*, ed. Donna McGhee (Wonder Lake, Illinois: MCOI Publishing, 2020), 72-73, 76-77 (69-81 chapter page range); Richard Rohr, "The Christification of the Universe," Center for Action and Contemplation (CAC), November 6, 2016, https://cac.org/the-christification-of-the-universe-2016-11-06.
25. Veinot, Veinot, and Montenegro, *Richard Rohr and the Enneagram Secret*, 70, 79-80; Center for Action and Contemplation (CAC), Living School Program Details, "Lineage and Themes: Themes," https://cac.org/living-school/program-details/lineage-and-themes/; Center for Action and Contemplation (CAC), Living School Program Details, "Non-dual Thinkers of All Religions," accessed June 30, 2020, Mp3 audio, 2:01, https://cac.org/wp-content/uploads/2015/08/Non-Dual-thinkers_LS-8-middle.mp3; Center for Action and Contemplation (CAC), Living School Program Details, "Wisdom Lineage: Orthopraxy in much of Buddhism and Hinduism," accessed June 30, 2020, Mp3 audio, 1:01, https://cac.org/wp-content/uploads/2015/08/Orthopraxy_LS-9-right.mp3; Center for Action and Contemplation (CAC), About (Who We Are), "What Is Contemplation?" accessed June 30, 2020, https://cac.org/about/what-is-contemplation/.
26. Veinot, Veinot, and Montenegro, *Richard Rohr and the Enneagram Secret*, 78-79; Richard Rohr, "A Change of Consciousness: Emerging Church," Center for Action

and Contemplation (CAC), November 29, 2017, https://cac.org/a-change-of-consciousness-2017-11-29; Center for Action and Contemplation (CAC), Living School Program Details, "Non-dual Thinkers of All Religions," accessed June 30, 2020, Mp3 audio, 2:01, https://cac.org/wp-content/uploads/2015/08/Non-Dual-thinkers_LS-8-middle.mp3; Center for Action and Contemplation (CAC), Living School Program Details, "Wisdom Lineage: Orthopraxy in much of Buddhism and Hinduism," accessed June 30, 2020, Mp3 audio, 1:01, https://cac.org/wp-content/uploads/2015/08/Orthopraxy_LS-9-right.mp3.
27. Veinot, Veinot, and Montenegro, *Richard Rohr and the Enneagram Secret*, 73-74; Richard Rohr, "What Do We Do with the Bible?" Center for Action and Contemplation (CAC), January 6, 2019, https://cac.org/what-do-we-do-with-the-bible-2019-01-06.
28. Ibid.
29. Veinot, Veinot, and Montenegro, *Richard Rohr and the Enneagram Secret*, 74; Richard Rohr, *The Universal Christ* (New York: Convergent Books, 2019), 27.
30. Veinot, Veinot, and Montenegro, *Richard Rohr and the Enneagram Secret*, 74; Rohr, *The Universal Christ*, 33 and 147.
31. Veinot, Veinot, and Montenegro, *Richard Rohr and the Enneagram Secret*, 74; Rohr, *The Universal Christ*, 225.
32. Veinot, Veinot, and Montenegro, *Richard Rohr and the Enneagram Secret*, 74; Rohr, *The Universal Christ*, 120.
33. Veinot, Veinot, and Montenegro, *Richard Rohr and the Enneagram Secret*, 75-76; Richard Rohr, interview by Rich Heffern, "The Eternal Christ in the Cosmic Story," *National Catholic Reporter*, December 11, 2009, https://www.ncronline.org/news/spirituality/eternal-christ-cosmic-story.
34. Veinot, Veinot, and Montenegro, *Richard Rohr and the Enneagram Secret*, 64-65.
35. Veinot, Veinot, and Montenegro, "Chapter 6: Reap the Whirlwind," in *Richard Rohr and the Enneagram Secret*, ed. Donna McGhee (Wonder Lake, Illinois: MCOI Publishing, 2020), 84-85 (83-97 chapter page range); Veinot, Veinot, and Montenegro, "Chapter 8: Can God Redeem Anything?" in *Richard Rohr and the Enneagram Secret*, ed. Donna McGhee (Wonder Lake, Illinois: MCOI Publishing, 2020), 124 (123-130 chapter page range).
36. Veinot, Veinot, and Montenegro, *Richard Rohr and the Enneagram Secret*, 109-110; Christopher Heuertz, *The Sacred Enneagram* (Grand Rapids, MI: Zondervan, 2017), Kindle Edition, 72.
37. Veinot, Veinot, and Montenegro, *Richard Rohr and the Enneagram Secret*, 85; Ian Cron and Suzanne Stabile interviewed by K. Mulhern, "Seeing the Face of God: A Patheos Q&A with Ian Morgan Cron and Suzanne Stabile," Patheos, October 21, 2016, https://www.patheos.com/blogs/takeandread/2016/10/seeing-the-face-of-god-a-patheos-qa-with-ian-morgan-cron-and-suzanne-stabile/.
38. Veinot, Veinot, and Montenegro, *Richard Rohr and the Enneagram Secret*, 86-87.
39. Ibid., 86-87.
40. Ibid., 123-127.

WORKS CITED

The Biographical Dictionary of Chinese Christianity. "Marie Monsen: 1878-1962, Norwegian Missionary in China." https://bdcconline.net/en/stories/monsen-marie.

Blunt, Emily (Mary Poppins). Vocal performance of "Can You Imagine That?" By Marc Shaiman (composer and lyricist) and Scott Wittman (co-lyricist). Recorded 2018 with Pixie Davies, Joel Dawson and Nathanael Saleh in *Mary Poppins Returns*. Burbank, CA: Walt Disney/Buena Vista Home Entertainment, 2018. DVD, 4:22.

Blunt, Emily. "Can You Imagine That?" Clip/*Mary Poppins Returns*. December 12, 2018. YouTube video, 1:03. https://www.youtube.com/watch?v=e_sV7hm179Q.

Botts, Philip. "Speaking in Tongues Workshop: The Benefits of Tongues for the Individual, Part 1." The River Room. August 31, 2019. YouTube video, 50:28. https://www.youtube.com/watch?v=xXCJk0d8A5c.

Browning, Elizabeth Barrett. "How Do I Love Thee?" (Sonnet 43) Academy of American Poets. https://poets.org/poem/how-do-i-love-thee-sonnet-43.

Center for Action and Contemplation (CAC). About (Who We Are). "What Is Contemplation?" Accessed June 30, 2020. https://cac.org/about/what-is-contemplation/.

Center for Action and Contemplation (CAC). Living School Program Details. "Lineage and Themes: Themes." Accessed June 30, 2020. https://cac.org/living-school/program-details/lineage-and-themes/.

Center for Action and Contemplation (CAC). Living School Program Details. "Non-dual Thinkers of All Religions." Accessed June 30, 2020. Mp3 audio, 2:01. https://cac.org/wp-content/uploads/2015/08/Non-Dual-thinkers_LS-8-middle.mp3.

Center for Action and Contemplation (CAC). Living School Program Details. "Wisdom Lineage: Orthopraxy in much of Buddhism and Hinduism." Accessed June 30, 2020. Mp3 audio, 1:02. https://cac.org/wp-content/uploads/2015/08/Orthopraxy_LS-9-right.mp3.

Clark, Randy. "Session 18, Healing and Disbelief: Cessationism." *School of Healing and Impartation Essentials 2*. Global Awakening. 2008. Audio teaching electronic download, 1:09:39.

Collin, Rodney. *The Christian Mystery* (Lent, 1952). Holy Books dot com. https://www.holybooks.com/wp-content/uploads/The-Christian-Mystery.pdf.

Craft, Corinna. "Casting Lots: Prophecies by Divine Design." The River Room. November 25, 2020. YouTube video, 59:38. https://www.youtube.com/watch?v=5ECisD3MQMI.

Craft, Corinna. "Interpreting Tongues (Part 1): Impressions of Meaning." The River Room. July 17, 2020. YouTube video, 1:46:23. https://www.youtube.com/watch?v=qzGcqb3KpBw.

Craft, Corinna. "Interpreting Tongues (Part 2): Comparing Multiple Messages." The River Room. August 9, 2020. YouTube video, 58:58. https://www.youtube.com/watch?v=AnR6pBkmXHU.

Craft, Corinna. "Interpreting Tongues (Part 3): Judging and Delivering an Interpretation." The River Room. September 20, 2020. YouTube video, 1:25:00. https://www.youtube.com/watch?v=H6HYywjzsRM.

Craft, Corinna. "Pentecost: the Gift of Tongues for Power Evangelism, Prayer, Prophecy and Spiritual Warfare." The River Room. May 23, 2021. YouTube video, 56:18. https://www.youtube.com/watch?v=e7kIwA4yYrQ&t=202s.

Craft, Corinna. "Singing in Tongues Part 1: Spiritual Songs." The River Room. January 15, 2021. YouTube video, 53:15. https://www.youtube.com/watch?v=gdZeFBI0t2w.

Craft, Corinna. "Singing in Tongues Part 2: Love, Transformation, Protection, Warfare." The River Room. February 16, 2021. YouTube video, 1:12:35. https://www.youtube.com/watch?v=6woH55dDhsE.

Craft, Corinna. "Singing in Tongues Part 3: Power Evangelism." The River Room. March 12, 2021. YouTube video, 1:02:29. https://www.youtube.com/watch?v=o-fzcoQkorY.

Craft, Corinna. "Singing in Tongues Part 4: A New Song." The River Room. April 9, 2021. YouTube video, 1:44:37. https://www.youtube.com/watch?v=hj7qrdb933s.

Craft, Corinna. "Singing in Tongues Part 5: Tonal Quality and Mood of Different Themes." The River Room. May 14, 2021. YouTube video, 1:27:48. https://www.youtube.com/watch?v=THCQGOSuqWg&t=4256s.

Craft, Corinna, "Speaking in Tongues Workshop: For the Common Good or Profit of All." Ray Boetcher/The River Room. January 17, 2020. YouTube video, 48:13. https://www.youtube.com/watch?v=bk_fo-1ZUeY&list=PLGYFMQ8WuIJB29bXH1e_nPiG1aHWz4Y3G&index=4&t=2568s.

Craft, Corinna. "Speaking in Tongues Workshop: Praise, Worship, and Prophecy." The River Room. February 21, 2020. YouTube video, 48:42. https://www.youtube.com/watch?v=0CRktERo80c.

Craft, Corinna. "Speaking in Tongues Workshop: Unity in the Holy Spirit and the Royal Priesthood." The River Room. March 20, 2020. YouTube video, 1:11:29. https://www.youtube.com/watch?v=8lf0NmHLoKc&t=1740s.

Craft, Corinna. "Speaking in Tongues Workshop: The Royal Priesthood of All Believers, the Laity as Clergy." The River Room. April 17, 2020. YouTube video, 1:16:15. https://www.youtube.com/watch?v=N4dGBQM9-58.

Craft, Corinna. "Speaking in Tongues Workshop: Public Purposes of Tongues, Part 1." The River Room. May 22, 2020. YouTube video, 59:38. https://www.youtube.com/watch?v=Iby9VB6S9vQ.

Craft, Corinna. "Speaking in Tongues Workshop: Public Purposes of Tongues, Part 2." The River Room. June 19, 2020. YouTube video, 1:00:11. https://www.youtube.com/watch?v=hj6WaGQtyps.

Craft, Corinna, Jutta Gay, and Sveta Spear. *Spirit Stairwell: A Cappella Voices Hosting the Presence*. CDBaby. 2019. Compact disc.

Cron, Ian, and Suzanne Stabile. *The Road Back to You: An Enneagram Journey to Self-Discovery*. Downers Grove, IL: InterVarsity Press, 2016.

Cron, Ian, and Suzanne Stabile. Interviewed by K. Mulhern. "Seeing the Face of God: A Patheos Q&A with Ian Morgan Cron and Suzanne Stabile." Patheos. October 21, 2016. https://www.patheos.com/blogs/takeandread/2016/10/seeing-the-face-of-god-a-patheos-qa-with-ian-morgan-cron-and-suzanne-stabile/.

Culpepper, C.L. *The Shantung Revival*. The Gospel Truth dot net. March 25, 1968. https://www.gospeltruth.net/shantung.htm.

Donnelly, Cassandra. "Speaking in Tongues Workshop: The Public Purposes of Tongues, Part 2." The River Room. June 19, 2020. YouTube video, 1:00:11. https://www.youtube.com/watch?v=hj6WaGQtyps.

Fitzgerald, Ella. "How High The Moon/Epic scat LIVE 1966 [RITY archives]." Archived from Reelin' In The Years Productions. Posted July 18, 2018. YouTube video, 6:34. https://www.youtube.com/watch?v=1GUmxnYheK0.

Hill, Evan, Ainara Tiefenthäler, Christiaan Triebert, Drew Jordan, Haley Willis, and Robin Stein. "8 Minutes and 46 Seconds: How George Floyd Was Killed in Police Custody." *The New York Times*. May 31, 2020. https://www.nytimes.com/2020/05/31/us/george-floyd-investigation.html/.

Heuertz, Christopher. *The Sacred Enneagram*. Grand Rapids, MI: Zondervan, 2017.

Horton, Greg, and Yonat Shimron (Religion News Service). "Southern Baptists Change Policy on Speaking in Tongues." *Charisma News*. May 15, 2015. https://www.charismanews.com/us/49661-southern-baptists-change-policy-on-speaking-in-tongues.

Jones, Andrew Zimmerman. "Albert Einstein: What is Unified Field Theory?" ThoughtCo. Last updated May 16, 2018. https://www.thoughtco.com/what-is-unified-field-theory-2699364.

Kim. "Hebrew Year 5780 (2020): A Year to Widen Your Mouth in Wisdom or Zip It Shut." *Sheerah Ministries - Waking Eve: Waking Sleeping Beauty* (blog). July 3, 2019. https://sheerahministries.com/?s=Hebrew+year+5780+2020.

LeClaire, Jennifer. "Remove the Bottleneck from Your Life!" Jennifer LeClaire @ propheticbooks. January 17, 2020. Periscope TV.

Matthews, Robert. "Is Anything Truly Random?" *BBC Science Focus*. BBC. Accessed October 16, 2020. https://www.sciencefocus.com/science/is-anything-truly-random/.

Medenwaldt, Jay. "The Enneagram, Science, and Christianity—Part 1." *Jay Medenwaldt: Psychology, Apologetics, and Theology* (blog). January, 15, 2019. http://www.jaymedenwaldt.com/2019/01/the-enneagram-science-and-christianity_17.html.

Moore, James. "The Enneagram: A Developmental Study." *The RunningFather* (blog). Last updated March 25, 2004. https://runningfather.wordpress.com/2013/03/25/enneagram-a-developmental-study-james-moore/. First published in *Religion Today: A Journal of Contemporary Religions* (London) 3 (October 1986-January 1987): 1-5.

Myers, Meghann. "Horrific Cable Mishap Caused by Maintenance Errors." *Navy Times*. July 14, 2016. https://www.navytimes.com/news/your-navy/2016/07/14/horrific-cable-mishap-caused-by-maintenance-errors-navy/.

Naranjo, Claudio. "The Origin of the Enneagram: Claudio Naranjo Speaks." June 18, 2010. YouTube video, 10:01. https://www.youtube.com/watch?v=wlO3KJWnNd8.

North American Mission Board. "Baptists and Speaking in Tongues." March 30, 2016. https://www.namb.net/apologetics-blog/baptists-and-speaking-in-tongues/.

Parke, Caleb. "From George Washington to Ulysses S. Grant: Statues, Monuments Vandalized Extend beyond Confederates amid Black Lives Matter Protests." *Fox News*. June 22, 2020. https://www.foxnews.com/us/statue-monument-vandalized-torn-down-protest.

Price, Paula. *The Prophet's Dictionary: The Ultimate Guide to Supernatural Wisdom*. Rev. ed. Tulsa, OK: Whitaker House, 2006. First published 1999.

Prima, Louis (King Louie) and Phil Harris (Baloo the Bear), vocal performance of "I Wan'na Be Like You." By Robert Sherman and Richard Sherman (songwriters), with George Bruns (instrumentals) and Walter Sheets (orchestration). In Walt Disney's *The Jungle Book* (1967). November 7, 2013. YouTube video, 3:49. https://www.youtube.com/watch?v=FOTZJ8EFgpk.

Rohr, Richard. "A Change of Consciousness: Emerging Church." Center for Action and Contemplation (CAC). November 29, 2017. https://cac.org/a-change-of-consciousness-2017-11-29.

Rohr, Richard. "The Christification of the Universe." Center for Action and Contemplation (CAC). November 6, 2016. https://cac.org/the-christification-of-the-universe-2016-11-06.

Rohr, Richard. "Richard Rohr says about Helen Palmer." Enneagram dot com. Last updated 2011. Accessed June 29, 2020. https://enneagram.com/helen_palmer.html.

Rohr, Richard. *The Universal Christ*. New York: Convergent Books, 2019.

Rohr, Richard. "What Do We Do with the Bible?" Center for Action and Contemplation (CAC). January 6, 2019. https://cac.org/what-do-we-do-with-the-bible-2019-01-06.

Rohr, Richard, and Andreas Ebert. *Discovering the Enneagram: An Ancient Tool for a New Spiritual Journey*. Translated by Peter Heinegg. New York: Crossroad Publishing, 1992.

Rohr, Richard. Interview by Rich Heffern. "The Eternal Christ in the Cosmic Story." *National Catholic Reporter*. December 11, 2009. https://www.ncronline.org/news/spirituality/eternal-christ-cosmic-story.

Rogers, Marcus. "If You Love Smoking Weed or Drinking You Will Really Love Speaking in Tongues." November 9, 2019. YouTube video, 25:12. https://www.youtube.com/watch?v=7xXgPgyI16c.

Roth, Sid. "God Talk: Doorway to the Supernatural!" *It's Supernatural!* FaceBook page. Posted on FaceBook (Live), January 9, 2018. Video, 11:55. https://www.facebook.com/its.supernatural/videos/10155253197347263.

Roth, Sid. "God Talk: The Key to Unlocking Your Destiny!" *It's Supernatural!* ISN. March 29, 2017. Television program, 43:14. https://sidroth.org/god-talk/.

Scully, Rachel, and James Bikales, "A List of the Statues across the US Toppled, Vandalized or Officially Removed amid Protests." *The Hill*. June 12, 2020. https://thehill.com/homenews/state-watch/502492-list-statues-toppled-vandalized-removed-protests.

Sheets, Tim. "Pentecost and Divisions of Angels." Oasis Church. May 24, 2020. YouTube video, 41:19. https://www.youtube.com/watch?v=ZkHYPbERhQM&feature=youtu.be.

Sheets, Tim. "Shoulder to the Wheel." Oasis Church. August 17, 2020. YouTube video, 51:25. https://www.youtube.com/watch?v=yeX5KhewHz8.

Swearingen, Chet, and Phyllis Swearingen. "The Shantung Revival (1927-1937)." Beautiful Feet. Accessed June 5, 2020. https://romans1015.com/shantung-revival/.

Veinot, Don, Joy Veinot, and Marcia Montenegro. *Richard Rohr and the Enneagram Secret*. Edited by Donna McGhee. Wonder Lake, Illinois: MCOI Publishing, 2020.

Zadai, Kevin. Interview by Sid Roth. *It's Supernatural!* ISN. January 5, 2020. Television program, 28:30. https://sidroth.org/television/tv-archives/kevin-zadai-5/.

INDEX

A

angel(s) 19, 27–33, 36, 39, 40, 77, 82, 84–85, 88–89, 92, 93, 98, 102, 130-31, 152, 164, 171, 200, 223, 224, 237
    armies 28, 29, 33, 36, 39, 40, 190
    assistants (servants) 29-30, 88–89
    evangelizers 32
    execute God's judgments 31
    guides 30, 31
    host(s) 28-29, 84–85, 132, 185, 187, 190
    messenger(s) 30, 31–32, 84–85, 88–89, 130–31
    strengtheners 30, 33
    warrior(s) 30–31, 37, 39
Appendix (The Enneagram) 66, 67, 203–13, 216–20

B

baby babble (tongues activation) 57, 64, 69, 70
Bapticostal (Baptist + Pentecostal) 8
baptism in the Holy Spirit (see: speaking in tongues impartation)
Baptist denomination 4, 5
    declining membership in America 5, 13
    International Mission Board of the Southern Baptist Convention 4
        policy disqualifying tongues-speaking missions applicants 4, 5, 9
        policy repeal 5
        view of tongues as non-normative 5–6
        view of tongues as a "private prayer language" 5
    missionaries 5, 8, 12–14, 16, 19, 22–25, 52
    North American Mission Board 9
        official position statement looks orthodox on paper 9
        position accomodates cessationist theology 4, 9
bi-locality (in the Holy Spirit vs. drug induced or mediated by eastern mysticism) 47, 48

block to the gift of tongues 65–68
Book of Life 57, 75–77
booth prophecies 121, 163
Botts, Philip 1
    a Southern Baptist from the womb 4
    an oddity within my own denomination 8
    change in theological view on tongues: "desperation" 7
    change in theological view on tongues: "fascinated" 6
    liquid love experience 8
    my mind clears when praying in tongues 1
    Navy ship deployment 2, 6, 8
    wife Amy 2, 8
Browning, Elizabeth Barrett: "How Do I Love Thee?" (Sonnet 43) 181

C

Catholics and the New Age: How Good People Are Being Drawn into Jungian Psychology, the Enneagram, and the Age of Aquarius 213
Cauthen, Baker James 23–24
Cessationism 4
Christian Mystery 211
Christians at New Age and occult expos 65–67, 86, 87–88, 89–90, 104–5, 116, 117, 121, 163–164, 165
    backslidden/drifted 117, 165
    nominal 116, 117, 165
    proto-Christians 165
    seeker sensitive 165
    suffered spiritual abuse 165–66
Clark, Randy 8, 9
A Closer Look at the Enneagram 213
Collin, Rodney 211–12
corona virus/COVID-19 78, 80
Craft, Corinna 107, 119, 242
    interpreting tongues testimony 107
    singing in tongues testimony 83
    speaking in tongues testimony 45
Crawford, Mary 14
Cron, Ian 207, 216, 217–18

Culpepper, C.L. 14–16, 18, 24–25
Cutrera, Eddy 133, 134

D

Daniels, David 213
"Daybreak," Maxfield Parrish 176
Dial, Andre 149
Discovering the Enneagram: An Ancient Tool for a New Spiritual Journey (1989 German language) 213
Discovering the Enneagram (1992 English translation) 208, 213
disqualified from missions by tongues 4
dissimilar interpretations 108, 204
divination (occult source of knowledge) 66, 86, 117, 123, 166, 211, 212, 219, 220
    a block to receiving or operating in the gift of tongues 65–68, 203, 219, 220
    caution against approaching interpretation like divination 123, 126
    examples of types:
        astrology (horoscopes) 66, 86, 211–12
        Enneagram 66, 67, 203, 210–11, 211–12, 219–20
        fortune tellers 66
        I Ching 66
        numerology 66
        palmistry 66
        psychics 66
        Tarot cards 51, 66, 86, 108, 116
    repentance and renunciation 66–67, 220
divine design vs. random or chance occurrence 121, 156, 158–62
divine design personal prophecies 156
Donnelly, Cassandra 39, 78, 80
    art therapist and prophetic artist 39, 40, 78
    vision-dream: outpouring 39, 40, 41, 42, 43
    dream: tornado 42–43
    sign and wonder: ten tattered pieces of a $50 bill recovered in a hurricane 42, 43
    survivor of parental abuse and Satanic ritual abuse 40
    "The Overflow," painting 38, 40–43
    "The Overflow," prophecy 39, 40, 42
    "The Overflow," scriptures 43
Dr. Seuss (child-like poetry) 197

E

ecclesia (city council; the church) 33–34, 36, 39
    applied to God's people 32, 34–36, 39
    definition 34
    deployed to disciple nations 36
    historic political meaning 34
    prophecies of God's ecclesia mobilized 33, 36, 37–38, 39–40
    tongues, the governmental language of God's ecclesia 35
Enneagram (see: Appendix)
    definition 203
    influence, New Age and occult 203, 210, 216, 217–18, 219–20
        astrology (temperament typing system) 211–12
        automatic writing (channeling a spirit) 212
        divinatory tool 210, 211, 219–20
        four humours (personality typing system) 211–12
        Hinduism (and yoga philosophy) 212, 214–15, 216
        New Age 203, 208, 212, 213
        occult 203, 210, 212, 213, 217–20
        transmission of information from the spirit realm 210–11
        psychedelics and shamanism 212
        spirit guides 212–13
        Universal Christ 214
        universal salvation 215–16
    not redeemable 219–220
    occult block to gifts of the Holy Spirit 65–68, 203, 210, 219–20
    opponents 213
        Medenwaldt 204–6
        Montenegro 203
        Pacwa 203, 213
        Ranaghan 213
        Veinot, Don and Joy 203
    origin, Christian myths 208–9, 213, 215
        Evagrius 208–9
        Lull 209
    origin, myths of antiquity 207–9
        Arithmologia 208
        Ars Magna 208

    Kabbalah 208
    Pythagorus 207–8
  origin, true 204, 207, 210–13
    Collin 211–12
    Gurdjieff 208, 210–11, 213
    Ichazo 212
    Naranjo 212–13
    Rohr 203, 208, 209, 212, 213–16
  popularity among Evangelical Christians 203, 208, 212–13, 216, 217–19
  proponents 206, 208, 211, 213
    Collin 211–12
    Cron 207, 216, 217–18
    Gaultiere 218–19
    Heuertz 216, 217
    Ichazo 212
    McCord 216
    Naranjo 212–13
    Rohr 203, 208–9, 213–16
    Stabile 216, 217–18
  psychometric analysis 204, 206
  scientific evaluation 204

The Enneagram: A Christian Perspective 208, 213

Esalen Institute 212

Eulo, Jill 148

Evagrius of Ponticus 208–9

eye contact 118, 151

F

falling under the power of the Holy Spirit 69
  catch 69
  courtesy drop 69

false religions
  a block to receiving or operating in the gift of tongues 65–68, 203, 210, 219–20
  examples:
    Buddhism 89, 92, 116, 166
    eastern mysticism (Hinduism, Buddhism, Taoism) 45, 47, 51–52, 91, 166, 211
    Egyptian mysticism 66, 207

Hinduism (and yoga philosophy) 47, 66, 89-90, 166, 212, 214, 216
  New Age 89-90, 166
  Paganism 50-51, 117, 166
  Taoism 66, 89, 92
  Wicca 66
 repentance and renunciation 65–67, 220
false religious doctrines (heresies) 4, 9, 47, 89, 96, 214–16, 217
 Cessationism 4, 9
 Non-dualism 47, 214, 215, 216
 Panentheism 214
 Pelagianism 217
 Perennialism 214
fish bowl prophecies 163
fishing for men prophecies 162-163
Fitzgerald, Ella: "How High the Moon" (scat) 64
Floyd, George 2, 43

G

Gaultiere, Bill 218–19
"God Talk!" *It's Supernatural!* television program (group intercession in tongues) 77, 78
Gurdjieff, George 208, 210–11, 213
Guy, R. Cal 23

H

Harris, Phil (Baloo the Bear): "I Wan'na Be Like You" (scat) 64
heresies (see: false religious doctrines)
Heuertz, Christopher 216–17
"How Do I Love Thee?" (Sonnet 43), Elizabeth Barrett Browning 180–81
Hudson, Russ 216

I

Ichazo, Oscar 212
International Mission Board of the Southern Baptist Convention (see: Baptist denomination)
interpretation(s) 4, 81, 87, 88, 107–9, 113, 115, 117, 121–24, 126–28, 132–34, 150–55,

160–66, 169–76, 178–82, 184–86, 189, 190, 192, 193, 195–201
interpreting tongues, ascertaining meaning 108–9, 124–25
    ask God to explain what He shows you or tells you 60, 129, 130–132
    divine show-and-tell 129–30
    hear a word or see a picture 128–29
    go with your first impression 124, 125
    impressions of meaning 81, 124–125
    latitude in interpreting 124–25
    not translation 108–9, 124
interpreting tongues, case studies 169
    closed vs. open-ended sessions 122–23, 169
    closed sessions 169, 177, 178, 183, 188–89, 194–95
    comfort and counsel 169, 182
        emotional healing 87, 201
        matters of the heart 201
    open-ended session 169, 170, 176
interpreting tongues, case study participants 169
    Clara 183–88: ministry ignored by church leadership
    Daisy 178–82: depression, isolationism; Shepherding Movement trauma
    Dana and Dasha 170–76: themes for 2020-2029
    Leonora 177–78: hormonal imbalances, mood disorders, generational sickbed pattern
    Sofia 188–94: schizophrenic, marijuana addicted, demonized son
    Wendi 194–201: failed tea shop business
interpreting tongues, comparing interpretations 127–28, 151–52
    a case in point 107–8
    complementary interpretations 126, 128, 152
    different interpretations 107–8, 126, 127–28, 152
    multiple interpretations 127–28
    similar interpretations 125, 127, 128, 152
    validity of diverse interpretations 152–53
interpreting tongues, developing an interpretation
    key word or key phrase search 125
    online resources 122
interpreting tongues, evaluating interpretations 128
    by scripture and by the Holy Spirit 126
    giving and receiving constructive criticism 126–27
    monitoring your internal response to an interpretation 128
    stewardship responsibility 128

interpreting tongues, kinds of interpretations 107–8, 115, 121, 124, 128–29, 132–34, 154–55, 160–64
    a picture - seeing what God shows, "seer" 128–29
    a word - hearing what God says, "Samuel" 128–29
    various ways Holy Spirit communicates 124
    visual impressions: simple to complex 129
        Amos 129
        Ezekiel 129
        Jeremiah 129–30
        Zechariah 130–32
interpreting tongues, introduction 124, 127, 152
    caution: do not approach as divination 123
    closed communication vs. open-ended 122–23
    length of time to speak in tongues for an interpretation 123–24
    observe silence after speaking 124, 125
    scribe tools to formulate and record interpretations 121–22
interpreting tongues, practice exercises
    art as a springboard to interpretation 128–34
    by yourself 123
    partners 125
    small group 128
    whole group 150, 151, 155, 160, 163
interpreting tongues, prophecy 105, 115, 121, 132, 154–55, 160–64, 201
    equals prophecy/reveals mysteries 132
    personal prophecy 154–56, 160–64
        All for One: all prophecy over one person 160
        audio recording or transcription of 122, 154–55
        Divine Design Drawings (vs. chance drawings) 156, 157, 160–62
        One on One: each person prophesies over another 161
        partners 155, 169
        small group 128, 155
        whole group 150–53, 155–56, 160–62
interpreting tongues, public outreach 121
    at the event 164
    before the event 163–64
    booth prophecies 121, 163–64
    conversions, re-dedications, and introductions to Christ 116
    examples of messages for recipients 115

    dream to found a wedding company 115
    future neonatologist's research and development 115
    good shepherdess 118
    rescue people from suicide 116
    validated discernment 118
    wife's concern about husband's emotional health 115
examples of types of recipients
    Capitol Hill worker 116
    channeler 87
    crisis counselor 116
    neonatologist 115
    software developer 115
    university students 118
    wife 115
    youth group chaperone 118
eye contact 118, 151, 164
fast and pray 163
follow-up 165
Fish Bowl prophecies 163
Fishing for Men prophecies 162
handling tricky cases 118
    ex-Catholic, Unity Church member 165–66
    Pagans 117, 166
    person of discernment 118
    wariness of some recipients 118
    youth group chaperone 118
interacting with specific populations
    New Agers or practitioners of eastern religions 116, 166
    Pagans 117, 166
inviting people to receive the ministry of heavenly languages, "May I Sing Over You?" 116
Mischief and Magic 108, 109
New Age and occult expos 86–89
New Age church 89–91
partner ministry 115, 119, 164,
whether to identify the spiritual source of the vocal gifts 88, 117, 165–66
interpreting tongues, purpose
    comfort and counsel 169, 182
        emotional healing/matters of the heart 201

      encourage 124
      motivate 124
      strengthen 124
      uplift 124
   confirming, redemptive, directive messages 115
   public outreach prophecy 105, 109, 112, 115–16, 121, 128-29, 162–65
interpreting tongues 81, 107, 108, 121, 124, 127, 128
interpreting tongues, solo presentation 150–51, 153–54
   before an assembly 153–54
   pointers 150–51
   practice 150–51
interpreting tongues, teaching and activation videos 124, 127, 128, 160

"Casting Lots: Prophecies by Divine Design," The River Room YouTube channel, November 25, 2020. 160, 233

"Interpreting Tongues (Part 1): Impressions of Meaning," The River Room YouTube channel, July 17, 2020. 124, 233

"Interpreting Tongues (Part 2): Comparing Multiple Messages," The River Room YouTube channel, August 9, 2020. 127, 233

"Interpreting Tongues (Part 3): Judging and Delivering and Interpretation," The River Room YouTube channel, September 20, 2020. 128, 234

interpreting tongues, testimony 107–119
"I Wan'na Be Like You," (scat) Louis Prima (King Louie) 64

K

kintsugi/kinsukuroi (golden joinery, golden repair) 41
   Buddhist view: non-attachment 41
   Christian view: redemption 41–42
   Japanese golden repair technique 41
   Japanese "wabi sabi" ("embracing the flawed") philosophy 41

L

language building blocks (tongues activation) 62, 69
laying on hands 59, 68, 96
LeClaire, Jennifer 74
"Love Lifted Me," lyrics by James Rowe 190–91
Lull, Ramón 209

M

magic (occult source of power) 66, 67–68, 108, 109, 111, 219
    a block to receiving or operating in the gift of tongues 65–68, 203, 219, 220
    examples of types:
        amulets 66
        shamans 66, 212
        sigils 66
        sorcerers 66
        talismans 66
    repentance and renunciation 66–68, 220
McCord, Beth 217
McGavran, Donald 25
Medenwaldt, Jay 204–6
mimicking (mimicry - tongues activation) 69, 70, 71
Mischief and Magic 108–19
Monsen, Marie 14–15
Montenegro, Marcia 203, 220
more than one/multiple tongues 57, 71

N

Naranjo, Claudio 212–13
New Age/New Agers 66–67, 86–91, 104–5, 121, 163, 165–66, 203, 208, 212, 213, 216
    Aikido instructor 92
    astrologer 86
    booth prophecies 121, 163–64
    channeler 66, 87
    New Age church 89–91

    New Age expos 86–89, 90, 104
    occult practitioners 66
    public outreach 121
    Sebastian (astral projection, succubus) 188
    similarities to Buddhists and Hindus 166
    Tarot card reader 108, 116
    woman who attended Unity Church 165
    woman who believed in universal Oneness 88
    woman who spoke of Atlantis 87
    vibrational attunement practitioners 90–91
Nixon, Wendi 194–201
Non-Dualism 47, 214–15
North American Mission Board (Baptist) 9
    official position statement looks orthodox on paper 9
    position accommodates cessationist theology 4, 9
numerology (Biblical) 40
    meaning of the decade "2010-2019" 170
    meaning of the decade "2020-2029" 170
    meaning of the number "5" 40, 80
    meaning of the number "8" 41
    meaning of the number "50" 41
    meaning of the year "2020/5780" 170

O

occult blocks to the gift of tongues 50–52, 65–68, 203 (Enneagram), 210–20 (Enneagram)
Ochs, Bob 213

P

Pacwa, Mitch 204, 213
Pagan(s) 30, 50, 117, 121, 160, 166, 210
    at booth prophecies 121, 163
    at public outreach 121
    hostile/contemptuous toward Christianity 117, 165–66
    Mischief and Magic 108, 109, 116, 117
paintings 3, 7, 10, 38, 79, 133–149

    by Eddy Cutrera
        "Deeper Waters" (2019) 133
        "Lunar at Big House Church" (2019) 134
    by Andre Dial
        "Liberty's Vision" (detail, 2016) 149
    by Cassandra Donnelly
        "Door of Hope" (4/6/2020) 79
        "Door of Hope, Collage Element" (4/6/2020) 10
        "Door of Hope, Colorful Burst of Sunlight" (4/6/2020) 7, 147
        "Door of Hope, Gray Scale" (4/6/2020) 3
        "Hope Arising" (4/03/2020) 144
        "Nightly Blooms" (2/21/2020) 146
        "The Overflow" (6/6/2020) 38
        "Seeds of Faith" (4/17/2020) 143
        "Tree of Hope" (4/17/2020) 145
    by Jill Eulo
        "Out of the Clouds 'I' Come" (2019), Jill Eulo 148
    by Alison Webster
        "Cleansing the Harvest" (2017) 141
        "Forgive Them" (2017) 140
        "Grafted Olive" (2017) 139
        "Job's Jar" (2017) 142
        "Open Heavens" (2016) 135
        "Refiner's Fire" (2017) 136
        "Unquenched" (2017) 137
        "Walk Ye" (2017) 138

Palmer, Helen 213
Panentheism 214
Parrish, Maxfield, "Daybreak" 176
Pelagianism 217
Perennialism 215
pet talk (tongues activation) 64
Pierce, Chuck 27
pretend dialogue (tongues activation) 69
Prima, Louis (King Louie): "I Wan'na Be Like You" (scat) 64
Priore, Louisa 119
prophetic actions 73–74, 96, 97, 100, 192
    laying hands on someone or something 96

lifting an offering 96–97
  lunging, leaping over, dancing on or around something 100
  placing feet on top of or standing on something 96, 97, 101
  raising the hands upward or extending palms outward 100
  stationing yourself at four corners; facing four directions 98, 100
  symbolic act 98
  walking around someone or something 98, 99, 100–1
  waving an offering 96–97
pseudonyms (aliases) for case studies 169–201
  Clara 183–88
  Daisy 178–82
  Dana and Dasha 170–76
  Leonora 177–78
  Sofia 188–94
  Wendi Nixon (real name) 194–201
Pythagorus 207–208

R

Ranaghan, Dorothy 213
Riso, Don 216
The River Room YouTube channel activation workshops 57, 78, 106, 124, 127, 128, 160, 163
The Road Back to You 216
Rogers, Marcus 62
Rohr, Richard 203, 208–9, 213–16
Roth, Sid 74–75, 77, 225, 238, 239
Rowe, James, lyricist: "Love Lifted Me" 191

S

The Sacred Enneagram 216
scat (tongues activation) 57, 64, 69, 70
The Shantung Revival 9, 11–25
  greatest Baptist revival 9, 23
  historic context 12
    Chinese modern history 12–14, 23–24
    compromised state of Chinese church 13, 15

    demoralized state of missionaries 12–13, 15, 23–24
key contributors 21
    Crawford, Mary 14
    Culpepper, C.L. 14–16, 18, 24–25
    Monsen, Marie 14–15
miracles 20–21
outcomes 21–23
prayer 14, 15, 20, 21, 22, 23, 25
reflections by Christian educators 23
    Cauthen 23–24
    Culpepper 24–25
    Guy 23
    McGavran 24
repentance 15–20
    testimonies of Christians repenting 16–17
    the Chinese people repenting 18–20
revival at hospitals 19
revival at country churches 19–20
revival at girls' and boys' schools 18–19

Sheets, Tim
    "A Mega Pentecost" prophecy 27–28, 33, 36, 37–38
    angels mobilized 29–33
    ecclesia mobilized 33–36, 39
    Exodus, historic and contemporary 28, 29, 97
    mass conversions 36
    miracles, signs, wonders 31, 37, 39
    tongues as the language of divine law and government 35

singing (or chanting) in tongues 68, 72, 83, 84, 87, 88, 91–93, 95, 104–6, 116, 164
    as a tool of power evangelism 106
    at Mischief and Magic 108, 111–12, 115–16, 118
    at New Age church 89, 90
    at New Age expos 86–88, 90–91, 104–105
    Compact Disc, *Spirit Stairwell: A Cappella Voices Hosting the Presence* 91
    corporate tongues in church 77
    disrupts occult spirit power 86, 89, 90–91
    hosts the presence of the Holy Spirit 84, 86, 91
    impassioned speech 84
    opens a stairwell to heaven 84, 91

    serenades people in the Holy Spirit 87, 88, 91, 105, 115, 116
    unseen singers in the sanctuary (heavenly choirs) 93
singing in tongues, practice 95
    corporate worship in church 104
    instrumental accompaniment guidelines 103, 104
    sing along to a familiar song 95
    sing by yourself 96
    sing in public as you shop or ride public transit 104
    singing: duet, trio, quartet, choir 103
    sing over a family member or friend 98
    sing over someone or something 100, 101
    sing over your neighborhood, city, state or nation 100
    sing over yourself 96
    tool of power evangelism 105–106
singing in tongues, teaching and activation videos 106

    "Singing in Tongues Part 1: Spiritual Songs," The River Room YouTube channel, January 15, 2021. 106, 234

    "Singing in Tongues Part 2: Love, Transformation, Protection, Warfare," The River Room YouTube channel, February 16, 2021. 106, 234

    "Singing in Tongues Part 3: Power Evangelism," The River Room YouTube channel, March 12, 2021. 106, 234

    "Singing in Tongues Part 4: A New Song," The River Room YouTube channel, April 9, 2021. 106, 234

    "Singing in Tongues Part 5: Tonal Quality and Mood of Different Themes," The River Room YouTube channel, May 14, 2021. 106, 234

singing in tongues testimony 83
    Craft, Corinna 83, 226
speaking in tongues 7–8, 46, 48, 49, 52-53, 57, 62, 68–69, 71–72, 81, 84, 111, 116, 124, 169, 170, 176, 220
speaking in tongues activation, stewarding the gift as a group 77–78
    a form of intercession and proclamation 77
    a governmental function of the church 77

    cycle through diverse tongues 81
    monitor impressions 81
    stand and move around 81
    suggested topics for intercession and proclamation 81
    volunteers "lead the charge" 81
speaking in tongues activation, stewarding the gift by yourself 71–74
    as praise 74
    as prayer 73
    as prophetic proclamation 74–75
    as spiritual warfare 73
    for discernment, understanding, revelation 73
    for divine destiny 73, 75–77
    for mental health/emotional stability 72
    for rest and refreshing 71
    for tense interactions 72
    Say Yes to Your Book of Life 75–77
    Sid Roth's testimony of a good outcome 75–76
    Take the 90 Day Challenge 74
    to counteract negativity/endure trials 72–73
    to redeem the time 72–73
speaking in tongues impartation, by yourself 58–61
    Biblical basis (Bible quotes) 58–61
    prayer to receive the gift of tongues 61
    sensations you might have 62, 69
    vocalization starters 62–63
        baby babble/pet talk 57, 64
        language building blocks 62–63
        scat 57, 64
        zany nonsense 65
speaking in tongues impartation, in a group 70
    immerse a recipient in the sounds of tongues 70–71
    logistics for small groups vs. large groups 70–71
    partner mimicry 70
    varieties of tongues 70–71
speaking in tongues impartation, with a partner 68–69
    carefree mood 68–69
    catch a recipient who falls 69
    immerse a recipient in the sounds of tongues 68

language building blocks, baby babble, pet talk, scat 68–69
laying on hands 68
partner mimicry 69
pretend dialogue 69
speaking in tongues, public outreach
    booth prophecies 121, 163
    conversions, re-dedications, and introductions to Christ 116
    examples of messages for recipients 115
        dream to found a wedding company 115
        future neonatologist's research and development 115
        good shepherdess 118
        rescue people from suicide 116
        validated discernment 118
        wife's concern about husband's emotional health 115
    examples of types of recipients 115
        Capitol Hill worker 116
        channeler 87
        crisis counselor 116
        neonatologist 115
        software developer 115
        university students 118
        wife 115
        youth group chaperone 118
    eye contact 118, 151, 164
    fast and pray 163
    Fish Bowl prophecies 163
    Fishing for Men prophecies 162
    handling tricky cases 118
        ex-Catholic/Unity Church member 165–66
        Pagans scornfully rejected ministry 117, 166
        person of discernment 118
        wariness of some recipients 118
        youth group chaperone 118
    interacting with specific populations
        backslidden, nominal or proto Christians 117, 165
        New Agers or practitioners of eastern religions 116, 166
        Pagans 117, 166
    inviting people to receive ministry of heavenly languages, "May I Sing Over You?" 116

    magic spells vs. tongues 111
    Mischief and Magic 108–09, 111–12, 115–19
    New Age and occult expos 86–89
    New Age church 89–91; capitalize New Age
    partner ministry 115, 119, 164
    whether to identify the spiritual source of the vocal gifts 88, 117, 165–66
speaking in tongues, solo presentation 150, 153
    before an assembly 153–54
    pointers and practice 150–51
speaking in tongues, teaching and activation videos
    "God Talk: The Key to Unlocking Your Destiny!" *It's Supernatural!* March 29, 2017. 78–79

    "Pentecost: The Gift of Tongues for Power Evangelism, Prayer, Prophecy and Spiritual Warfare," The River Room YouTube channel, May 23, 2021. 57, 234

    "Speaking in Tongues Workshop: For the Common Good or Profit of All," Ray Boetcher/The River Room YouTube channel, January 17, 2020. 78, 234

    "Speaking in Tongues Workshop: Praise, Worship, and Prophecy," The River Room YouTube channel, February 21, 2020. 78, 235

    "Speaking in Tongues Workshop: Public Purposes of Tongues, Part 1," The River Room YouTube channel, May 22, 2020. 163, 235

    "Speaking in Tongues Workshop: Public Purposes of Tongues, Part 2," The River Room YouTube channel, June 19, 2020. 164, 235

    "Speaking in Tongues Workshop: The Royal Priesthood of All Believers, the Laity as Clergy," The River Room YouTube channel, April 17, 2020. 78, 235

    "Speaking in Tongues Workshop: Unity in the Holy Spirit and the Royal Priesthood," The River Room YouTube channel, March 20, 2020. 78, 235

speaking in tongues, testimonies (baptism in the Holy Spirit) 45–55
    Craft, Corinna 45–50
        bi-locality/womb of God experience 47–48
        laughing, sobbing, wallowing on the ground 48
        many tongues 48

        practical and versatile gift 49
        tongues sustained her through years of self denial and sacrifice 49
    Spear, Sveta 50–55
        asleep, sounds emerged 52
        barrier of mistrust and control 52
        cobbled together phonemes (sound units) for weeks 53
        gateway to revelation and supernatural musical skills 54
        Russian assemblies practiced corporate tongues 53–54
        tongues helped her cope in a dysfunctional society 52
    woman who spoke in tongues for four days 50
    woman who was catapulted backward 50
speaking in tongues, troubleshooting blockage 65
    occult blocks 66–67
    soul blocks 65, 66
    step by step deliverance overview 65–68
Spirit Stairwell: A Cappella Voices Hosting the Presence (singing in tongues CD) 91
Stabile, Suzanne 216–18
symbolic/prophetic actions 98
    laying hands on someone or something 59, 68, 96
    lifting an offering 96
    lunging, leaping over, dancing on or around something 100
    placing feet on top of or standing on something 96, 97, 101
    raising the hands upward or extending palms outward 100
    stationing yourself at four corners; facing four directions 98
    walking around someone or something 98, 100, 101
    waving an offering 96

T

"Tell Me Who I Am, O Enneagram," in the *Christian Research Journal* 213
tongues, baptism in the Holy Spirit (see: speaking in tongues impartation)
tongues, interpreting (see: interpreting tongues)
tongues, more than one/multiple 57, 70–71
tongues, singing (see: singing in tongues)
tongues, speaking in (see: speaking in tongues)

U

The Universal Christ 214

V

Veinot, Don and Joy 203, 220
voice projection 81

W

Webster, Alison 135–42
witchcraft (occult source of power) 49, 50-51, 65–68, 78, 88, 178, 188–189, 212, 219–220
    a block to receiving or operating in the gift of tongues 65–68, 203, 219–20
    examples of:
        astral projection (Sebastian) 188
        channelers (mediums) 66, 87
        Feng Shui 66
        fantasy role playing games 66
        shamans 66
        spiritists 66
        sorcerers 66
        succubus encounters (Sebastian) 188
        Wiccans 66
    repentance and renunciation 65–68, 220

Z

Zadai, Kevin 75–77
zany nonsense dialogue 65

ABOUT CORINNA CRAFT

Corinna Craft received a bachelor's degree in communication with an emphasis in print journalism from Stanford University; a master's in English literature from Old Dominion University; and a doctorate in jurisprudential philosophy from Regent University School of Law. For two decades she maintained two trade certifications, one in massage therapy and the other in group exercise. Corinna taught English composition, literature, and argument and research as an adjunct instructor at the college and university level. She also taught group exercise at gyms; massage therapy at trade schools, and worked as a massage therapist at a clinic. In her youth, she performed as a cabaret jazz dancer in Nevada, Utah, and Japan and was trained in classical ballet.

Corinna is a licensed minister of the gospel through The River Room in Virginia Beach, Virginia, where she teaches activation workshops on the gifts of tongues and interpretation. She loves fostering worship arts and facilitating prophetic intercession for reformation in the United States and for the emergence of the royal priesthood of all believers worldwide. She enjoys test driving creative forms of power evangelism in the marketplace.

Corinna also teaches on the subject of deliverance and demonology, particularly eastern mysticism and the occult, including yoga and energy medicine. Two decades of her own life were hijacked by these practices due to her own presumption—a widespread misconception!—that such practices can be selectively censored, secularized, and even sanctified for personal use and communion with Christ. Yet many Christians like herself have become demonized through gym yoga, Asian bodywork, and even Christian yoga and Christian martial arts.

Corinna maintains an anti-yoga website (currently through the Word Press platform) entitled, *What's the Matter with Yoga?* The website presents chapters of her forthcoming book on the subject and educates visitors about the non-dualist and Hindu spirit power inherent in the yoga posture system, breathing techniques, chanting, and meditation, even so-called demystified, exercise-only formats and Christian formats. Corinna plans to write another exposé on the Taoist and shamanic spirit power inherent in Traditional Chinese Medicine and its many derivatives entitled, *What's the Matter with Energy Medicine?*

Corinna senses that the body of Christ is being reconstructed and is also reconstructing the world around itself. She notes that two thirds of reconstruction is demolition and one third is building:

> God reached out, touched my mouth, and said, "Look! I've just put my words in your mouth—hand-delivered! See what I've done? I've given you a job to do among nations and governments—a red-letter day! Your job is to pull up and tear down, take apart and demolish, and then start over, building and planting."—Jeremiah 1:10 MSG

www.ingramcontent.com/pod-product-compliance
Lightning Source LLC
Chambersburg PA
CBHW081614100526
44590CB00021B/3440